D0875269

LIMELIGHT

LIMELIGHT

RUSH IN THE '80S

MARTIN POPOFF

LIBRARY AND ARCHIVES CANADA CATALOGUING IN PUBLICATION

Title: Limelight : Rush in the '80s / Martin Popoff.

Other titles: Rush in the '80s | Rush in the eighties

Names: Popoff, Martin, 1963- author.

Description: Series statement: Rush across the decades ; 2 | Includes bibliographical references.

Identifiers: Canadiana (print) 20200232436 | Canadiana (ebook) 20200232754

ISBN 978-1-77041-536-2 (hardcover)
ISBN 978-1-77305-586-2 (PDF)
ISBN 978-1-77305-585-5 (EPUB)

Subjects: LCSH: Rush (Musical group) | LCSH: Rock musicians—Canada—Biography. | LCGFT: Biographies.

Classification: LCC ML421.R95 P85 2020
DDC 782.42166092/2—dc23

The publication of *Limelight* has been generously supported by the Canada Council for the Arts which last year invested $153 million to bring the arts to Canadians throughout the country and is funded in part by the Government of Canada. *Nous remercions le Conseil des arts du Canada de son soutien. L'an dernier, le Conseil a investi 153 millions de dollars pour mettre de l'art dans la vie des Canadiennes et des Canadiens de tout le pays.* Ce livre est financé en partie par le gouvernement du Canada. We acknowledge the support of the Ontario Arts Council (OAC), an agency of the Government of Ontario, which last year funded 1,737 individual artists and 1,095 organizations in 223 communities across Ontario for a total of $52.1 million. We also acknowledge the contribution of the Government of Ontario through the Ontario Book Publishing Tax Credit, and through Ontario Creates for the marketing of this book.

PRINTED AND BOUND IN CANADA   PRINTING: FRIESENS   5 4 3 2 1

TABLE OF CONTENTS

INTRODUCTION

et any pile of Rush fans together at, say, one of the many legendary RushCons over the years, and you can quickly elicit strong opinions on what parts of the band's '80s catalogue are valid and which are not.

It was an action-packed decade for the boys, as they finally found themselves, by dint of their own wiles and will, in the top quartile, not so much with *Permanent Waves* but for sure come *Moving Pictures*, a red-and-black record accepted as the band's masterpiece.

With *Signals*, Rush started challenging expectations. The '80s will mess with your head, and Rush took to messing about with all the decade had to offer, enthusiastically so, given the guys' predilection toward explorations of modernity. Keyboards and hairstyles in tandem, Geddy, Alex and Neil took the mile when offered an inch, and by the time we get to *Power Windows* and

Hold Your Fire, Rush was an astringent, high-strung pop band, trendy keys and synths in excess.

Most fans went along for the trip, and if they weren't always happy with records like *Presto*, the concert halls were still filled, as the band had no problem delivering the power trio power the fans expected during a show, aided and abetted by a deep catalogue of hits more analog.

And the productivity was impressive as well. Most '70s bands couldn't hold a candle to Rush's tally of seven studio albums and two double live spreads in the '80s, even if the guys decided to notch back on the mega-tours. Rush were regulars in Europe, but, never a world band, they began to visit less frequently, also cutting back on how much of the U.S. and Canada they would hammer at repeatedly.

As you may or may not know, *Limelight: Rush in the '80s* is the follow-up tome to *Anthem: Rush in the '70s*. That book looked at the long ramp-up to the Zeppelin-esque debut album in 1974 and the arrival of a transformational force in the guise of Neil Peart, sadly and shockingly deceased from brain cancer just as that book was getting ready to go to print. Peart, of course, became heralded as one of the greatest rock drummers of all time — and certainly one of the most air drummed — as early as his third record with the band, *2112*. Anthem then examined the band's first live album, followed by *A Farewell to Kings* and *Hemispheres*, and all of a sudden, the '70s are over and it's time for something fresh, including technological innovations as well as the rise of MTV and the age of video.

Limelight: Rush in the '80s is the story of these subsequent years, beginning a couple of weeks into the "haties" (as voiced by Morrissey) with the robust if brief *Permanent Waves* and bowing out in November of 1989 with *Presto*, a record that bucked so many trends, the band found themselves kind of marginalized, or more positively, defiantly singular, sounding like no one else while still essentially playing a form of mainstream pop.

Along the way, we hear from the myriad producers Geddy, Alex and Neil brought into the circle, not so much desperately but avidly, curiously, looking for inspiration from industry peers. Essentially what Peter Collins and Rupert Hine (and slightly less so Peter Henderson) brought was pop modernity, with the guys all too happy to push buttons on the latest toys to craft a sound more in keeping with what they saw as valid and au courant, the music of grown-ups. A contentious dynamic of the book, which I argue is borne out in the music and lyrics, is that the band was seeking the respect of folks they thought were smart, folks who had good taste. You may look at that as a negative, or you might see that as the guys enthusiastically participating in the hustle and bustle of the modern world, growing intellectually, not conceding that they themselves couldn't be new world men.

And becoming new world men meant that Geddy, Alex and Neil would develop interests outside of music, because, after all, wasn't music itself moving toward the idea of multimedia? Toward this end, toward becoming well rounded — in effect, Renaissance men — as the '80s wore on, the guys pulled back from touring, spending more time on family, travel and other creative pursuits. The business of Rush is very different in this book versus the first one, reflected in the vast difference between *A Show of Hands* and *All the World's a Stage*.

But this isn't the end of our story. Because of course Rush didn't stop at *Presto*, even if the band had slowed. More joy and much more heartbreak were to star-cross the lives of Geddy, Alex and Neil, and the story wouldn't be complete if we didn't march forward and meet the heroes of our tale at their own individual completions. Stay tuned as we continue this loud and loving march through time toward a conclusion that now, with the recent passing of the Professor, is very, very different and darker than when this trilogy began.

MARTIN POPOFF

CHAPTER 1
PERMANENT WAVES

"Most promising keyboard player of the year."

For all the turmoil in the music industry in the late 1970s, including the changings of the guard (from rock, quickly past punk into post-punk) to the recessionary year that was 1979 (saved barely by the arrival of *The Wall*, *In Through the Out Door* and *The Long Run*), Geddy Lee, Alex Lifeson and Neil Peart — a.k.a. Rush — kept moving forward from strength to strength. Their sixth album, *Hemispheres*, proved that the band could sell, and on tour excel, despite a record that was as anti-commercial as they get. Broken down, that record gave up a side-long song about Greek gods and a long instrumental, leaving room for only two short pieces, one of them heavy slide-rule metal ("Circumstances") and the other hummable enough, but about trees fighting each other. But the awards kept coming, allowing for even more of the autonomy and validation the band attracted. By the end of the decade, Rush was undisputedly the biggest band from Canada.

Still, the band wasn't making a lot of money. Rush had moved away from the days of hit singles like "Closer to the Heart" and "Fly by Night." But the financial situation wasn't dire, and there was a sense of generosity within the Rush camp. They wanted to give back, often playing B-city gigs that might not be particularly profitable. The band also poured a lot of their profits into making their show bigger and more extravagant any chance they got. It's a strategy that paid off: it made Rush, a still-small band in 1979 and 1980, look huge.

In tandem with the band's expanding maturity as a live act was their consistent growth from record to record. *Permanent Waves* would demonstrate a number of advancements, but these would be subtle, and in part driven by the guys changing up the environment in which they worked.

"We were torn at that point with what kind of music we wanted to make, in terms of its length," recalls Geddy. "We had fallen into this pattern of writing these really long pieces and that started to seem formulaic to us, predictable. Complicated musical part here, this is where we do the chorus, and it kind of got boring. So we thought, we still like to play long, complicated pieces. If we had our druthers, that's all we probably would do. And then there is the lyric thing. How do we bring that in and how do we keep improving? So we came up with this idea of trying to make the long pieces but have them much quicker. So over five, six minutes, as opposed to twenty."

Permanent Waves did not let up on the quick edits, the progressive virtuosity, the rapid arrival and dispersal of action points, but as Geddy says, it's almost as if the result was long songs defying the space-time continuum, somehow being as long as they've always been, but then there's time left over (maybe that's also why *Permanent Waves* is such an irritatingly short album).

"It was a conscious thing, to not write really long songs,"

seconds Alex. "And what resulted from that would be fine. I remember that when we wrote these songs, it seemed like they were songs within songs, just smaller pieces. 'The Spirit of Radio,' for example, the sequence was a very key part to it. That led to the signature guitar riff, off the top of the song. We all connected to that one thing as the center, and all these other little pieces branched out — the same thing but much more condensed."

"There was something about the record that was really fresh for us," continues Geddy. "It was written quickly. And the recording session was so smooth — or maybe it was just in comparison to the horrible pain of *Hemispheres* — but it seemed so fresh and energetic, and there was a really good vibe to the whole session. We weren't so far from home, not so isolated from family, in a new studio. You walk in and there's this beautiful view of this lake and the Laurentian Mountains. So it was a very happy, good-vibe record. And we finished it very quickly, I think five or six weeks."

Leading up to the sessions at the iconic Le Studio, in Morin Heights in rural Quebec, the band had taken their longest break yet; they'd had six weeks to recharge. The band enjoyed a rural retreat before entering the studio, with writing and rehearsals taking place at Lakewood Farms, near Flesherton, Ontario. This mirrored their approach to *Hemispheres* and was something they also did for the next album. The sessions ran in September and October of 1979 toward a release date of January 14, 1980. At the farm, the gear was set up in the basement, and Neil had some space for lyric writing, which he could do in a cottage nearby. The songs were further honed during a handful of warm-up tour dates as well as demo sessions at the Sound Kitchen, Terry Brown now presiding.

"It was the first album we did at Le Studio, and it was such a treat to work there," notes Alex. "We set up a volleyball net and court outside of the front door of the house we were staying at, which is by a lake. We put lights up so we could come back at two in the morning when we were finished recording and play volleyball for a couple of hours and drink and all that stuff. It was about a mile to paddle or row from the lake to the studio from the house.

"That's before Le Studio became a big complex, so it had a very homey vibe to it. [Owners] Yael and Andre Perry were just wonderful people. We had some great dinners; I have very fond memories of it. That was a very traditional period. We had just gone from that last concept, *Hemispheres*, and we had been recording in England, but that one we recorded at Le Studio but mixed it in England, at Trident. It was an attempt to condense our songs a little bit, be more economical, try to get as much as we could in that four- to five-minute framework rather than eight to eleven minutes."

"That became a regular thing, an obsession," says Geddy, keying in on Alex's mention of volleyball. "That was one of our early introductions to sport activities [laughs]. We'd finish at one in the morning or whatever, and we kind of perfected the art of night volleyball. And we played even in the winter. We'd have a few drinks and get a bit fortified after the session and go out on the volleyball pitch. We built light standards and had it lit so we could play at night. And sometimes we'd even play after dinner a little bit, but then we'd get back into the studio, and our hands would be all swollen from punching this stupid ball. We were like, I don't know if we should be playing like this, after supper."

"It's on a kidney-shaped lake, called Lac Perry, after the founder, Andre Perry," explains Neil, as, years later, he walked through the burned-out ruins of the studio, at this point consigned to be taken over by nature. "And at the other end there's a beautifully appointed guest house that we would stay in, month after month over the years. And it's only six hours from home. All of us lived in southern Ontario at that time. So it was convenient; we could even have our families up to visit. It was very much a home away from home. In wintertime I would cross-country ski between the guest house and the studio. I would get up in the morning and go cross-country skiing, and then ski right in to work, because all the trails link right along here. It became such a nice escape. A lifetime passion was formed here. The assistant engineer taught me how to cross-country ski — the late Robbie Whelan.

"What a workplace to walk into every day," reminisces Peart. "I mean, I'm a lifetime nature lover anyway. And to be exposed to this view, changing through the seasons . . . We worked here, first time in fall, which was glorious. And then later in winter and summer and spring as well. There's a mountain that goes up opposite the guest room, dining room, and every morning we'd watch the autumn colors change on that hillside. And the three of us, we actually hiked up there one time. We often have subgroups that we write as. And one of them, our new wave romantic group, was called the Fabulous Men. And the three of us hiked up to a high ski trail called the Portageur. I'd ski by it in winter so I knew it was there, and I led us up there and I carved it into the tree, the Fabulous Men. Probably still there [laughs].

"In the summertime there were paddleboats on the lake, or a little rowboat," continues Neil. "Oh, and there were Alex's radio-controlled planes. There were many stories of him crashing and us chasing them. One of them went down way across the lake in the woods, and all we heard was 'bzzzz, crash.' So we went across there in the boat with the radio-control thing, and he worked the servos, and we'd all be creeping through the woods listening for a 'beep beep' and, you know, sure enough, there it is up in the tree. So all kinds of personal, friendly adventures like that.

"And being immersed in the French-Canadian scene was for me life changing because in 1980, I bought a cabin and have had a place here ever since. I loved the cross-country skiing and snowshoeing in the winter, and the rowing and swimming in the summer. It still really speaks to me, this area. In the autumn, of course, the colors are spectacular. There's so much history here, both personal and professional. Thinking of those first few records, *Permanent Waves*, *Moving Pictures*, *Signals* and *Grace Under Pressure*, so much that happened here."

About *Permanent Waves*, Neil says, "In those days, we all recorded together in the room, all of us. All of us were learning the song and interacting with each other's parts. So a lot of stuff was hammered out — is the best way to put it — here. You know, by playing it over and over again; that's the way we worked in those days."

"Everything on the *Permanent Waves* record came together in a relatively short period of time," adds Geddy, surveying the whole experience, but reflecting on how prepared the band was. "In fact, it was one of the most pleasurable and easiest albums for us to record. It was just one of those great writing sessions. At that time, it was still three of us sitting around, throwing ideas together and writing together in typical garage band style. We would write two songs, rehearse them, take them into the studio and lay down live backing tracks. Everything just clicked. Morin Heights was beautiful, and the engineer was terrific. It all came together in a very quick and spontaneous way, which I think is reflected in the songs. Subsequently, we've tried to maintain that over the years.

"It's much more interesting to try to take that idea of being progressive and not do it in a way that people expect you to be progressive," continues Geddy, further attempting to articulate what was different about the songs on this album. "What is a progressive band? Oh, you do a concept album that has space involved, and here's the long instrumental portion, here's the overture. That, to me, just seemed less interesting than saying, okay, let's do ten individual songs and each one of them can be a mini concept unto itself. And it's okay that there's a thread that connects all those songs, and the thread is the concept, right? It's not the repeating melody lines or the repeating elements that keep reappearing. To me, that was a step forward. That was Rush progressing and not just staying in the same mold we had cast on *2112*.

"But it was a challenge. Can we write a song that's five, six, seven minutes long — those are short songs by our standards — and still deliver something really interesting musically? Is there enough time to be musically adventurous in five minutes and yet tell a different kind of story? That was the whole key, and that began ten years of experimenting. And it's a never-ending experiment, still to this day, really. Structurally it was interesting to see if we could be very aggressive one moment, very melodic another. Still have those instrumental sections that have a climax and a peak — that's the way you would structure a ten-minute piece — but shrink it all down and see . . . does it sound edited together? Does it still have a flow? Does it still have a rhythm to it that feels good to listen to? Those are all things every writer of that genre of music has to deal with, and we were obsessed with it.

"But I think we spent five weeks, six weeks making that record. It was just boom, boom, boom, and then we went to England and mixed it at Trident. Without the difficulty of *Hemispheres*, we never would have found Trident Studios. So everything happens for a reason. All the crappiest experiences of your life prepare you for the next step."

"They came very well prepared for that album, with a lot of preproduction," says Terry, obviously pleased with the contrast to the previous project. "They had spent an inordinate amount of time rehearsing, so they came to the table with things finished, as it were. We didn't spend as much time together as they spent together preparing the songs. That was a big change. It was a fun record, but it wasn't easy. It was hard from a playing standpoint, but again, they were really starting to push the envelope as players."

"There was a strong division between *Hemispheres* and *Permanent Waves*," reflects Neil with respect to the compositions, "even though we still had long pieces and a lot of extended arrangements and instrumentation and so on. But there was a change of attitude in the late '70s and in the music we were responding to. 'The Spirit of Radio' incorporates stylistically and again, implicitly, what all that was about.

"And from *Permanent Waves*, that set us up to be able to do *Moving Pictures*. What we decided to do at the end of *Hemispheres* was realized with *Moving Pictures*. Very often, that's the case; there'll be a whole album's growth necessary to take us to where we're going. And I remember a critic around that time in the '70s saying he just wished he could give us a big kick in the direction we were going. And that was a nice criticism, you know? And one of the few worthwhile ones we ever received. That was really thoughtful. I remember Geddy pointing it out to me, how great that was. He was acknowledging that we were going in the right direction, but it was taking too long."

"When they came up with the material for *Permanent Waves*, it was pretty exciting," says Terry, "because it was so different. But I hadn't had the conversation, 'We need to come up with something shorter or more concise or different.' *Hemispheres* was a hard record to make, and it drained everybody creatively, so it seemed only natural that the next record was going to be quite different. You couldn't do two of those in a row."

The engineering credit on *Permanent Waves* went to Paul

Northfield, who begins his long association with the band at this point.

"It was September of '79 and I was working in Morin Heights, Le Studio. At that time the studio's reputation was built on not just the equipment, but the people who worked there. Its reputation had already started to rise as there had been some great hard rock records done there. And it was convenient. It's in Canada and it's a beautiful area. When people came to the studio, either myself or Nick Blagona, the other engineer, would be assigned to engineer the projects. There would be myself and an assistant, and in this case, it was Robbie Whelan."

In terms of Paul's history, he explains: "In the case of the studio, I was hired because of my credentials, because I'd worked in London for four or five years, and I'd gotten a track record of working with people like Gentle Giant, Emerson, Lake & Palmer and Yes, and to some degree, Steve Howe. I had a resume, so I think they suddenly saw an opportunity to have somebody in the mix who had a different point of view, and a point of view they really liked.

"And people often used house engineers. So when they walked in the door, I kind of assumed I was going to be sitting in the engineering seat and Terry was the producer — I made that assumption from day one — and I sat down and talked to them about it: 'This is how things work out here,' 'This is a good place to set up drums.' And I think in that moment I probably sold them on the idea of, 'Oh, okay, let's have Paul sit in the engineering seat and Terry will sit in the producer's seat and this will be a change.'

"It wasn't until later that I realized Terry did a lot of the engineering himself. That's the way it was. I guess at the end of the day, they probably came and met me and realized I had a lot of experience that might be interesting to bring to the table, and so

Terry decided to take the producer's chair, rather than doing both jobs, and we worked from there. I did all the hands-on stuff, and he would be overseeing the whole project as a producer often does.

"There was a lot of camaraderie with the band and with Terry," continues Northfield. "It was very much like a boys' club. Becoming part of the recording process with Rush was entering into their world. Because they spent so much time together on the road, working a ridiculous amount of time, and when they were not on the road, frequently either writing or recording. They had a sort of insularity about their environment, and so obviously that included Terry, and subsequently included us — myself and Robbie. We would often eat with them, most times, actually, for dinner, essentially for two months during the recording from beginning to end. We were recording twelve hours plus a day, seven days a week. So that's the atmosphere at the time."

About his role as engineer on *Permanent Waves*, Paul says, "I made a lot of suggestions as to what the best places in the studio were, because I knew the room and the basic setups and the idiosyncrasies of the equipment we had. Because at that time, there wasn't the same level of standardization you have now in studios, and there wasn't the rental aspect of recording. Now you can pretty much go anywhere and have any equipment, and if you don't have it, you can get it within a day or a few hours; you can have it shipped to you as a day rental. That didn't exist then. Each studio had its particular strengths and weaknesses, and those contributed toward how records sounded.

"And even the monitoring and speakers we used, I mean, we were mixing and recording using very large speakers that were mounted in the wall, in the ceiling, above the control room window. And that has a profound impact on the sound. There was no uniformity. These days, there is relative uniformity. If you don't like the speakers when you walk into the studio, sitting on the console, you go and get the ones you like. But those small high-quality speakers didn't really exist in '79. That's not to say none existed, but it wasn't until probably the mid-'80s or the early '80s that things like the Yamaha NS-10 became popular. But at that time, part of my role was to be like, 'Okay, I am familiar with this room, this is the equipment we have, these are the good things we have, try this, try that.'"

Paul also understood the narrative the band was writing for itself concerning the previous album and this one.

"It was just fairly explicit. I think they had decided they'd indulged themselves to such a degree in doing anything they wanted to do, musically. If they felt like they wanted to stretch a certain section out for five minutes because they really enjoyed playing it and wanted to experiment with it, they just did it. I think after having done that with *Hemispheres*, they wanted to say all of the important things in a smaller, more concise way. And obviously it has its benefits, because it makes it easier and more accessible for people. If they want to be heard on the radio, it's very hard to play a twelve-minute song and get any airplay.

"Although that seemed to be very secondary," Paul continues. "It seemed to be the challenge of being able to say something concisely that appealed to them. They were very much an idealistic band, probably driven by the fact that in the early days when they did what other people said, it always went invariably wrong. And when they just did what they wanted to do, they got a really great response from their fans and their career blossomed. So they were very idealistic about what they did. Now we're doing this because we want to — this is the direction we're going because we enjoy it.

"Their desire to change and be different and challenge themselves was even down to the recording process. I remember it driving me a little crazy in the early days, for *Moving Pictures* and

Permanent Waves. They had this idea that whenever we recorded anything, even if we got it and everything sounded good, particularly the drums, then we would change all the microphones on the next song, for the purpose of not wanting to repeat themselves and to be creative. Which, in theory, is very interesting. In practice, there are certain microphones that are really excellent for doing certain jobs, so to change them for creative reasons, for change's sake, was actually like, 'Oh, really?' Some of it may have been a certain naïveté, but it was very heartfelt. This is what they do. They're not really interested in conforming to anybody else's preconceived ideas of what they should or shouldn't do."

Paul says Geddy took a particular interest in the production side of things. "Yes, Geddy did take a more hands-on approach. He was there all the time, sort of watching, sitting at the side, present pretty much every step of the way. Sometimes when Alex was playing a solo it would just be Terry, Alex and myself in the control room. But even so, I think Geddy was there lapping it all up and being a part of it. He was like a sponge, trying to suck up everything that was going on in the studio. He was there in the control room for almost every minute of making *Permanent Waves* and *Moving Pictures.*

"One other thing about Geddy: he was the first bass player I've worked with that came in with an overdrive kind of amp sound. Although Chris Squire was also doing that at that time, using a Marshall head and a Marshall 4x12 for the growl part of it. That may have also been a bit of an inspiration for Geddy because they were both Rickenbacker players."

But Paul and Geddy never really talked about Yes. Northfield says that was more an "unspoken thing, the fact that Rush were playing progressive music, albeit a more metal-driven kind. They really liked the arrangement depth that was there with the best of the progressive stuff, and the experimentalism and the indulgence that works both ways. It can be indulgent in a negative way but also liberating. It's like creatively, you just do what you like rather than what is formulaic and what fits for a pop song or a successful song. You go, 'I love the way this thing plays, I love playing this riff, I want to play it for five minutes' because I love it.'

"Extended jams, even if they're highly structured, they're part of what Rush was all about. That ignoring the formulas of the record business, to just do what they like doing and what they were getting a response from their audience with. Geddy came in with his bass sound and with his attitude and his playing and was looking for us — Terry and the new studio and me — to actually capture that, and sort of surprise them maybe with something new."

Addressing Geddy's temperament, Northfield reflects on "his humor and his focus, which kind of flipped back and forth. One minute he's being very relaxed and irreverent when everything is going smoothly — the humor is flying, the side comments, the relaxed banter. But if at any moment it seems like something is not quite where it's supposed to be, he can turn on a dime and be very intense, for want of a better word. That's happened to me a couple times, where we go from being very easygoing, and then for some reason he felt like something was getting missed or overlooked, he would turn into a different kind of personality. Not Jekyll and Hyde but fairly substantial swings.

"Humor is important for the whole band. They egged each other on. Alex is a natural comedian, but Geddy has a sense of the absurd. A good example is when we did the vocals for *Permanent Waves*, he had a mandolin. It might've been one that was lying around at the studio. But he would be doing vocals and holding a mandolin, and every time he would stop singing, he would play the mandolin, just to mess with us. Normally when you're recording vocals, you want to keep everything quiet. So what that meant was we had a lot of work. One of the albums he had the mandolin and on another it was a harmonica, and on one of them he had a set of congas set up. And he did that to fuck with us, you know?"

As Paul emphatically explains, Rush at this point wasn't particularly well versed in keyboard and synth technology.

"No, when they first came in to do *Permanent Waves*, it was a three-piece band with a synthesizer that just played one note, you know, one big string 'deeee,' like this, and Taurus pedals that played the big, deep 'oooooh,' like that. And Geddy could just flick a switch and play a super-low note on the Taurus pedals and have this orchestrated, high, almost stringlike sound, which was preprogrammed. He had this Oberheim synth, like four-voice Oberheim, that's not programmable. You set everything up. And it was basically set to one sound. He might have had two sounds on it, but all it did was go 'zing,' and then the Taurus pedals would be like that thunderous low end.

"It gave them this kind of dimension, because sometimes Geddy wanted to riff with Alex, high up the neck on the bass. When you do that, suddenly all the bottom end is gone out of the track. They could play as a three-piece, almost like two guitars, but then the Taurus pedals would give the thunderous low end. And then there's the little zingy string stuff that would sometimes come in on the chorus or on a section, which would give it this orchestra feel. And that is not particularly high-tech. That's just one note from a pedal with a complementary high. And then, obviously, he did a bit of Minimoog stuff, simple Minimoog melodies, not technical playing. He knew how to program the Minimoog for what he wanted; he was just a basic programmer. He wasn't a tech head about it.

"But then as time went on, just by nature of his desire, first of all, polyphonic synths came in where you could play chords — and interesting ones. The first really interesting polyphonic synth he used was the OB-Xa. And that was funny, because that was on *Moving Pictures*. And at that time, there was like, not a battle, but a running gag between the guys in the band. Because Neil would win drummer of the year in *Modern Drummer*, like regularly. And Geddy was winning bass player of the year, and Alex was coming second to Eddie Van Halen. And it was a source of much . . . I'm sure for Alex, it was a bit of a tough pill to swallow, even though those things being what they are, they're more like popularity contests.

"But the thing that was really funny was that Geddy won most promising keyboard player of the year," chuckles Paul. "For *Moving Pictures*. And that was when he'd just gravitated to chords. And so he'd probably have a sense of irony or humor about that because obviously he's not a keyboard player of the year by anybody's imagination.

"But the use of them in the arrangements was a different matter. You could argue that their arrangement sense was, between all of them, really powerful. But in terms of his technique, like I say, he'd just graduated from playing one note at a time or Minimoog melodies to actually playing chords. And that's when, suddenly, the technology started to come in. And then for a while there, I was very involved because I used to do programming as well. I was more of a technical kind of person. A lot of my strengths in recording and music come from a technical background, an obsession with the technology, if you like.

"We had a big meeting at one point. I had latched onto somebody who was a great electronics designer from the video side of things. We talked a bunch, and for a while, there was the possibility that we were going to be building a programmable way of playing chords from his foot pedals, which was basically before MIDI. Now that is very easy to do; you can just buy an off-the-shelf set of foot pedals and have preprogrammed chords under every pedal. But that was something we actually almost did back then. And at the last minute, Geddy kind of decided no, because it was gonna cost quite a lot of money when you do something like that from scratch. But he was very intrigued by that. But I think what stopped him wasn't how much it was gonna cost. I think it was that he prefers to just play bass and sing, not pressing this foot, that foot, this hand, singing, playing bass. That's been one of his frustrations as a musician, sometimes he was so busy playing three or four things at once."

Northfield calls Geddy a natural bass player. "He's got very good instincts. And on the aggressiveness of his bass playing, the interesting thing is, he's the only bass player I've ever worked with who broke an E string on his bass in the studio. And when it happened, I was like, 'You what?!' It has a lot to do with, I think, the power in his right hand, the way he flexes his hand. You see that right hand sort of twisting, and sometimes he's really snapping the strings, whereas other people that have great technique hardly move their hands at all, and they can maybe play insanely great or they slap and do all kinds of stuff. But his hand kind of rotates as he plays, and he digs in. He uses his whole wrist to get the power, rather than just his fingertips. Very few players play with that kind of real digging-in, super-aggressive right hand. To me, that's where his power comes from. Plus a lot of conviction and commitment. And then, obviously, in the early days, that growly Rickenbacker tone, with the sort of fret buzz and the particular . . . it was like Rotosound strings with the Rickenbacker and the fret buzz and the aggressive playing. He built this really chunky, growly, kind of Chris Squire–like sound."

Hugh Syme wasn't particularly happy with his cover art for *Hemispheres*. On *Permanent Waves*, the man redeemed himself fabulously, creating a stunning cover image that went the extra unknowable, abstract and magical mile, helping to define the contents of the record, in this case conjuring words like *austere* and *modern*. This is underscored by the arty shot of the band, as well as the typestyles.

But it is the Hipgnosis-like cover image that is the real treat. Canadian model Paula Turnbull is pictured, oddly lit, unconcerned about the carnage behind her. (Turnbull would come back to represent this cover on *Exit . . . Stage Left*, which features references to all the album covers up to 1981.) There are permanent waves in her hair and a wave in her skirt. Behind her is a big wave crashing over Seawall Boulevard in Galveston, Texas, during Hurricane Carla, September 11, 1961, from an iconic photo by Flip Schulke, who used to put himself in harm's way getting these shots. Also oblivious to the weather is a tiny Hugh Syme, waving. A newspaper flaps and waves in the atmospheric turbulence, with the famous incorrect advance headline from the *Chicago Tribune* announcing Dewey Defeats Truman. The paper complained, and Hugh altered it to say Dewei Defeats Truman (some later reissues delete the headline altogether).

The red electrocardiogram-like pattern into which the name of the album is artfully incorporated is a remnant of Syme's original idea, related to Neil in a phone call to his country home. Syme wanted to tape electrodes to the heads of the guys while they were performing and get ECG readings, which would be reproduced in reds and perhaps embossed golds. Originally, the record was to be called *Wavelength*, but the band found that title had been used too many times. *Permanent Waves* was a bit of a dig at the music industry, constantly announcing new waves in music.

Once the needle drops on the music, one is instantly confronted with a bracing Alex Lifeson lick, which sounds like Eddie Van Halen–style tapping but is in fact Alex picking rapidly. Geddy and Neil punctuate in unison cascading fills, and we are off to the races. A couple more intro riffs are tried on for stadium-rocking size, and we are efficiently placed in the verses, where Neil tells a nostalgic tale of the magic of radio. "The Spirit of Radio" also features a brief tip of the hat to reggae, all the rage around the world at the time and revived into a new context by the Police, whom Rush admired. The band had added a reggae intro to live renditions of "Working Man" and thought it would be a fun touch in this song about the magic of music. And the song continues to surprise — there's even a part designed to represent the turn of a radio knob and the quick sampling of different stations one might hear.

"Yeah, it worked," says Geddy of "The Spirit of Radio," which hit #22 in Canada, #51 in the U.S. and an impressive #13 in the U.K. "I don't know whether it was just a relief for people not to have to sit through twenty-five minutes to get to the end of a song, but we just took all our ability and all that experimenting we'd done and focused it in a smaller time period, and the songs really had a lot of power. We still had some longness going on there on 'Jacob's Ladder,' but 'Spirit of Radio' was one of those songs that proved to us we could take a five-minute format and make it complex and make it melodic and make it all work, so that was a big learning moment for us."

Explained Neil, speaking with *Modern Drummer* back in 1980: "It's not about a radio station or anything; it's really about the spirit of music when it comes right down to the basic theme of it. It's about musical integrity. We wanted to get across the idea of a radio station playing a wide variety of music. For instance, 'The Spirit of Radio' comes from the radio station at home called CFNY. That's their slogan. They play all great music from reggae to R&B, to jazz, to new wave, everything that's good or interesting. It's a very satisfying radio station to me. They have introduced me to a lot of new music. There are bits of reggae in the song and one or two verses have a new wave feel. We tried to get across all the different forms of music. There are no divisions there. The choruses are very electronic. It's just a digital sequencer with a glockenspiel and a counter guitar riff. The verse is a standard straight-ahead Rush verse. One is a new wave, a couple of reggae verses, and some standard heavy riffing, and as much as we could possibly get in there without getting redundant."

Reflects long-time road manager for the band Liam Birt, the song is about "how radio can make or break people. And of course, radio loved that song because they seemed to think it was a pat on the back. I don't think it necessarily was — you can read those lyrics more than one way — but radio seemed to get very attracted to that song. To me, it was also a shot at radio. With them, they've always wanted to take the hard way around doing something. If they see an easy way out, they almost instinctively know it must be the wrong way. The joke is you can never find a Rush song you can dance to — reasonably true. Even if you could dance to 'Tom Sawyer,' you'd be exhausted halfway through. As far as what attracts people to their music, I really don't know."

"I think individually we all thought it would be nice to have more success at radio and sell more records," opines Terry. "Because records at that point were the backbone of the business — for me as a producer, very important. So we all thought it would be nice, but we didn't want to make a 'hit' single. Because a hit single is kind of like selling out. Whether you like it or not, that's the way it's viewed. But I think we did very well with 'Spirit of Radio.' That's a hit single, but it's a pretty wacky hit single. It was fine-tuning in order to be slightly more commercial. All the parts were there, and when it was finished, it had a sound to it and an appeal that worked at radio.

"I would always meet with Ray [Danniels] prior to making a record. We'd have lunch and we'd talk about the upcoming record, and he'd always give me the impression he would like to make that commercial nugget. But he never said to me, 'If you don't make it, you're fired.' Or 'Get those boys to knuckle down.' There was never a conversation like that. And sure enough, we did, from time to time; we came up with little nuggets that were radio-friendly and gave the boys another lift. But we did it in a really smart way, I think, and kept the integrity.

"But we would talk about his needs as manager of the band. You know, 'I need something to go to radio with. I need something that is going to get me FM play.' And we would talk about the United States and world markets, and he'd give me an idea of what was lacking in the previous record and where we would go with the new one. I would absorb it and try to do something with it. Sometimes I knew what was coming down the pike. So then I would meet with the band and we'd start working on it. I'd be thinking about my lunch with Ray while I was working on the production of the records, knowing full well there was only so much I could do to change the course of history.

"But the kind of records we were making, I can still listen to them and hear details that excite me. It might be something really subtle, but that's a good thing. When you can keep playing records over and over again and still relate to them, that's what you want. And that song is totally different. I mean, you use this term *progressive* sort of euphemistically, but it was something out of the ordinary. I saw it as very commercial, but it had amazing potential at radio, not least of all because of the title. But it was also outrageous in terms of the construction. But I thought it had enough that it could tip the balance in being a hit record."

As Terry says, "The Spirit of Radio" started breaking on the radio — after all, it glorified and validated the jobs of DJs. "It definitely broke into new areas, and people were starting to take notice who hadn't before. And it was getting so much airplay that we were starting to get good reports back from radio."

And it's not just about the lyrics; any DJ will tell you the song is attention getting, and its instantly recognizable intro makes "The Spirit of Radio" a great broadcast track. And not only because of Alex's kaleidoscopic guitar lick but the quickly arriving air drum moment, which remains one of the toughest to get perfect in the catalogue to this day, much like the intro to Led Zeppelin's "Rock and Roll" a generation earlier. The song also quickly becomes relaxing, yet it's still buoyant and loud, easy to work out, a toe-tapper for Rush fans of any aptitude level.

"It was long overdue, and it was so nice to hear something that outrageous on pop radio," continues Brown. "I'm not really a big fan of modulating key changes coming in and out of a song just to give it that extra lift. But if it's done properly, sometimes it can be a really exciting thing to add to a tune. If there's a sudden change that goes on in the way a tune moves, but it's not jarring, you don't have to work hard to figure it out. I think that's the good thing. If you've got to start thinking and wondering why and how and when, then the tune is not working. But if the tune makes you feel good and takes you somewhere and sort of pinpoints a time in your life, that's pretty special. At the same time, they had that ability to put something together that's not pop pablum, shall we say — as you're listening to it, there's a story to be told. It's not just banal time-wasting stuff."

And speaking of banal, the song ends with the word *salesmen* sung once, sung again with more feeling and then shouted in exasperation. This is laden with a couple of meanings. First, Neil has talked about how the song is lined with a touch of irony, that maybe for him as a kid, all seemed more than right with radio, but now that golden age is being lost, the salesmen taking over, going for the cheap playlists that seem the easy route to ad sales.

The idea that concert halls echo with the sounds of salesmen ties in with the guys' idea of "the sickness," of bands knocking out the same gratuitous blather to crowds everywhere, barely aware of what town they're in for the night. Driving home both points is the substituting out of the word *prophets* for *profits* — Hugh is proud of the band's never punning with the word *rush* in album titles, but that doesn't mean Neil doesn't sometimes sneak puns into his lyrics. In fact, he's a serial offender. Redeeming this section's pun somewhat is that this configuration of words seems to be a tribute to Simon & Garfunkel's "The Sound of Silence." And there's interesting similarity and contrast between the titles of the two songs.

Despite any animosity from the Rush camp regarding what was going on in radio in the era of *Permanent Waves,* Terry is adamant the medium still mattered.

"I was certainly interested in commercial value. I've had hits over the years, and to have a band that you're working with on a regular basis and not hear them on radio is not success to me. If we were making a record just for the band, something very creative we all loved that nobody could listen to, that to me is not a successful record. It has to work on all levels. So the challenge of putting something together that was sufficiently different, and yet could hit radio and inspire people, I thought was fantastic. Very exciting."

Drilling down a little further into this balance, Terry says, "I think the band was only too aware of what was going on. There are two ways of doing things in the music business. You either write for success and radio, or you write for yourself and success. And if you want success as a writer, as a creative person, then you do it one way, and if you are doing it for the record label, you do it another way. And since you have to live with that for the rest of your life, I think it's important to do it for yourself.

"Now if you can combine that success, then obviously you've got the best of both worlds. I've worked with artists over the years, and some have been doing stuff not really for themselves, but for their career, and it falls flat on its face, generally speaking. Not always, but years later, when your career is waning, you have to live with the stuff that you did, that you weren't happy with. To me, that's not an option. I like to do stuff I'm happy with and the artist is happy with. And to make records and coerce artists into doing stuff purely for commercial success, to me, is a bad move. It's doomed to failure. So we were very lucky with 'Spirit of Radio.' There's a tune that by all rights should never have gotten onto radio. It's off the wall, it's long and it had crazy parts in it, but it was exciting and told a story. And couched in the sounds and the way it was put together, the editing and all the stuff that goes into making it what it is, it came out and proved it could actually have commercial success."

Terry confirms the song's pickup by radio. "I found it interesting that they had written a song about radio, or Neil had written a song about a radio station in Toronto that wouldn't play them. That was a little out there, but it was his artistic license to do that. At that point, I was getting used to the idea that we would start to have more and more radio airplay. And my focus was not just on the stations we had it on, but where we didn't have it. And 'Spirit of Radio,' I don't think there was a city in North America where we couldn't get airplay with that."

Rush prove this new commercial success was no fluke with the next song on *Permanent Waves*, "Freewill." It's insanely catchy, yet still tricky, and it's relatively brief, at 5:23. Like "The Spirit of Radio," this was worked up early. Played live for the first time at Varsity Stadium in Toronto, September 2, 1979, the song as performed there and then is virtually identical to the studio version, right down to Neil's drum fills (Geddy might have sung the odd different word). "The Spirit of Radio," played on the same night, was also quite similar, although a little loose, especially come the reggae section, which is amusingly chunky and laid-back.

"Freewill" is particularly strong in melody, cheerful even, with a vocal melody that follows the riff — which alternates from 7/4 to 6/4 but is easy to follow after a few tries. "Conceptually, the heaviness of *Hemispheres* made us want to run away from that kind of album," says Geddy. "So we ran from *Hemispheres* straight into those songs. They were still long songs, but it had a very different spirit. We just avoided the heaviness and the dark vibe of *Hemispheres*, a total reaction to the darkness of that period." On a musical note, Alex has remarked that his solo on the song, occurring during a 3/4 time break — with Neil shuffling feverishly and Geddy firing off gnarly distorted licks — is one of the most challenging for him to play.

Lyrically, "Freewill" (curiously rendered as one word) is championing atheism, with artful, succinct yet direct shots at belief in various gods. The arguments for and against atheism are many, but here the focus is on the concept of free will, the idea that man has control over and responsibility for his actions. It's an extension of Neil's core beliefs as expressed across earlier records. And this song features one of Neil's most celebrated lines — from what in aggregate are some of his best lyrics — namely, "If you choose not to decide, you still have made a choice." Interestingly, the original version of that line was "If you choose not to decide, you cannot have made a choice," which was already gone by Varsity Stadium. This of course expresses an opposite meaning and might be read as a denouncement of agnosticism as dithering.

Next up is "Jacob's Ladder," a gorgeous and artful prog rocker, ominous of melody, somewhat more in the spirit of the *Hemispheres* album. Synths are prominent but sensibly woven into what is a typical expression of the band's "progressive metal." Concerning the succinct and exquisite lyrics, Neil told *Modern Drummer* that the band "built a whole song around a picture. We wanted to build a song around the phenomenon called Jacob's Ladder, where the rays break through the clouds. I came up with a couple of short pieces of lyrics to set the musical parts up. And we built it all musically trying to describe it cinematically, as if our music were a film. We have a luminous sky happening and the whole stormy, gloomy atmosphere, and all of a sudden these shafts of brilliance come bursting through and we try to create that musically."

Adding meaning past playing weatherman, Neil ends his brief poem with the idea that man can take inspiration from the beauty of this phenomenon. Indeed, the name "Jacob's Ladder" comes from an Old Testament story of Jacob seeing angels ascend and descend these shafts of light between heaven and earth. There's a subtle continuation of the debate started on "Freewill" there, with Neil essentially hijacking a scriptural concept in the name of humanism. Neil recalls Geddy's mother using the term, and he's also intimated that the lyrics were almost secondary to the concept and challenge of the music, as if added later to underscore the painted picture. Indeed starting at 7:28, there's a long passage of music without a vocal and a dramatic build in tension up to the last vocal, evoking similarities to the guitar solo section in "La Villa Strangiato."

Over to side two, "Entre Nous" is another of the record's more conventional songs, a sort of mid-paced, even poppier amalgam of "The Spirit of Radio" and "Freewill." There are Styx-like synths, and Alex is busy building his narrative as a guitarist who will switch between electric and acoustic on a dime, on top of his propensity to layer them atop each other. Another nice touch finds the band playing a verse at half-time, Alex changing it up by switching from the jazzy power chords of the first go to picking the individual electric notes. Later there's an ebullient, sublime break section, over which Geddy applies one of his languid synth "solos."

Neil's "Entre Nous" lyric is yet another triumph on this record. Here it becomes apparent that arguably, the main advancement of the band with *Permanent Waves* wasn't this surface idea of no side-long songs, but a coming of age for Neil as a lyricist. He tackles relationships, repeatedly coming up with metaphors for the distances between two people, while searching for some sort of potential positive outcome, that "the spaces in between leave room for you and I to grow."

Comments Alex on "Different Strings," the next track on the album: "There's usually one song per album that is produced in such a way that we'll never play it live. 'Madrigal' is one of those; so is 'Different Strings.' There are some good songs on that album. 'Natural Science' is one of my favorite songs to play live, at this point. 'Jacob's Ladder,' 'Entre Nous.' And 'Spirit of Radio' and 'Freewill'; those are really two Rush classics."

"Different Strings" is the record's lone ballad, and the simplest song on the album, but as Alex alludes to, it is produced with a few extra textures, including synth and piano, the latter courtesy of Hugh Syme. Essentially, however, it's vocal, bass, drums and acoustic guitar. Lyrically, this one is Geddy's alone, and it's easy to draw comparisons in that respect to *2112*'s "Tears." It drills down further past "Entre Nous," into the subject of commonality in a relationship. Structurally, there are basically two parts: verse and chorus, and an atmospheric, bluesy fade section that is nearly a quarter of the song, featuring spare electric soloing from Alex. A request from Terry Brown to Neil with respect to making a tempo change on this one went over like a lead zeppelin — the song remained as worked up before Terry was brought in.

"There was always one song they used to do in those early days that wasn't intended to be played live," says Paul, although, contradicting Alex, he thinks on *Permanent Waves* that song would have been "Natural Science" (note: Paul is wrong here and Alex is right). "This is so they could layer things and play parts they wouldn't be able to reproduce because there would be too many different parts. They'd go, 'Okay, we don't care whether we can play it live or not. We're just gonna go for it, just do what we feel like doing.'

"Geddy always had this sort of battle, wanting to just play bass, sometimes even not wanting to sing. And I could sense that — because I mixed a number of live albums of theirs. When you listen to his bass playing, the difference between the power and the force of his playing when he's not singing versus when he's singing is noticeable. And not surprisingly so. Because once you're trying to sing, you're concentrating on your phrasing and your vocals. Obviously, your bass playing tends to follow the vocal. Whereas as soon as he stops singing, he goes back to digging in much harder. And he's an aggressive bass player; part of his sound, as he always used to say, comes from fret buzz, and to some degree a bit of overdrive. Which is not so noticeable these days because people use overdrive on bass guitar a lot more than they used to."

Permanent Waves closes with a nine-minute prog epic that tackles everything from the randomness of the universe to man's effect on the world, Rush perhaps presaging today's concerns about climate change. Both part one, "Tide Pools," and part two, "Hyperspace," address this theme. Late in the sequence, following increasingly urgent musical passages, we arrive at part three, "Permanent Waves," and the sense of melody becomes triumphant. Hope is expressed for science, art and the honesty of man, which brings us back to the moral of "The Spirit of Radio," past the reminiscing. However, at the end, the message is more that of "Freewill," with the inexorable quakings of the universe ultimately sweeping over Earth like an ocean wave erasing the accomplishments of man and other life-forms — natural science.

Essentially then, Neil has ended the record with the start of the record. Not only is the last four-minute "song" the title track, but it recycles, in order, the truths of tracks #1 and #2, first how both creativity and honesty matter, but then how, in the end, nothing matters. Underscoring this is the fact the song both opens and ends with water sounds, but at the beginning, man is clearly there — that's Terry and assistant Kim Bickerdike making splashing sounds with oars — and at the end, it's just roaring surf.

Reflects Neil on "Tide Pools," "It's lost on musicians, a band, to be able to go away to a place like this where they eat, sleep, drink, work. When I think of the lake, it's boating around the lake and skiing around the lake in the winter, and the volley-ball games. Down in that lake we recorded the intro of 'Natural Science,' called 'Tide Pools,' with an oar. I remember we ran a mic cable all the way down to the water.

"There was a raft out on the lake. They put my drum kit out there for a Tama ad, and it was a big cloth banner — it's very collectible now, I think. But people said, 'How did you do that?' Well, the raft happened to be exactly the same size as my drum riser in those days, probably 4' x 8', standard plywood. And we used a rowboat and paddleboat, and we took the drums out a piece at a time, and pieces of the drum boards, and set it out there, and I played and we recorded it too. Somewhere there are tapes of that. We recorded it from the shore, just to get different effects that someday, you know, you might use, because I was doing it anyway. It was done just on a lark, really."

To clarify, it was something that took place the following year, with the photo shoot handled by regular Rush photographer Deborah Samuel.

Terry remembers this fondly as well, saying, "The lake was surrounded by a mountain on one side and a hill on the other side, so when you fired something off, it just came back seconds later with a huge reverb response. I thought the drums would sound amazing. I wanted to record the whole band out there, but it would upset the neighbors. We got the drums set up on the floating dock. It just fit — you know Neil has this big kit, and his stool was right at the back of the floating dock. Right on the edge. We got him out there in the boat. He gingerly climbed out and sat at the drums. I heard later that he was not happy."

"That's one of my favorite songs," says Geddy of "Natural Science." "It's one of those songs that kind of went away in our live show for many years [note: it was played on the *Moving Pictures* tour but not again until the *Test for Echo* tour]. And when we brought it back, we changed the arrangement a bit. There were things in the arrangement that were a little shortchanged in the original song. Like in the second part for the main 'wheels within wheels' part. It's not a traditional song; there's no real verse/chorus/verse/chorus, but I remember certain melodies that I felt deserved to appear more than they did, and I thought it would give the song more resonance. So we did those things, and the last section is made shorter than it was in the original version. I felt we had kind of overdone it on the record. So sometimes there's that opportunity to fix a mistake or an arrangement that may be shortchanged in some way. And I think our current version live is the best we've ever played it."

Notes Paul, "One of the really exciting parts of 'Natural Science' is that middle section, which is guitar with the bass side by side, an octave apart, playing the same riff. Geddy with the growly, aggressive bass tone and Alex with a power guitar, you know, riff sound. And when you're doing that, you're so far up the neck that everything — half of the sound of what's involved in an arrangement for a rock band — is gone. So you have to use all of these tricks. I think Geddy probably decided early on that he liked the opportunity of not being restricted to holding down the bottom end, to being big and fat on the bass. I can play something on the bass pedals that keeps the bottom end so it suddenly isn't all missing. And I can play right up the octave on the neck, on the high strings on the bass, and be up there closer to Alex. I think, because of the arrangements, they developed an interesting dynamic. And originally that was very simplistic. It was just one note, one bass note or one single high note. It would have been very easy to do. It would just involve putting the foot on the pedal to hold the root down, whilst you're raging away on the bass. It wouldn't require a lot of thought."

"Natural Science" is probably the most *Hemispheres*-like track on the album, musically speaking and arguably lyrically. A number of time signatures are utilized, and the multipart structure is very prog. In fact, some of this music was to be used with an even proggier lyrical theme from Neil. He had originally planned to write a song based on *Sir Gawain and the Green Knight*, which might have opened him up to all manner of ridicule. Better instincts prevailed, and instead we got a bank of lyrics that were head and shoulders above any of his previous wordsmithing.

Continuing the legacy of U.K. scribes being on board with Rush, Malcolm Dome reviewed *Permanent Waves* for *Record Mirror*. After remarking that it was the first Rush album to be made in Canada in four years, he says, "Happily, however, a change in studio setting doesn't mean a change in musical direction, as Geddy, Alex, Neil and co-producer Terry Brown (almost the fourth member of the band these days) deliver a set of six modern, battle-hardened epics which exhibit enough technical proficiency to satisfy Yes fans, contain sufficient lyrical talking points to win over Floyd freaks, yet never become overbearing or stifling. I strongly recommend those who think intelligent heavy metal is the figment of a half-crazed reviewer's warped sense of humor to get hold of a copy of the album and surprise their ears. If they don't do anything for you, then go back and wallow in the sounds of boredom from Genesis and The Eagles. You deserve nothing better."

The *Permanent Waves* tour commenced in mid-January of 1980, preceded by a warm-up tour in August and September of 1979 called Semi-tour of Some of the Hemispheres. Acts opening on select dates included Blackfoot, Streetheart, New England and FM — like Max Webster, these Canadian progers were also somewhat of a "baby Rush." At the tail end, in the U.K. for two shows at New Bingley Hall in Stafford, the guys reacquainted themselves with erstwhile drinking buddy Brian Robertson and his new band, Wild Horses. Support on the 1979 dates came most consistently from the Pat Travers Band, who had played with Rush on the two previous tours as well.

"Yeah, I loved Pat's style," says Alex. "It's a really blues-based style of playing, but he was a super-confident guy, to the point of being cocky. I was really impressed. You know, not so much in the last so many years, but I used to be very self-conscious and a little lacking in self-confidence. When I watched guys like him, it was like, 'Oh, I wish I had the balls to just go for it.' I didn't always feel like that about my guitar playing specifically. I felt there was so much more to improve on. Yeah, I'd go and watch him, and we got along really, really well with the whole band; Tommy Aldridge, great drummer. He and Neil got on really well. He was a lot of fun to be with."

"That was one of the things we liked about having an opening act," seconds Neil. "We always liked to have a good opening act, and we got things off to a high standard. And certainly, I liked having good drummers to work with, which we often did. Tommy Aldridge, wonderful drummer; I always liked watching him. And again, having that caliber of band on the same show was much nicer than having a not good one. We had Rod Morgenstein with the Steve Morse Band on one tour. In the early days there was Gary McCracken with Max Webster, Marty Deller with FM and later on, Herb [Tim Alexander] with Primus."

The *Permanent Waves* tour proper spanned six months, January through June of '80, throughout the U.S. and Canada (conspicuously with no Ontario dates). June found the band playing England — nineteen nights out of twenty-two — with no trek to continental Europe included this time out. Support for the tour came most substantially from Max Webster and 38 Special, with new wave of British heavy metal stalwarts Quartz called up for duty in England.

Back home, manager Ray Danniels was pleased that the new record "made them more competitive. There were more doors open. We were going to bigger venues in some markets. We were in arenas in some places. There was definitely momentum, but there has always been momentum with Rush. Rush had records that didn't sell as well as previous records, but when those records weren't as big, we didn't simply go, 'Oh, we can't play the NBA or the NHL arenas anymore; we've got to go back to the theater.' It wasn't that kind of band at all. We may have done ten or eleven thousand people, where we had thirteen or fourteen before. But pretty much, once we were there, we kept it there."

Despite a couple of songs from the record becoming Rush staples, success on the charts this time out was more about the album itself. *Permanent Waves* reached #4 in the U.S. and #3 in the U.K.

For extracurricular fun while on tour, the band and crew would watch hockey games whenever possible. Alex used to quip that sound check was going to be late if there was an afternoon game on. And if circumstances allowed it, the guys would take over the local rink and play a game themselves, sometimes with real NHLers (former Montreal Canadien Steve Shutt is a friend of the band), and sometimes even taking over the ice at the arena they had just played, trotting out in full uniform for a quick game during tear-down, before driving on to the next city. As well, there were always racetracks and amusement parks, not to mention backstage roller skating. For Neil there were his books — he'd usually devour one every two or three days — and, especially for Geddy, many, many movies, sometimes three a day.

"Different Strings" and oddly "Entre Nous" would not be taken from the album to the stage. "'Natural Science' is always a real challenge to play live," remarks Alex, years later. "There's a lot of intricate, hard playing in it; the tempo's quite upbeat. You sort of step up into it and just go right until the end. So that's always a challenge for all of us. And when we play that well, it really feels great."

Yet again, hometown friends Max Webster were called on to support dozens of dates. Max, of course, was the second most prominent Anthem Records act after Rush; they were produced by Terry Brown and in some respects they were Rush-like. Their lyricist occasionally collaborated on Rush songs with Neil, and keyboardist Terry Watkinson was key in teaching Geddy what he knows about the ebonies and ivories. For Max Webster's final album, *Universal Juveniles*, Rush teamed up with the band on July 28, 1980, and roared their way through the heavy and heaving Max epic "Battle Scar," a song the band knew all too well because Max had been playing it live. In fact, Neil Peart himself was already playing it, having by this time adopted the habit of warming up to the last few songs of Max's set shortly before Rush was to take over.

"Yeah, behind Sticksy," explains Alex, referring to consummate Max drummer Gary McCracken. "There was a scrim that went across the stage. Max was out there. Neil's kit was directly behind Sticksy, and he'd go up and that was his warm-up. He'd go up and play the last few songs with them. I think he might have done it a couple times later with Primus, but it was a nightly thing with Max. We did so many dates with them. In fact, we were on tour when Kim [Mitchell] had had enough and decided to go home. I remember pulling into that gig and all the guys were sitting on the grass, and they looked so despondent. 'What happened?' 'Kim's had enough. He can't take it anymore. He went home.' 'He went home?' 'Yeah, he went home. He was on a flight this morning.' So they were stuck there. And we had taken them to Europe and all over America. They were really starting to catch on in the States too. They were starting to develop a fan base. But I think Kim . . . it's a little much for him, to travel that much and be away; it was a lot of pressure, and I don't think he dealt with pressure that well. I think he was much happier to be here where everything was a given. At least, that was my impression then."

Max photographer and designer Rodney Bowes remembers Neil shadowing Gary in concert. "I loved Neil Peart. Those guys are really the nicest men in the world. There's another example of a band where there's just a real brotherhood there. They're all absolutely lovely, lovely people, like U2 are — they're real. What they would do is they would have Max Webster on the stage, and they would have the black curtain with all the huge Rush setup behind it, right? And Neil used to warm up, not amplified, but right behind Gary, right behind the fucking black curtain. And what he would do is fuck with Gary. So he'd speed up the beat and he'd double-time it and he would play along. But he would just do all of what Gary does. It was like, he used to have to go into this Gary McCracken world and count out loud. And then afterwards, Neil would have a huge smile and go, 'Hey, good, I only made you fall twice.' Gary says, 'You gotta stop doing that!' He goes, 'Nope. It's good for you.'"

"Yeah, at that time, my drums were under a tent on the stage," clarifies Neil about his odd warm-up routine, "so I could go up under there and hang around and listen to the band do the song. And sometimes I would just play along with Max Webster songs. Nobody could hear me, I don't think. I would be backstage and then go in. No one knew I was there. It was a tarp, and it would hang off this rack system I had with all my bells and blocks, so the tarp went over that. I don't think anyone was looking at the covered-up drum set. I remember also, one of their songs had the Max Webster dancing in it, and we used to put weird costumes on and go and dance around the stage for thirty seconds. You would hear the call backstage, 'Come on, it's Max Webster dancing coming up!' And everyone would fashion costumes out of whatever we could find and go up there."

"Battle Scar" is indeed a remarkable piece of Rush history, in that it finds the entire band playing — Geddy singing as well — along with their long-time friends, and not just on any song, but a classic, crunching hard rocker, and an interesting one at that, given its slow sixty-two BPM pace (Rush would soon have their own "slow" hit in "Tom Sawyer").

"That was actually hard to set up, technically," begins Kim Mitchell, on a demanding track that is a concert highlight to this day, played as part of his solo set. "It was a case of getting enough microphones, getting a console large enough, enough channels; all the logistics were kind of hard to work out technically. We opened for Rush, fuckin' forever it seemed, in the States, and it was amazing for us.

"Neil would play drums, every night, to our set. He would be behind a scrim and playing drums. And he said, 'Man, we really gotta record "Battle Scar" together; we should do something like that.' And we always thought, 'Okay, yeah, right, whatever.' So when we went in to do the album, they were like, 'Are you guys recording "Battle Scar?"' And we said yeah. And they said, 'Well, can we join you?' Like, they asked. So it was like, 'Holy fuck, okay.' So we did it all live off the floor, two bands just fuckin' plowing, two drummers; man, it was fun. No headphones, nothing, just amps in the room, like, bleahhh! Let's go! It was pretty powerful. It sounded like six Harley Davidsons in the studio all revving up.

"To this day I'm always correcting people about that song," says Kim. "It's like, no, Rush wanted to do it with us. They asked us — they came down to our studio. There is a lot to be said about the creative process, and how some of it came from Rush, and how a lot of their ideas came from us. There was a point when we were on the road with Rush and they started dressing like us, and their manager flew down and gave them shit. But really Alex started going onstage with helmets on and big flight suits; it was getting crazy. And they took a lot of their attitude from Pye and me."

"Oh yeah, I was there for almost everything in a recording situation, and that one was pretty wonderful," laughs Max Webster lyricist Pye Dubois, who wouldn't miss a rock summit like this one for anything in the world. "What can you say? Max was playing this song live. I think that's why Rush said absolutely. Because they loved the song. You technically don't want to put twenty-four-tracks together, and the electricians did that. A great tune. You know it's going to be heavy. You know it's going to be loud. I have a vague memory of how they set up, on the soundstage. They played together. There wasn't a lot of, 'Okay, Geddy, you go do your part,' and the band would sit there waiting for Geddy to do his part. It was like, set up, 'Okay, guys, play the song.' Live off the floor."

"I had pretty much equal opportunity on all of them to blow," says Gary when asked about the most active drum performances in the Max Webster catalogue, "but when you look at 'Battle Scar,' right, you look at doing that thing with Neil — that's a good drum show right there. If you're going to consider anything a drum tour de force, there it is. That was exciting and it was historical. More than exciting. Because nobody else has ever sat down and double-drummed with Neil on a song. He's only considered the best guy on the planet. So I feel pretty good being the one guy that did jam with him, and we got it on a record.

"First time two bands ever tried to record with two twenty-four-track machines, ever. Jack Richardson brought in two twenty-four-track recording machines and linked them up so they would be in sync. And then they recorded one band on the one machine, and they recorded the other band on the other, and it was unbelievable. We recorded 'Battle Scar' all day. We did like fifteen or sixteen takes. And it was live."

Prompted to indulge in a little comparison with Neil, McCracken figures, "Yep, it's pretty funny that way. Just being in the same sentence as Neil, that's insane. Let alone somebody thinking that maybe you play better than him. It wouldn't be me saying that, but there are people who really like my style. People tell me I'm a musical drummer, I'm a musical guy. And when you're in Rush, you've got three people, so you're going to have more room with the drums.

"When you're in a band like Max Webster, you have to always remember there is that fourth guy who has quite a lot to do with it. There's the keys and the guitar but there's always that extra, that fourth dimension. So when you're playing drums you have to click to that format. As opposed to with the trio, you've got more freedom to go loony. Neil couldn't play like that in a normal band. Normal bands, you just have guys play normal drums with a good singer. But when you play like Neil, it's that environment in Rush, you have to be in Rush to play that way."

To prepare for the session, two weeks prior, Gary had driven out to Neil's rural home in Beamsville, Ontario, where, in Neil's drum room over his garage, they worked out some of the parts they would unleash upon their unsuspecting bandmates, some parts unison, some diverging. Neil recalls driving to the recording session in his black Ferrari 308 GTS and pulling up to Phase One just as an epic thunderstorm struck.

Bassist Dave Myles has fond memories of the "Battle Scar" session as well. "You know, here I am, I traveled with Geddy, we come into the studio, and I thought, 'I'm not going to get into a bass lick shootout with Geddy Lee. I'm just not gonna do it.' I know when to pick my battles. So I thought, 'I'm gonna do the background thing, and I'll let Geddy blow.' And that was a good thing."

"'Battle Scar,' the thing with Rush, was genius," comments Mike Tilka, Myles's predecessor. "And it was wonderful that the guys in Rush did it. And it became a huge FM hit. I personally don't think it's much of a song, but it's kind of neat. The recording is amazing."

"We had the tune together already, without Rush coming in," continues Myles, asked if for such an occasion, the guys figured they would turn it into a party atmosphere. "No, when you're recording like that, you don't party. You're straight and you're clean; you're there to get the best you can get down on tape. And of course, those guys are confident professionals too. Man, I remember when we were listening to the playback, after putting the bed tracks down, we came back in and listened to Geddy wailing. Wow, really great."

And from a business standpoint, it was pretty easy getting the bands together, says Capitol executive Deane Cameron. "That was all done at the Anthem/SRO level, because both bands were there for management. So my recollection was that it almost popped up out of nowhere. I mean, it did and it didn't. I heard what was going to happen. But yeah, it's really handy when you have both acts with the same management company."

Despite management and two bands pulling "Battle Scar" off, as alluded to, it all turned out for naught in terms of Max Webster's career. Kim would soon walk off, moving on to a successful solo career in Canada. Still, Rush's generous gesture of trying to help break Max Webster in the States would have reverberations. Seeing the two Canadian bands out there year after year inspired other Canadian artists.

The example of Rush was instructive: Hit the States hard and never let up. Serve the Canadian bases but be reasonable about it, respectful of the limitations of population bases and the long gas station fill-ups between them. Moxy found themselves regional stars in Texas after Rush had opened that door. This typically started in hard rock town San Antonio and fanned out. Same thing happened for Triumph, another trio, on a bigger basis. April Wine, with many records before Rush, finally found themselves with a career in the States by 1979's *Harder . . . Faster* (recorded at Le Studio) through to its follow-up 1981 album *The Nature of the Beast*, which sold platinum. One could say that Randy Bachman's The Guess Who and his subsequent louder crowd, Bachman–Turner Overdrive, were the first Canucks to break the States, but no one had gotten the response Rush had both commercially and with respect to the love — despite all the complaints about bad reviews, Rush never had any real problems at *Circus* or *Hit Parader*. And *Creem*? They made fun of everybody.

And now, having become at least stable with *Permanent Waves* — as far as the music industry was concerned, the record was one song deep — Rush would be in a position to capitalize. But the guys were not going to sell out to sell up. The next record would prove to be as dense, action packed and intellectually challenging as the one before it. But no one could ever gripe that it was only one song deep.

CHAPTER 2

MOVING PICTURES

"The right time, the right place,
the right song, the right parts."

Pleased with the living/working arrangements for *A Farewell to Kings*, Rush tried it again for *Hemispheres*. Pleased with the living/working arrangements for *Permanent Waves*, Rush tried it again for *Moving Pictures*. Fortunately, the sequel effort this time didn't disappoint, and the guys found themselves more Canadian than ever. Living and raising families in Canada, writing on Canadian farms, recording immersed in the Canadian forest, bridging the divide between English Canada and French Canada, winning Junos and paddling canoes . . . Rush were celebrating everything it meant to be Canadian.

"We went out to Ronnie Hawkins's farm, out in the Stony Lake area," begins Alex, on preparations for the record that would serve as Rush's *Machine Head* and *Paranoid*, or *Fragile* and *Not Fragile*, as it were. "I guess it's just north of Peterborough. He had a really nice little home up there, nice cottage with a big barn on it. We converted the barn into the studio, and set Neil's

45

drums up, and had areas for Geddy and myself. And it was a really nice location.

"We were there in the summer, and everybody was in good spirits. There was a good energy to the work. We started writing there and basically wrote everything in rehearsal there, and then moved into Le Studio later that fall and started recording. There was a real positive energy, not unlike what we went through with *Snakes & Arrows* years later. But at that time, there was just something that was very strong and positive about where we were with that record. I don't want to say it was effortless, but the effort seemed to be very smooth. We had some guests visit, and we had a lot of fun across the whole process. It wasn't just in the studio — it was a really nice place to be at that point in our lives."

The guys were enthusiastic about carrying on the concept kicked off with the last album. "Yeah, it was great, really exciting," Alex continues. "Because instead of one story you had five stories in the same time span, but you could link them with a sentiment or with an idea. A little bit less so with *Permanent Waves* but more so with *Moving Pictures* — that whole idea of a collection of short stories is what we were after and that's what *Moving Pictures* is."

Consensus is that *Moving Pictures* is the record where Geddy toned down his patented high shriek. "I bought it at Kresge's," laughs Lee on coming up with it in the first place. "I keep it downstairs in my studio for when I need it. Lifetime guarantee.

"I think I can still shriek if the music requires it," figures Geddy. "I have no conceptual adverse feelings about it. As the music changed, it became more interesting for me to write melodies as opposed to shrieking. It was basically used for cutting through the density of the music. And sometimes we would write without any consideration for what key we were in in the early days, and I would find myself with twelve tracks recorded in a key that was real tough to sing in, so I didn't have a choice at that point. Re-record the record in a different key or just go for it.

"Alex started getting really heavily into model airplanes," says Geddy, offering further glimpses into Rush's release valves during writing and recording. "It started when we were writing *Permanent Waves*, when we were at Lakewood Farms, in a little farmhouse out of the city. And even Terry Brown got into it. In fact, we had a lot of fun. In August of '80, writing *Moving Pictures*, we were working on Ronnie Hawkins's farm out near Stony Lake, and Alex was really into these remote control airplanes. He would spend hours building them. And of course, they would always go haywire, where they would get up too high, or lose control or something. And I remember, there was one that went completely haywire and ended up crashing and exploding on the top of Ronnie Hawkins's truck, put a big hole in the top of it.

"And then Terry Brown had this fantastic giant one, this giant plane he had been working on. It was so big you had to have this kind of tether so it would fly around in circles. And it had a huge engine on it. And I remember he finally cranked it up and man, it took off! And suddenly, we all had to hit the deck! It was like this charge went out, and everybody is diving for the ground, and poor Broon is holding onto this thing going around in circles. He's going around and around and around [laughs]. Finally the plane ran out of gas and landed, and he basically fell over in the grass. He was completely dizzy; it was hilarious.

"And we continued that at Morin Heights. Alex, and in fact, Tony Geranios, who is also known as Jack Secret, started working on rockets, and we would have these rocket launches, sometimes at dinner, sometimes at breakfast. I remember one time he launched one in the backyard, and the thing just took off the wrong way completely and missed exploding in Alex's brand-new Mercedes by inches. It was always great fun. And Alex got into water planes at Morin Heights, because they had a lake. He would land it in the water and take off from the water."

Notes Terry, on the way the band had been evolving at this juncture, "We went for a bigger sound. But then looking at the instrumentation, there were more keyboards. So the guitar needed to be textured differently. But then we used chorus for many, many years; this was not something new. It was just the way it was used. Alex was always into delays. I loved working with him for that reason. He had all these delays he would put through the amp, so we were always getting these great guitar sounds right through the amplifier — we weren't adding delay afterwards. But yeah, the guitar sound changed, and it needed to change. The material was different. You can't go back in and do the same thing every time. You've got to move forward.

"We were working forty-eight tracks," continues Terry, "and we would cut the drums and some guide guitar and bass parts on one twenty-four and put it away until we were finished, and then put a guide track on another twenty-four-track and then fill it up with all our overdubs. So we didn't really approach it a lot differently than we had before, but there was some magic going on, certainly that day when we loaded in and set up the drum sounds for 'Tom Sawyer,' and it just blew everyone away. It was very, very exciting. It's a hard thing to break down though. It's a combination of the right time, the right place, the right song, the right parts and the energy that was around us at that time. But it definitely has a magic to it."

Geddy explained this process further to CHUM-FM's Rick Ringer: "What it really did for us was we were able to get a bass and drum sound that we like, put it on one twenty-four-track. On one of the twenty-four-tracks we recorded bass and drum tracks, and then we transferred from one machine to a couple of tracks on the other on a fresh piece of tape. And then we took the original bass and drum tape and we put it away so that we would not lose any quality in running the tape over and over again, because the more you run a tape the more quality you lose, the more oxide you lose. This might be getting a little technical but anyway that was the process we utilized, and it enabled us to preserve the bass and drum tracks to as close to the original sound as possible. That was really the whole concept behind this album, to try to preserve the sounds as much as we could, the way they were originally recorded. Because as most albums are done, by the time it gets to the consumer through the various means and methods of tape copying and mixing down onto another piece of tape and dubbing this and that, you end up losing a lot of quality, and so we wanted to avoid that loss."

Moving Pictures also represented another step with respect to the band's use of keyboards. This was an incremental evolution — at this point more textural than anything but still present in greater quantity and quality. "Tom Sawyer" serves as a perfect microcosm of this idea.

"That's right," reflects Terry, "and keyboards were Ged's department; he was always on top of the new keyboards. It was cutting edge, as far as having everything we needed. If we wanted a particular sound, we just needed to find it. Keyboards were already becoming more and more important, and they had been right from the days of *Farewell to Kings*, I think. We had lots to work with in the studio, in preproduction, and parts were now being written specifically for keyboards. I know Geddy was using keyboards to write."

"The thing that was probably the most significant was that the studio had changed," explains Paul Northfield, comparing the recording of *Moving Pictures* to *Permanent Waves*, "because we had just got in a brand-new SSL console, one of the first in

North America. Which, although it's just a recording console, was a step toward a more high-technology approach to recording. The automation on the computer was superior, and we were using forty-eight-tracks. *Permanent Waves* was twenty-four-track. We moved to forty-eight-track, or two twenty-four-track machines locked together. We added more tracks to the drums, more tracks to everything.

"In terms of their mood, I think they were excited to be back. *Permanent Waves* had been such a successful record for them that there was a buzz. They came in fully prepared. Preproduction had gone well, and they'd gotten great stuff. They came in and we did that record in ten weeks, every day, seven days a week, from beginning to end. Recording and mixing. Because they'd had such a good experience before, and also because of the nature of the new console that was in the studio, they decided they were going to do the whole thing then, from day one. I think had the mixing not gone as well as it had, they would have done other things. But they liked the studio environment so much, and we all got along great, so we just did the record and that was it.

"It's only in retrospect that you deconstruct the record and go, 'Well, why was *Moving Pictures* so significant?' And I think it's just a time and place that the band was at musically and where tastes were at. Plus that simplicity and power of the three-piece at the same time as the sophistication, just the right balance between new technology and the raw power of the band. And their more refined song approach and finding it to be a fruitful direction for them. So even though they had some longer songs on *Moving Pictures*, I think the difficult part of the album was technical. At that time, when you did forty-eight-tracks of recordings, you had to lock machines together to do it. All the technology was relatively new and unpredictable, and we had nightmares trying to keep everything together."

As for the increased use of keyboards, Northfield theorizes that "everybody involved in making music was interested in what new things were on the horizon. In retrospect, we see keyboards as being in some kind of conflict musically with the raw three-piece drums, bass, guitar situation. But at that time, that wasn't even the discussion. It may have come later, but in the early days, it was really, 'This is interesting stuff.' There were some profoundly unusual sounds, and when I say profoundly, some of the sounds these keyboards were able to produce had never been heard before. And for that reason alone, we were all excited about it. We were all waiting for the latest, newest toys that we could add to the arsenal. And that was true in the studio and it was true for the band.

"It's only later that you realize maybe there is a pact with the devil. When that technology starts to be more important than the music or the songwriting or the basic performance, then you start to realize there is a place for it. I think the recording industry has matured to the point where we no longer really care what the latest toys are. Some of our favorite toys are old toys that have existed from thirty, forty years ago. But at the same time, we wouldn't be able to make records without some of the new toys, computers being a major part of making music now. But that was just the way it was. We were all waiting for the latest, newest thing, and that became part of the record; very straightforward, really."

Album safely whacked together, it came time for packaging it and putting it in the shops, which in hometown Toronto meant big chains like Kelly's, A&A, Sam the Record Man and Records on Wheels. The cover shot, featuring movers actually moving pictures, was the Ontario Legislative Building at 111 Wellesley Street West. Toronto is the capital of the province of Ontario, and this is the government's front door — it was shot on Sunday when the building was closed. The guys liked the power trio symmetry of the building, consisting of three arches and three pillars between each arch.

We don't see that the scene of the movers is being filmed until we flip over to the back cover. The sense of plush class exuded is very much on par with *A Farewell to Kings* and *Permanent Waves*, with the listener tacitly feeling the quality, also represented by the staunch fonts and the regal red and black theme. The cost of putting together the cover was about $9,500 according to Hugh Syme, and the label was none too pleased, charging back some of it to the band. Hugh was validated when it won him his first Juno for cover art. Years later, it became apparent that the front cover shot was actually a still from a film that was made of the scene (by the crew on the back), when the scene suddenly became animated in a video montage.

At the far left of the image is Hugh's design assistant, Bob King, who was also the model for *2112*'s Starman as well as Dionysus on the front cover of *Hemispheres*. Mike Dixon, the man with the bushy mustache and high forehead, would reprise his role on *Exit . . . Stage Left*; he got involved at the behest of King, as the two were friends. Carrying the Starman painting (ergo King is on the cover twice) is the lead singer of '70s Toronto mainstay Crowbar, Kelly Jay. The model in the Joan of Arc painting is photographer Deborah Samuel, who was also working the session — Neil has acknowledged the tie-in of this painting with the record's "Witch Hunt." Hugh explains he couldn't find a Joan of Arc painting, so they staged the scene over a half-hour session with Samuel, photographing her in burlap with lighter fluid being lit in pie plates in front of her. Another artwork being moved is less serious, one of the famous kitsch paintings of dogs playing poker; the guys chose this simply because it was silly and cliché.

Also a nice touch, the album got custom thematically consistent record labels, as was the case with *Hemispheres*. Also included were artful black-and-white live shots, which perpetuated the upper-crust presentation of the band as seen within *A Farewell to Kings* and on the back of the *Permanent Waves* jacket.

Moving Pictures opens with a song that would go on to become the biggest and boldest of the band's long catalogue. "Tom Sawyer" began life as a synthesizer lick that Geddy would play at sound checks. In its final form, it would be a Neil Peart showcase. Ironically, Neil has to play fast on a very slow song, at least when it comes to hi-hat. His part during the surging, languid verses is notable, but it's his fills on this track that propel this song to the top tier of air drumming classics. "Tom Sawyer" would become a huge hit in no small part due to the drama Peart creates, although really, the track's big hanging chords repeatedly create thespian thrills.

"I love that song, and I never get tired of playing it," muses Geddy. "The fact that it is so popular still just confuses the hell out of me. I love the fact that it begins with such a great backbeat and there's this kind of faux rap part. To me the song is just about innocence more than anything, and I think that comes through. And it still holds up somehow; the slightly inscrutable lyrics still deliver that message to people, and people identify with it and they dig it. And it's got this weird middle part. And if you can get away with that in a popular song ... geez, it's a major victory."

Geddy may love "Tom Sawyer" now, but at the time of recording, the band thought it was one of the weaker tracks slated for the album.

"The drum part for 'Tom Sawyer' — infinitely detailed — and I played it five thousand times," laughs Neil, who said he was red, raw and aching after the day and a half it took to get the song acceptably down on tape at Le Studio. It never lets up for him; Neil says in particular that his toes were all mashed because he was hitting the bass drum so hard. Alex was all too aware of that, marveling in his playing at the beginning, where it's essentially just drums and synth, and then drums and synth and vocal.

Touring the ruin of the complex, Peart says, "I would be set up over here, and going into it again and again, and the next time I'd add one detail, add a detail, relate this detail to the third . . . all those things happened that way by playing the songs over and over again. Nowadays my approach is the opposite, where I go for as much spontaneity as I can. But I was about composition then. And it was, of course, a great way to come up, through composition to spontaneity. But really, we had the idea and we had to all get a good take. And then they might redo bass parts and guitar parts and the overdubs and so on. But the idea was that the basic track was all three of us. So those songs were played over and over again, some of them, and I think those are the triumphant ones."

Neil confirms that "Tom Sawyer" is one of the tougher Rush songs to pull off properly from a drum standpoint. "It's more so due to feel, always, the subtleties of music. The more sophisticated your knowledge and tastes become, then the subtler are the things you're looking for. And there's a fundamental feel thing that I'm always seeking in it and in all songs. It's the reason I keep listening to live tapes on days off on the road, to make sure I'm nailing that tempo. A small shift in feel affects everything so much, and I'll hear where Geddy's having to sing that line too fast — I should pull the tempo back a bit and let it breathe. There are subtleties like that that are hard-won, to nail that every night onstage.

"A movie called *The T.A.M.I. Show* is one of my earliest influences, from '65. It had everybody from Chuck Berry to James Brown to Lesley Gore to the Beach Boys to the Rolling Stones, who headlined. And I noticed the bands with their own drummers playing live on TV, they're all a little bit speedy and the singers are getting a little breathless. It's subtle; I don't mean that everything was raging fast. But it was just on edge. Whereas, Hal Blaine, who played in the orchestra that was backing up all the singers . . . the tempo was just perfect, just laid right down, you know? So there's a hard-won mastery of a guy like Hal Blaine who can do that, all the time, anywhere, as opposed to seeking that and trying to achieve it, recognizing it even, those kinds of subtleties. It's that kind of a subtle, overall consistency in the feel that I'm looking for.

"To me, a lot of it is ambition that makes me accomplish things," continues Neil. "The drive factor. I really want to play the drums, so I'll put the time in it takes to play the drums. I really want to write a book, so I'll spend a year writing a book, and make it the focus of my life and reward of its own, a daily satisfying work in progress. It's a matter of character. Once somebody said, 'No failures of talent, only failures of character.' Those are character issues."

The "Tom Sawyer" lyric is wonderful, the definition of enigmatic, as Geddy says, "slightly inscrutable," and incidentally, a cogent precursor to that of "New World Man." It was the first collaboration between Neil Peart and Max Webster lyricist Pye Dubois, and it paints a piecemeal portrait of an edgy, cynical outsider who just may have found some good within himself.

The working title of the piece before Pye handed his bits over to Neil was "Louie the Lawyer." "Pye's method is that he just kind of sends me pages of scribbles and I impose order on them," says Neil. "So it's a perfect meeting of personalities, in that he dwells in an imagistic universe and an impressionistic universe and expresses it as such, whereas I live in a much more ordered universe and impose that structure and rhythm and parallel construction on it. I think right from that foundation, it's a collaboration of personalities, as much as it is of words. For example, I'll start with the way he set up the framework for a song like 'Force Ten,' and I'll respond to that. I'll start creating images in his voice, as it were, just because that's the character of the piece. And I adapt it like a language. I translate my thoughts into his kind of images or his images into my kind of language, and it becomes a kind of interwoven, interpersonal collaboration."

"I think we do the song injustice if we start to pick it apart," demurs Pye. "It doesn't make any sense. It was just two people painting a picture, wasn't it? The original was 'Louie the Lawyer,' sixty, seventy lines or something, very typical of what you see here," Pye says, stopping to show off his journals. "I had this idea, had 'Louie the Lawyer' at the top of the page, and I was just writing these lines. Here was 'Louie the Lawyer,' and over here was maybe 'All We Are.'"

Pye confirms the handover happened when the two bands got together to work on "Battle Scar." "Yes, that's where it started with Neil. But it wasn't, 'Oh my God, I hope Neil wants to read this.' We were just in the studio hanging out. It may have just been a simple social situation of Neil saying to me, 'What are you writing there?' Or me saying, 'Hey, Neil, wanna hear this line?' It was very innocent. It was never meant to be a song. All I can say is there were four or five minutes of, 'What are you writing?' 'Well, I'm writing 'Louie the Lawyer.' And Neil said, 'Well, that's nice.' He probably didn't mean all of it's nice [laughs]. There were probably just a couple of ideas in there he liked.

"There was a lot of editing before I gave Neil a new 'Louie the Lawyer' version," continues Pye. "It never came back to me. It was 'Louie the Lawyer,' when I gave those pages to Neil, and then it was 'Tom Sawyer' all of a sudden. He didn't like 'Louie the Lawyer.' It was completely different. Well, not completely. It was the same with respect to some of the lines I had written. I had just grabbed lines from the original that I thought were nice. I don't remember putting them in any kind of order. In some respects, that's how we wrote songs subsequently too. I would have the general idea, but I would have it very modular. I would just change the syntax or the verb, and it shows up in a new form.

"But the original was, I'm sure, eighty lines. Those eighty lines didn't go to Neil. I might've given him twenty-five or thirty lines, and two or three versions of the one line. And then it came back to me in finished form."

Pye says of the finished classic lyric: "There is a wonderful, steely Rush sense to it. It's a bit ambiguous but hard-edged. If you use the word *government* in a song, you open up the door to feedback, in that you're making a comment, a political statement. Or a comment about politics. I think the lyric really speaks for itself. 'Today's Tom Sawyer, today's warrior.' Tom Sawyer had his own battles back then, probably just the waves in the river and the marsh. And I was young enough then to have people in my life that were lost and confused with things in our culture, or with the way their life was going. It was a fight or flight kind of experience growing up at that age. You know, how do you not buy into the system, or how could you be different from the system? That's all."

Though Kim Mitchell at times has offered a different version of the "Louie the Lawyer" / "Tom Sawyer" story, implying a little more forethought, Neil recalls the situation much the way Pye explains it.

"I saw real love and respect," recalls Max Webster manager Tom Berry, on the interaction between Rush and Max. "And the 'Tom Sawyer' thing, I remember when that went down. I know that Neil always respected what Pye did with lyrics. And I think, actually, the band wanted to work out a tune with Pye, and there you go, they did, and it's one of Rush's biggest songs."

Geddy speaks of his own necessary collaboration with Neil regarding phrasing, turning Neil's musings into something rhythmically sound and linguistically possible within the context of the song at hand. "I just think the style changed over the years," Geddy says. "But it's not quite as simple as that. In the early years the music was ambitious and adventurous and, yes, sometimes the lyrics were unwieldy, but it didn't seem to be a problem in the context of the bombast we were throwing together. But of course as songs became more melody-oriented and less of a furious onslaught, the requirements lyrically and melodically changed as well. Neil's great to work with in that regard. After the first draft of lyrics are given to me, obviously I have to shape them into a melodic thing. And I have to feel comfortable with them. And if I don't sound comfortable, it's obvious. So the two of us have always worked closely."

Terry recalls the magic that happened with "Tom Sawyer" once the band presented it at Le Studio. "Morin Heights is a beautiful environment and it suited the boys because they don't get distracted. I was talking to other bands that went to Morin Heights, and all they did was party their brains out and then make the record in the last week — and it sounded like it. Whereas with Rush, we would start day one and we would work. 'Tom Sawyer' was cut on the night we loaded in. We were all excited about this new tune, the new drums and getting started on this five- or six-week journey. We were all blown away with the drum sound and we just cut the track.

"Everything would be perfectly in place from the time we kicked off, say two in the afternoon, which was their usual start time. We worked from two to two every day. If it was vocals, Ged would be there and he'd be ready to sing. We'd vet parts as we went through it, but he would know the songs. I have had artists that would come through and they'd sort of look at me like, 'What am I doing?' But Rush were always hard workers.

"Obviously 'Tom Sawyer' was an amazing song and has a real signature sound to it. We mixed it digitally. I know that doesn't really change the fact that the songs and the material on that album have a certain sound to them. But we did take that step, and I think it made a subtle difference to the way things sounded, to the way the drums sounded. I finally felt I had gotten the drums captured optimally. Which we'd done really well before, yet there was just something subtle about the way the drums and the bass and the guitars projected on that record. When you listen to the record they did after me, *Grace Under Pressure*, it was done in an analog way and has a completely different sound to it. So, you know, we had something on *Moving Pictures*."

Neil spoke to Jim Ladd back in 1981 about the song. "There's a lot of different ingredients in that song lyrically. It began as a song by another writer, a friend of ours who writes for a group called Max Webster. His lyrics we've always admired very much, and we have a close working relationship with that whole band. So he gave me this song and suggested it might be suitable for us. I added a certain amount of rewriting on it and it came out to be 50/50 his and mine. The stance of it does definitely have a modern day's rocker persona about it.

"It always surprises me how certain songs tend to become more popular than others," continues Peart, "and you can never predict the ones. It was always one of my favorite songs, right from the rhythm track of it, because that's the part I really liked. And that song exemplifies a change in our writing style that we've tried to institute on this album. We've tried to write more from the standpoint of rhythm; we'll establish a rhythmic feel that we like and work the musical changes around that. In the past we would often find a musical pattern we liked and then work rhythmic changes around that, which made the strata of our music very much different in that respect because there'd be shifting rhythms all the time, and it gave the music a certain twitchiness. 'Tom Sawyer' is an example of a really steady, confident song."

Asked about his favorite Rush song, Neil's father, Glen, picks this one. "I like a couple of the old-fashioned ones, of course, but especially 'Tom Sawyer,' which really gets the audience going whenever they're at a concert. Plus a couple of their older songs that everybody knows all the words to. I really enjoy those songs because you've heard them so often, they feel like old standards now.

"Funny story, when I went to the local dentist in our town here, when I gave him my name, he said, 'Would anybody in your family be a relative that's a drummer?' And I said, 'Well, yes, there happens to be. Our oldest son Neil was the drummer in Rush.' And he said, 'Well, do you want to hear my Rush stories now or at your next appointment?' And I said, 'No, let's hear them now.' And he had actually studied Rush lyrics and was given one of Rush's songs in a class project. He said their teacher was a Rush fan and he took the lyrics of one of Rush's songs and he said, 'Now I want you to study these lyrics and I want each of you to give me the impression of these lyrics.' And I've heard that story more than once. Maybe it was more academic than Betty and I were into, I don't know, but obviously there was a point there where people were reading what he had wanted into these lyrics."

When informed that Neil has called "Tom Sawyer" his favorite song to play, Glen says, "Oh, is it really? Well, that rhythm gets me going. I'm surprised to hear him say that because I never knew that. I guess that's one thing we're thinking alike on."

Next up on *Moving Pictures* is "Red Barchetta," an exquisite little futuristic story, not so much science fiction, but Orwellian fiction like *2112*. It seems it's not music that is outlawed in this one but cars, which, in the days of fees to enter the city, speed-limiters placed on trucks (and now Volvos) and self-driving cars, no longer seems too far-fetched. The Rush guys have always had a weakness for fast cars, and so this is right up their "one-lane bridge." It's not clear if the "gleaming alloy air-car" that swoops over the mountain is in fact the authorities, but it's probable. Still, it's nice to hope it's merely another auto enthusiast driving a sanctioned car that has just buzzed by to admire this ancient ground-and-pound Barchetta.

Neil's tale was inspired by "A Nice Morning Drive," a short fiction story by Richard M. Foster that appeared in the November 1973 issue of *Road & Track*. In the story, the car is an MG, but Neil chose to go with a Ferrari 166 MM Barchetta, which Geddy pronounces wrong. In 2007, Neil wrote about meeting Foster (he had tried to find him in 1981 but to no avail) and discussing motorcycles, in an article called "The Drummer, the Private Eye and Me."

At the musical end, like "Tom Sawyer," "Red Barchetta" lays down a solid, headbanging 4/4 foundation (with a few added and missing beats here and there). Essentially this is a vigorous, melodic hard rock workout along the lines of "Freewill," "The Spirit of Radio" or this record's "Limelight."

Alex told radio legend Redbeard that the intention with "Red Barchetta" was "to create a song that was very vivid so that you had a sense, if you listen to it and listen to the lyrics, of the action. It does become a movie. I think that song really worked with that in mind. It's something I think we've tried to carry on — become a little more visual with our music — since then. But that one in particular was very satisfying. It was always one of my favorites. I think it's probably my favorite from that album. I like the way the parts knit together. I like the changes. I like the melody of the song. I love the dynamics of it, the way it opens with the harmonics and creates a mood, then gets right into the driving, right up to the middle section where it's really screaming along, where you really feel like you're in the open car, and the music's very vibrant and moving. And then it ends as it began, with that quiet dynamic, and lets you down lightly. It picks you up for the whole thing and drops you off at your next spot."

What Alex says there is very much in keeping with Geddy's stated concept for the whole album, that each song is like a short film, hence the title *Moving Pictures*. "Red Barchetta" was not issued as a single, but because of the ensuing popularity of the album and the radio-friendliness of the song, it become an airplay staple from the record, along with the rest of side one.

"YYZ" ranks as one of the most popular rock instrumentals of all time. It even garnered a Grammy nomination, which is no surprise, as it's clever, humorous, an air drumming classic and mercifully short. Plus it's energetic and electric — this is the work of a power trio, a progressive one at that, getting to the point and staying on point. Bass players especially love it because Geddy really gets to blow, sometimes in unison with Alex's riff but most of the time peeling off riffs, licks and fills that are every bit as central and hooky as anything Alex is doing.

As Geddy explained to CHUM-FM's Rick Ringer, "We wanted to do a short instrumental. After we did 'La Villa Strangiato' on *Hemispheres*, we really enjoyed working in an instrumental framework, so we wanted to do a shorter, more concise one for the past couple of albums, and we decided that now was the time to do it. Basically it's a rhythmic tune. It was written by Neil and myself, by and large, and was just a lot of rhythmic ideas that we'd had floating around. We tried to emulate the feel of an international airport, namely Toronto International, 'cause that's the one we fly out of all the time. The opening of the tune starts with this very bizarre rhythm, and all that is is the Morse code for YYZ translated into bass, drums and guitar. So we threw a lot of different little things to emphasize some of the different moods of the airport. I mean an airport is sort of a door to many, many places. That's basically what the tune is about."

"I always felt we were moving forward all the time," comments Terry, on the idea of doing songs that were outside the norm, if Rush even had a norm. "And it was only one or two tunes; it wasn't the whole album. 'YYZ,' for instance, is a whole different kettle of fish. That was an exciting song to work on, plus it was instrumental and something totally new. We hadn't done one of those for some time, a number of years. So it was only a part of the whole. I could live with that."

"'YYZ' is an interesting test case in quite a few different ways," reflects Neil, "and in ways that resonate forward. Because often our most troublesome songs are the instrumentals, because we want so much out of it. We used to joke, we just took our leftovers at the end of writing the songs and put those into an instrumental. Which is partly true. Of course, there was a part we loved, and we decided, okay, we love that riff, but it doesn't belong in this song, take it out. And then it would bother us.

"I have that with lyrics. My scrap yard. Things that I hate to set aside, but I save them. And these were things we would save and stick together. But the defining thing was that all three of us have to love it. In everything we do. So an instrumental can be quirky, it can be highly technical, but all of us also want it to be textural and made up not of a bunch of pieces. I think 'YYZ,' if you compare it to 'La Villa Strangiato,' is definitely more compact and more tightly arranged. Because we were learning. That's one of the biggest things about that *Moving Pictures* period: we were really learning about arranging and really spending a lot of time on it, becoming more concise and more deliberate about that aspect of what we do. 'YYZ' definitely benefited from that.

"And it had an overall theme, with the YYZ rhythm at the beginning being the Morse code. We were flying into Toronto, and I heard that Morse code beeping, and I thought, hmm. So I thought that would be an interesting rhythm. And then we took the theme of airports, so there's some exotic character to the music, deliberately. There's the big sweeping, emotional middle A part, which is like the joy of reuniting, or the sadness of being separated. All of that was deliberately put in there.

"Then there's the other stuff like the bass and drum interchange. That was so much fun, when we designed that, when we would trade the patterns, and I said, 'You go first.' 'YYZ' is a perfect example of the way Geddy and I work together. And I kinda think there's three ways it comes about. One is direct communication where we talk about things. He'll say, 'Okay, I wanna do this little figure; it would be great if you could nail that for me.' Or I remember like in the song 'Force Ten,' I was cutting short accents. He says, 'This particular accent, I want to let the note ring, so, boom, don't jump in.' And we would talk about things like that.

"The other kind is paying attention. Listening to each other. And I'll hear him hint at a figure and then I'll jump on that. Then maybe the next time we play it, I'll hint at something and he'll hint back, and then we'll soon have built a little figure out of nowhere. So I can always nab that inspiration for where that came from. The two of us were exchanging things, and again, just playing it over and over again. You know, working out those little details together. And Geddy is very responsive to little figures like that. He loves them as much as I do. And if I put a little kick in somewhere, or a little off accent, he's all over that, with pleasure, same thing. I was thinking about the first time we ever played together, like in the auditions in July of 1974. I can remember him across the little rehearsal room with his eyes closed, just into it. And that's one of my first and fondest memories of the relation that we would build, you know, sensing that he was so inside what he was doing. And that's me too.

"The third is almost telepathic. There's sometimes we look at each other, 'How did you know I was going to do that?' Or a song like 'YYZ,' again, there's so many little decorations and the fills don't repeat and the choruses, for example. That was a big thing for both of us at the time. Don't play the same thing twice. Well, why should you? There's lots of stuff to play. Repetition has its value, and it does appear in that song, with the power of the choruses coming back. Repetition is a tool, but it's also too easily abused. There's no reason why I have to play the same drum fill in three choruses, where I've got two other perfectly good ones.

"There's also the building aspect that both of us are really into. Because I think both of us are a bit organizational in that sense. And both of us come out of that compositional idea. In recent years, all three of us are becoming much more spontaneous and improvisational. But especially in those times, when we were focused so much on arrangement, the two of us just sometimes looked at each other, were always listening to each other, and then were stopping to talk about it. And so the riffs like that would come through it, they'd become an expression of your personal taste, as this band is so much. You know, what we do is what we like, and we hope you like it too.

"We were trying to please ourselves all the way through, with parts that were technically fun to play," continues Neil, "back specifically on 'YYZ.' It's not just that they're hard to play — they're fun to play. Any young musician knows, as you start gathering new tools, it's not just showing off or demonstrating that you have this new toy — it's really fun. It's really exciting. And there were things I was learning around that time rhythmically, and influences that I was building on, in the construction of the drum fill. For example, the opening drum fill, and the little drum/bass interchange, came from us opening for Frank Zappa, when Terry Bozzio was drumming for them. We had to leave and drive five hundred miles to the next show, so I only saw a couple songs. But I watched Terry doing this stuff, that I know now comes from Miles Davis, from Tony Williams. But at the time, I was like, what is that?! But I was hearing him doing this triplet feel over the time signature and I kind of took that away and had my own go at it. It's nothing like what Terry did, nothing like what Tony Williams did, but it led me somewhere."

Closing side one of the original vinyl is "Limelight," one of the band's most beloved songs, despite it's being about Neil's discomfort with pressing the flesh with fans and industry folk.

But as Peart explained to Jim Ladd, a fair bit of the focus within the lyrics is more about the oddity and stress of the job in general, the presentation of self in front of thousands every night, not just the socializing backstage. Asked by Jim what "the fascination, the real relation, the underlying theme" is, Neil says, "That's coming back to music again. How difficult sometimes it becomes to maintain music as a focus. When you're on the road, for instance, it's two hours of every day that you spend onstage, and the rest of the day leads up to that or winds down from it. And it is definitely the focus of your life.

"When the day gets more complicated, there's more and more demands on your time. Instead of time on your hands, you have hands on your time — I like that! That's the question involved there: you have to put aside all that, and it's songwriting that's important, and that's going to make the difference between feeling good and not feeling good. If I walk offstage knowing I haven't played as well as I can, I feel bad. And it doesn't matter how many thousands of people are telling me it was good — it wasn't. On the other hand when I walk offstage knowing that

I've played well or close to as well as I can, then I feel very satisfied. And it's a sort of peace of mind that nothing can intrude on, negatively or positively. You just feel good about it and you don't need external ratification or external approval for that."

There's an additional subtext in what Neil says. Peart is uncomfortable not only with the fawning but also with just being complimented. I've heard this from many famous people — they become exasperated because everybody always says they played well, the album is great, you killed. It's hard for artists to solicit any good advice or invite blunt criticism. Everybody wants to be your friend, and they won't risk ticking you off. And in the case of a fan interaction, it's usually so brief, the typical course of action is a quick compliment and maybe an expression of connection or commonality. After about a thousand of those, Neil said enough, and left it to Geddy and Alex to do the glad-handing.

Late in the lyrics, Neil says "All the world's indeed a stage." It's as if when that Shakespeare reference was used to title the first live album, it was all happy and with wide-eyed wonder. Now, adding the word *indeed*, Neil's being a bit more rueful and ruminating about it.

"He always was very uncomfortable with the media," says Glen Peart. "He would be much happier sitting here visiting with the group of us. Neil is still very much a sit-down type of guy who likes to talk with people. And unfortunately, a lot of the media people — and no insult intended — tend to be very pushy. Neil can't stand that. I don't think he's ever changed over the years. That's still his personality today and still the way he feels about people who try to push their way into his life. He's uncomfortable with that."

"Most definitely, he is more of a recluse," adds Liam. "He just enjoys his privacy. We're all different in that perspective. Neil may appear to be standoffish or rude to people, but that's not the case. He just doesn't feel obliged to be as open as some people think he should be, or to be as approachable as some people think he should be."

"Neil's a super guy," agrees Terry, "but he doesn't like to be thrust into the limelight when he's not on the stage. But that's his prerogative and I admire that in him."

"That was kind of the turning point for Neil," seconds Alex. "I think that's when he started to really have a difficult time with being on the road, and being in the limelight, obviously. I'm a little, you know, softer in that way." On a more positive note, Alex adds that onstage, "the solo in 'Limelight' is probably my favorite solo to play, and if I feel I've really got the fluidity nailed, then it's very, very satisfying, personally. The whole thing is just very elastic. It's not always easy to get everything to be very circular from one part to the next. But when it happens, it's really a treat. Also Geddy's vocals settled down a little bit. They weren't so screechy and screaming as they were in the '70s. There was a wonderful energy when we made that record. We were still quite young. I guess we were in our late twenties, so there's a lot of positive stuff going for it."

Adds Neil on the music itself, "They were not commercial songs per se. Perhaps only one — 'Limelight' — has verses and choruses in a sort of conventional way. But the rhythm is all off; the other guys are playing 6/4 and I'm playing 4/4 over top of it."

On top of the second use of the Shakespeare *As You Like It* quote, Neil also references the next song on this very record when he writes "caught in the camera eye." In the song "The Camera Eye," the photographer is celebrated, whereas in "Limelight" he's a source of irritation.

Four songs in and, surprise, it's been wall-to-wall hard rock. "It's funny you should say that because I never thought of it quite that way," continues Neil. "They *were* heavier. But the whole attitude was always this, you had to make it fatter and tougher. It was heavy in a very controlled way, I thought. The sounds weren't ugly; they were sophisticated. It's like that balance between progressive and pop — it's all part and parcel of it."

Side two of *Moving Pictures* opens with "The Camera Eye." At 10:55, it would be Rush's final song exceeding ten minutes. Fading in peacefully with piles of synths, Neil soon joins with snare rudiments, slowly building the drama with cymbals, bass drums and toms. Interestingly, Neil admits to being "a bit of a bluffer" with rudiment work, despite appreciating marching band drums.

"The latest equipment tended to drive creativity," notes Paul Northfield, "because it was an opportunity to play with a new palette, whether it be recording equipment or actual instruments. *Moving Pictures* was the first time we had a polyphonic synthesizer, because Geddy had gotten an OBX, which makes its presence felt on 'The Camera Eye' in particular. That was the first time any significant keyboards were happening. There was a piano overdub done by Hugh Syme on 'Different Strings,' on *Permanent Waves*, but that was a guest appearance. In the case of the band themselves, all the keyboards prior to *Moving Pictures* had been just a Minimoog melody line, single high strings and Taurus pedals, which provided a backdrop for a three-piece. Once we got to *Moving Pictures*, the OBX appeared and gave them the opportunity to have more textured keyboard sounds. That was what was current then. That was one big change, although the three-piece guitar, bass, drums dynamic was very strong at that time."

Nearly four minutes of music elapses before we are into the lyrics, placed atop an odd time signature, distinguished by Alex's acoustic guitar strumming. Ascribing to the theme of the album, the song is quite cinematic, expressing the hustle and bustle of New York in the first part, and London in the second. The image of a street photographer freezing the motion is lightly suggested. Underscoring the film theme, the band made use of a crowd sample from the first *Superman* movie. The title of the song is a nod from Neil to John Dos Passos, who used the phrase in his U.S.A. trilogy of fictional works, the third of which is called *The Big Money*, also the title of a hit song by Rush.

As Neil wrote in *Modern Drummer*, "A good example of the principle of editing is the pair of long fills that introduce each vocal section in the second half of 'The Camera Eye.' I wanted something really special and exciting there, but I didn't want it to be organized and prearranged. The only way to capture that spirit of wild abandon is to be that way. Every time we did a take of the song, I would close my eyes to those sections, let go and flail away. This ranged from the ridiculous to the sublime, but I was able to choose the most successful, exciting fills for the finished track. What it really boils down to is that it's always you playing. Editing just gives you the opportunity to choose the very best you can do. A good analogy between playing live and recording in the studio is the difference between talking and writing. When you're writing, you can cross out unnecessary or inaccurate words and replace them or shift them around until you arrive at the essence of what you wanted to say. They are still your words. They're just refined and distilled into their ideal form. In the case of 'The Camera Eye,' I had to go home and learn how to play the 'accident' so I could play it that way live!"

"Witch Hunt" is subtitled "Part III of 'Fear.'" Neil posited three theaters of fear, this one relating to mob mentality, "The Enemy Within" relating to internal sources of fear and "The Weapon" relating to "how fear is used against us." Way up into *Vapor Trails*, there would be a part IV, called "Freeze."

Remarked Peart in the *Moving Pictures* tourbook, "'Witch Hunt' was the winner of the most re-written song award, being very difficult to get a handle on. But our intention had always been to use it as the 'production number' of the album, in the tradition of such pieces as 'Different Strings,' 'Madrigal' and 'Tears.' This frees us from our usual practice of writing as we would play live, maintaining the discipline of a three-piece band. It would serve as a sort of vehicle for experimentation and indulgence. For instance, we would be using Hugh Syme's talents on the keyboards, and my entire drum part was recorded twice (as two drummers) in one verse, while in another, a percussion section was created by recording each sound differently. The introduction was a very strange endeavor, as we assembled a 'Vigilante Choir' out in the snow, and the sound of the 'haunted child' at the beginning. Although the main thrust of our work has always been directed towards its live presentation, it is nice to take a small dose of studio indulgence!"

Poking through the ruins of Le Studio in 2014, Neil explained: "These old, crumbling stairs here . . . on that stairway we stood on a night in early winter and recorded the intro for the song 'Witch Hunt.' And I was the rabble-rouser — 'We're here to protect our children!' — all this stuff. There were a bunch of us from the crew and the studio staff and so on, all standing up on the stairs recording that intro to 'Witch Hunt,' right there." Alex remembers the session as being bitingly cold, soon made tolerable by a bottle of Scotch that was passed around.

Musically, this one is slow and fairly heavy metal of riff, oscillating between anguished and then atmospheric when Hugh joins in on synth. Neil gets to play with how to make a slow track interesting, panning fills between speakers, changing up accents.

Explained Neil in *Modern Drummer*: "Being a cinematic type piece, 'Witch Hunt' also allowed a lot of atmosphere for unusual percussion effects, which I took full advantage of! I emptied my armoury using the gong bass drums, wind chimes, glockenspiel, tubular bells, conga, cowbell, vibraslap, various electronic effects and in one section I double-tracked the whole drum kit. It was fun. The 'percussion ensemble' in the second verse was very interesting to do. When we recorded the basic track, I left that section largely blank, and went back and overdubbed each drum separately. I used different sounds and perspectives on each drum to create the dramatic effect of things alternately being very distant and very near. I also removed the bottom heads of my toms on this track to get a darker, more primal sound."

Moving Pictures closes on a futuristic note, with "Vital Signs" sounding like Gary Numan or Joy Division — a post-punk marriage between traditional heavy instrumentation and electronics. The Oberheim is used to create a sequenced lick that Geddy sometimes mimics on bass, sometimes not. Guitar is used to give the song a reggae twist, as is Neil's slightly Stewart Copeland–like percussive construct.

Writes Neil in the tourbook: "We had purposefully left one song still unwritten, with a view to writing it directly in the studio, as we have had such good results from this previously. Songs such as 'Natural Science' and 'The Twilight Zone' have benefitted from the pressure and spontaneity of this situation, although then it happened by force of circumstances, where now our planning includes a space for no-plan. 'Vital Signs' was the ultimate result. Eclectic in the extreme, it embraces a wide variety of stylistic influences, ranging from the '6os to the present. Lyrically, it derives from my response to the terminology of 'Technospeak,' the language of electronics and computers, which often seems to parallel the human machine in the functions and interrelationships they employ. It is interesting, if irrelevant, to speculate as to whether we impose our nature on the machines that we build, or whether they are merely governed by the same inscrutable laws of Nature as we are (perhaps Murphy's Laws?). Never mind!"

"Usually on every album there's one song we write spontaneously, just at the last minute, and that's the one for that album," seconds Geddy. "And those songs usually end up taking us in a totally different direction, as that one did. It's kind of a precursor for us getting more involved with sequencers. It's a last-minute tune, and I love those last-minute tunes, because you write them and record them in a short period of time and it's kind of minimal brain work. Lots of spontaneity — you just kind of go for it — and it ends up being a lot of fun."

Terry, perhaps because he'd seen it all in the U.K., was not on board with the creeping reggae influence on rock and Rush — see tour mate and fellow Canuck Pat Travers and the ganja vibe applied to his 1980 album, *Crash and Burn*.

"No," laughs Brown. "Frankly, it had been done before. But I think by the time we finished producing the tunes, they did have their own unique Rush qualities. The reggae thing was just . . . The Police were doing it, and doing it really well, and having a lot of success with it, so I wasn't totally convinced it was something we should spend too much time developing. But I think what we did, we did well. It wasn't the mainstream thing; it's just that I wasn't sure it was uniquely Rush and original at that point. I had doubts, but the tunes were good, and it was just a question of massaging these influences into something that was more uniquely Rush. I think we achieved that in the end."

Says Neil, "In 'Vital Signs,' I wanted an electro sound for that one verse of it. So yes, *Moving Pictures* I used electronic snare for the first time; I must have had pads to play that on. Before that, *Permanent Waves* still has a lot of organic percussion on it — no electronics." It's an interesting gesture, which actually serves to make Geddy's and Alex's unison chug sound heavier. Quite amusing really, because it's the most twee of snare sounds, with no hi-hat, electric or otherwise, and just the faintest suggestion of bass drum. By the end of the track, Peart's back on a massive kit, demonstrating what progressive heavy metal reggae will sound like in the future.

Explains Neil, addressing these new musical avenues: "Not to discount the late '70s, because there was so much ferment around us. The fact that we survived that was only because we were young enough. I was a huge fan when I first started to hear Talking Heads, and when I first started to hear the Police and Ultravox and all these new English bands. I loved them. As a music fan, this was now the music of my generation. I was still only in my early twenties then and a huge music fan, listening to new music all the time. So I went with that right away — we all did — and it became a part of our sensibility. Geddy was a big Elvis Costello fan.

"And unlike other musicians a little older than us who went, 'That's just trash. What am I supposed to do, forget how to play?' We wanted to write shorter, punchier songs, but we still really wanted to riff out. We wanted to use the crafts we had developed individually and among ourselves. We didn't see that as mutually exclusive. We could grow into 'The Spirit of Radio' and shorter songs then, after having put together the epics. But electronic music and reggae, that's all the stuff I was listening to, that we were listening to.

"We all had agreed that's what we were going to do. And yeah, that did lead us to *Moving Pictures* where, as I define it, that's when we became us. All the rest of it was great — some of it I'm very fond of and some of the songs we still play and I'm glad we did it that way — but *Moving Pictures*, we rented Ronnie Hawkins's farm in Ontario, worked there on the week and went home on the weekends, very civilized. And now when I look back on those songs, I can remember a lot about how they were born. The emblematic song in that way really is the last one, 'Vital

Signs.' All those other songs, again, we still loved playing them; there's no closed loop on that. 'Red Barchetta' is a joy to play always. It's always hard and it's always satisfying to get it right. But the most different song was 'Vital Signs,' where we used a sequencer for the first time and used a lot of reggae-influenced, ska-influenced beats, and drew upon what was around us. That is the critical part of the band as a synthesizing unit of drawing upon what's around.

"What I learned to do more and more lyrically," Neil continues, "and what we did stylistically, was listen and learn from a lot of other great music. I remember reading at the time Ray Davies saying, 'I never listen to music because it might influence me.' And that's such a weird thing to say. It's weird in the same way as when Eric Clapton said, 'When I heard Jimi Hendrix, I wanted to burn my guitar,' or some trumpet player say that 'When I heard Miles Davis I wanted to . . .' That's so wrong. When I hear somebody great, I want to go home and practice, and you know, not out of any intimidation. It's like, 'That's how good I want to be.' I really do feel like that.

"I remember groups like the Thompson Twins and all these elitist British artsy bands saying, 'Oh, guitar music is dead,'" continues Peart. "You know, nothing against them, but it was a transitory thing. But the pop music of the '80s I loved at the time, as it went through the Trevor Horn phase of orchestrations, and when sampling came along and they could do all these amazing things with production. I loved all that, and some of it even stands up now. And yes it did influence us in a way, but we were still us. We were still basically a rock band and we were still going to use our chops that we won with such difficulty. The intricate stuff was never going to go, but it could be framed differently. As we learned more about arranging, we would admire someone's style in arranging, and we'd be influenced by that.

"I was interested in African music at the time, so I would hear King Sunny Adé — who was a Nigerian artist — and I would bring those rhythms into Rush. That's one reason why there'd be so little solo activity from all of us, because we really get to do everything we want. If I got interested in African drumming or reggae drumming, I could bring it into this band. Or if I got interested in the British New Romantic bands or big band drumming, what have you. If Alex wants to play classical guitar, he can have that. If Geddy wanted to create a keyboard symphony, he can do that. Everything fits.

"So none of us have had the frustration of someone being the songwriter, for instance. It's all collaborative. Everyone feels equally appreciated and equally fulfilled and those are both important. A lot of bands have been torn apart by either a sense of aggrieved lack of appreciation — 'No one appreciates me; they just look at the singer' — or the fact that on the other hand, they had all these songs that no one wanted to make as part of the band. All of those things going on at that time were part of the ferment that kept us healthy as a band. We could be drawing broadly and opening ourselves to all experiments."

"It's the job of every musician to keep their ear to the ground," agrees Geddy. "You've got to learn what's going on, especially if you want to consider yourself to be current, topical. You have to listen, and you have to absorb. I'm still influenced by people I listen to. But there's so much of my own personality in what I do that as I absorb new influences, it just gets swallowed up in our own thing. The Rush sound is established, so now we can bring influences in and shift direction or move here, with it not being very obvious, because our influences are so diverse and sometimes obscure, sometimes not so obscure. But I listen to certain things. Sometimes I hear a vocal phrase and I'll go, 'Fuck, I sang that just the way Björk would.' But nobody's going to make that connection because why would they associate? But I love Björk and I listen to her vocal stylings all the time, so it's natural that it would come out subconsciously. It's not intentional, but your influences aren't intentional generally. So I think it's important to keep your ear to the ground. I also think it's important that it not be obvious."

With "Vital Signs," Rush's quirkiest and most cutting-edge track to date was now in the books, and it was time for mixing. Here, the album experienced a bit of a hiccup.

"We had problems with a bad batch of tape," explains Paul Northfield. "At that time, we were using Ampex tape. At the mixing process, it started to shed oxide. So every time the tape would pass the heads in the tape recorder, on the multi-tracker, you would have to clean the heads, because the oxide would be scraped off onto the heads. And that's a scary proposition because the more times you play the tape, the more it's going to deteriorate. Fortunately, it was only a few reels that it happened to, and we managed to get through the whole process. But it was quite disconcerting and tended to cause huge headaches. I remember the last few days of mixing were torturous with downtime and technical issues with the machines not working, and the tape shedding, and the console playing up — all teething troubles of new technology."

Continues Paul, "I remember Alex and I got profoundly drunk at the end of it. When they were putting the album together, I was completely incapacitated. I was just sitting in the chair the day after we had finished mixing, while it was being sequenced and chopped into order, because I could barely stand. When we were making copies to take home and everybody was packing up, it was pretty intense. It was the combination of ten weeks of twelve hours a day. Aside from the twelve hours a day at work, we invariably played volleyball until sometimes four or five in the morning, to get back into the studio for twelve or one o'clock to start the next day. Nobody questioned the sanity of working twelve to fourteen hours a day and playing two or three hours of volleyball at one o'clock in the morning. It seemed like a good idea at the time, and so that's what we did."

Moving Pictures was an immense success, hitting #1 on the Canadian album charts, #3 on Billboard in the U.S. and #3 in the U.K. The album currently sits at four times platinum in both Canada and the States. Rush had arrived on a grand scale, and that was reinforced by the band's lighting director, Howard Ungerleider, who made the show bigger and more beautiful.

Notes Vic Wilson, co-founder of Anthem Records with Ray and manager of touring duties back at headquarters, "The money went up, and of course the production went up too. We used to produce albums very, very reasonably. But then they started doing the trips to England, and it started to get expensive, but there was enough money to cover it. The show got more intense every tour. The stage show was one of the best out there at that time. We were using aircraft landing lights before anybody. Flash pots too, although everybody had those in those days. But Howard was the best light man in the business. And he did all the lights and road managed the band."

"We were feeling that with *Permanent Waves.* 'Spirit of Radio' was a pretty important song for us, if not all over America, in pockets of America and pockets of Canada and pockets of Europe," explains Geddy, putting the success of the new record in context. "Commercially and as a touring band, our reputation was being cemented and we were becoming a headliner through that. So when *Moving Pictures* came, it just started moving faster. Records kept selling and our audience just kept uniting and we were clearly a headline act then. It was really gratifying. Because we expect failure with everything we produce [laughs].

I don't know whether it's my background, as someone who's torn between being a pessimist and an optimist, or just so many disappointments as a young musician, but you just stop expecting success and expect the worst, and anything you get makes you feel good. It's a very Jewish way to be, I have to tell ya that. I know it's a little depressing if you think about it. But we didn't expect it really, and yet it just kept going. That record just never stopped. There was no turning back after that."

But that didn't mean the band would be accepted by the critics. Neil got into a famous row with *Creem* magazine, and the simmering war just continued. Now there was occupational jealousy to contend with. Not only were Rush ridiculous, they were rich and ridiculous.

"Yeah, I mean critically, we're put in a category of unhipness," reflects Geddy. "And that has prevented us from being overtly mainstream, strange as that sounds. It's also prevented us from getting any real critical acclaim, because the hip factor is really important from a critical point of view, from a writer's point of view. We were designated terminally unhip, and no writer was really going to change his view of that. Now mind you, I've gotten letters from writers since then that said they finally get it. I got one letter recently from an ex–*Globe and Mail* writer who was apologizing for all the bad reviews he'd given us because he finally gets it; it took him a long time.

"So you're saddled with terminal unhipness, and that prevents you from getting mainstream press and mainstream radio acceptance. Our songs were too long to go on mainstream radio, so what the hell are we? We're a touring band that is reaching out to more and more people, yet not mainstream. In Canada, I think we were viewed more as a mainstream band. We didn't have quite the same barriers on radio due to the Canadian content thing — CanCon."

What Geddy is referring to here is the government mandate that radio in Canada play a certain percentage of Canadian content, which was determined by a few factors. Rush checked every box, being as Canuck as they get. This mandate is a spot of ingenious protectionism that allowed many Canadian bands to flourish, though many critics and radio programmers gripe that certain bands don't deserve the attention.

"Our radio was friendlier to Canadian talent, so we got the benefit of that," continues Geddy. "We got the bounce from the CanCon thing. You know, with all good intentions they tried to legislate Canadian music to be more featured, but what it does in essence is feature more successful Canadian music more often, so the successful bands in Canada become more successful due to CanCon, but the smaller artists still have the most difficult time getting in that thirty percent range.

"So you've got a band that's got a different image in a lot of different regions of the world and yet not able to be a kind of collective mainstream band. And it's an interesting point, but in a way, not worth lamenting over. Critics aside, one way to feel comfortably part of the mainstream is ticket sales, and in this department, Rush was certainly a people's band. A people that were trying to better themselves, to learn some stuff. What's wrong with striving from whatever level you are starting from?

"We're kind of our own stream," muses Ged, "and it wasn't the main one, but it was not too far away from the main one. I always like to consider us the world's most popular cult band, in a way. But it all seems to be changing now. We're leaking into movies and magazines, and I think that's just our fans coming of age and now being in positions of power."

And it all started with *Moving Pictures*, says Terry. "That was the record, wasn't it? Certainly, for the mass audience that weren't diehard Rush fans. That would be the record they would mention, probably above all of them. That's the one that really hit radio and became part of the mainstream. It made a huge difference to the way the band was going to progress from there."

But Alex brings us back to the reality of the situation. Fact is, *Moving Pictures* came out at a time when the band was crawling out from under a mountain of debt due to the expense of making their records and then plowing all their profits back into their show. Not only is touring costly and marginal at every level, now the stakes were higher, with as much downside as upside and wilder mood swings between risk and return.

"To say it didn't make a big difference would probably be inaccurate, but at the same time, I don't recall really changing that much. Yes, we got a slightly bigger paycheck, we moved into a bigger van, or into a bus, I think, from a motor home. But we still worked a lot. We were still dead tired by the end of the tour, as ever. It was great to play to full houses and to go that next level up, where you are playing larger venues and filling the place through multiple nights. That was certainly exciting. We were still so young. I'm just trying to put myself back in that time. It was really, really exciting, now that I think about it. We did some really big gigs, Texxas Jam and some of these enormous shows.

"I paid off my mortgage," laughs Lifeson, looking for more good news. "The house we moved into, we had no furniture for two years. I had two kids at the time, so it was nice to get the start of some financial security. I bought a station wagon, I think. As a second car [laughs]. I didn't go buy Ferraris or any of that. But you know, there were six, or maybe four, very lean years. We incurred an enormous debt in that period, touring as much as we were. Because we were losing money every night, and we were being financed by management. I mean, we went a whole year without getting paid, and that was hard. With family, apartment rental, all that stuff — in my case, we lived off our wedding proceeds, you know, wedding gifts that we got, and had five bucks at the end of the week for cigarettes and whatever. You just didn't do anything. You walked to a park and played with the kids — that was what you did. And it was fine, I was perfectly happy, that's just the way your life is.

"But it took us a while to reduce that debt and get on a solid footing. It really wasn't until the end of the '70s that we managed to reach that point. Of course, it felt great, but we were worried. I mean, I bought a house in 1977 with my first royalty check, and it wasn't that big. I used the full amount to put a down payment on a house. We had no money other than our salary, which was quite modest at the time. And I remember we had cases with burlap boxes, cardboard boxes with burlap on it, and we had a little tiny twelve-inch black-and-white TV, and we had a couch in our living room, a kitchen table and a couple of beds. And really, that was it. Two mortgages and worrying that if anything happened, we're going to be in a little bit of trouble. But fortunately, everything worked out fine."

To represent how hard the band continued to tour, Vic recalls getting a pen set from the guys with a little plaque that said, "Can we come home now?" "Yes, my pen set," laughs Vic. "They knew they had to tour, as they knew that's what sold the albums. It was never a problem. Maybe making demands like, 'Okay, we only want to work four days of the week instead of seven.' You know, that's not unreasonable [laughs]. But they were easy to work with."

There were clues that *Moving Pictures* was making a big impact, according to Alex. "Well, we always had good relationships with the promoters we worked with. They became very generous around that time, and so that was one tangible thing you could see — all these gifts. And not that no one does that anymore, but the smiling faces. Crowds had changed. The fans had changed. They hung around the hotels a lot more."

But, says Alex, the press stayed critical. "We were used to the majority of our reviews being negative. Not all of them, but the typical stuff, Mickey Mouse on helium for Geddy's voice."

When you talk with the guys, you really get a sense that the bad reviews ticked them off. At least for Alex and Geddy, since Neil didn't read them. At the same time, Neil was getting into tussles with critics about politics and this very real debate: What constitutes good music? The classic example of this was his back-and-forth in *Creem* about the Rolling Stones. Essentially it came down to whether artists were people who tried really, really hard, like Rush, versus those who wrote songs that obviously connected (otherwise, why talk about the Stones?). In a sense, in this context, Rush was realism and the Stones were abstract art. It's a debate that is impossible to resolve. And yet the public was clearly on board.

"I think *Moving Pictures* entered the charts at #2 or something?" Alex says. "Which was a really big deal at the time. And the record company was quite excited, as management was. But honestly, for us, at the end of the day, we were just on the bus going to the next gig. And that's what counts, or that's what we're focused on. In so many ways, we're still just that little band of some friends that got together. That's what it feels like at sound check when the three of us are just up there goofing around. We might play something, whatever, before we get into the song for sound check, and it reminds me of when we were younger goofing around. That's still that essence of who we are."

Continues Alex, on the new success: "We were still touring as much as we ever toured. We could now take a nicer holiday, to the Bahamas or something, with the kids. But other than that, it didn't really change that much. It's just that some things got a little easier."

Alex eventually got to help out his parents as well. "I don't really like talking about it, but you just feel, certainly with your parents, you try to give them back something. Eastern European parents coming from the war, they are always so focused on feeding their kids and giving them a good home. Money was always an issue. Money didn't become much of an issue after that. Giving is a wonderful thing to be able to do, whether it's a big thing or a small thing. It's very rewarding."

"*Moving Pictures*, in particular, was a godsend," reflects Ray Danniels, clearly remembering the financial relief the album brought. "It was the right place and the right time. When I got the record, Geddy and I, and my girlfriend at the time, and his wife, went to Barbados. I had it on a cassette Walkman, and I listened to that record for a week while we were down there. And my partner and I weren't getting along very well — he wasn't working as hard as I was, and a lot of other things — and I listened to the record, and I thought 'It's now or never.' I came back home, bought him out, and I basically had to start over again."

"They changed," muses Vic Wilson. "Everyone changes. What can I say? They all change. You start making money, things change! Everybody . . . it happens to everyone. They were making the money, and we were all using the same accountant. They didn't like that, and then they got their own accountants. It was all there. Their money was all accounted for."

According to Liam, it got to the point where Geddy started to learn accounting, implying that maybe he didn't think the business was being run optimally. "In the late '70s, Ged and I were sitting around a hotel room on an unusual off day. He had his bass with him and he was practicing, and I think I was just doing up my receipts for the week. And Ged approached me with a novel concept: if I was to teach him how to do the books on the road, he'd teach me how to play bass. And I thought, 'Well, I've always wanted to learn to play an instrument.' I was never satisfied with the one year of trombone I had in high school, which should have been drums but the teacher didn't listen to me. At any rate, for a few days, I think Ged and I toyed with the idea of me teaching him a little bit about bookkeeping and he actually gave me a couple of bass lessons, but that was the end of it all.

"All three guys are that way," continues Birt. "They're all in some ways restless individuals and they're always pushing themselves to the extreme. Geddy got involved more on the business end of the band. It's partly because of a lack of interest from the other two; they'd rather not deal with it. Not truly a lack of interest, but they'd just rather let Ged deal with that side of it, you know, let him deal with Ray, let him push those buttons, just come back to us with answers we like to hear.

"Ged also likes to oversee the big picture of the tour prior to it going out, all the preproduction aspects, dealing with Howard and Alan and the filmmakers to make sure all the elements are there and that they all fit. And also dealing with the sense of humor that all three of them have, sometimes coming up with different prop ideas for the tour. Geddy's had his dryers at certain phases, the vending machines, the chicken rotisseries. There's always something just to make people think, and more so to make them laugh. They all kind of assign themselves roles inside the band. Neil works very closely with Hugh Syme on the album artwork and the credits and that type of thing. Alex is probably the funniest person you'll ever meet in your life. He's just naturally funny. He can put anyone at ease, anywhere. He's the most approachable of the guys if you're just a man on the street coming up to say hi. Alex will sit down and talk, and he's very open. None of the three of them have a pop star personality, but Alex is Mr.

Man on the Street, he really is. They all just take a little niche and it all blends together and it results in an end product."

For Vic, leaving the Anthem mothership was more of a personal decision. "December 1980," begins Wilson. "Our last child, James, my son, was born in October of '80. The two girls, Tanya and Heidi . . . Tanya had just started school and Heidi was two and a half years younger than that. And I just made a choice — step off. Because it's always nice to step off on a high. And that's how I spent the rest of my life. I was there for breakfast and lunch and dinner, with my children. They grew up with their father at home. And I got to go out on all the school trips, because I had a van at that time. I would drive all the kids.

"But I was a lot older than them too," continues Vic. "I had just had enough. I told Ray I was leaving. So we sat down, hashed out a price and that was it. I left. Got in my car, drove home. Left all my furniture there. Not difficult for me at all. It was a business decision. Family decision, I would say, a personal decision. Not many people can do that. And I was fortunate enough to be in that position."

As for how Ray reacted, Vic says, "He had everything then. How would you react? [laughs] He had to get the money together."

Now Danniels was running the show himself. Ray says, "Listening to that record, it was obvious that this was a hit. I was so blown away by that record — as a fan and as a manager, I just knew it. I can't say I knew *2112* would be as big as it was, but I knew *Moving Pictures* was going to be huge. And rock radio had gotten to the point where, for a band who had to fight to find a station in every market, suddenly that was the dominant format in the early '80s. And to use Toronto as an example, there were two stations like that, plus one just outside the city. And in other markets there were two, sometimes three stations we could get played on at the time the band delivered a record that would have 'Tom Sawyer' and 'Limelight' and some of the most successful songs they've ever written.

"And we'd started to get out of the debt from the *2112* era," continues Ray. "It got better, no question; it was night and day. We could do arenas. Rush was not a mainstream act, but Rush was starting to become big enough that there were other acts that wanted to sound like Rush. And there are younger bands coming up that are citing Rush as one of their favorite bands, or one of their influences. That starts happening around that era. So you see a shift. You're not in your late teens anymore; you're suddenly closer to thirty, and you are a man, not a boy, and you're starting to get back some of what you used to get as a fan. You're getting it back from young guys now."

On the other hand, Neil was not as confident as Ray that the album would be a hit. "We didn't expect it to be any more successful than the others," he figures, looking back at *Moving Pictures*. "You never do, you know? Like I said, we loved every record we ever made, but it doesn't mean other people are going to. You hope they will, and you put all that into it, thinking, 'Well, how can people not?' You know, we love this so much, other people should too. You really do tend to see it that simplistic. The upshot of that is, well, when people don't, you don't ever take that for granted again, and honestly I still don't. But the bloom of popularity: where previously if we had done one night in a city, suddenly we were doing two nights in the arena."

Neil essentially makes the point that in 1980 and 1981, Rush was sort of the "it" band, the band everyone was talking about. And it's kind of true. The tail end of the '70s had been kind of fallow for rock and prog — the old decade becoming the new really did represent some kind of demarcation. On the rock side, Van Halen was keeping the flame, AC/DC was renewed and doing well and suddenly, improbably, so was Ozzy Osbourne. There was also the new wave of British heavy metal (NWOBHM), and where Rush fit in this was weird. In essence, they'd run completely the other way from it in terms of influence. But for now, as Ray alluded to previously, they became a prime influence and a beloved legendary precursor.

In prog, Genesis was doing good business, but Yes was in transition and would not make a strong return until 1983 and *90125*. But both Yes and Genesis would modernize drastically — maybe prog really was dead. Asia wasn't particularly prog, and out of the new wave of British progressive rock movement, only Marillion made a dent. Running parallel was the founding of MTV in 1981, and then a couple of years later, a massive uptick in heavy metal's prospects with the rise of hair metal and thrash, primarily in California. Rush would run away from all of this (save for MTV — in this they would participate), even if what they were about to embrace possessed its own '80s tropes.

Continues Neil with respect to the band's moment in the limelight: "It really was only those couple of years, as it kind of dwindled away with *Signals*, a record that people didn't like so much because that was a keyboard experimental album with a lot of bizarreness on it. And from there to *Grace Under Pressure*, which is even more of a polarizing album. But *Moving Pictures* just hit the right summer with the right kind of music. And I remember being all kinds of places and hearing 'Red Barchetta' on the radio and thinking, 'That song's on the radio?!'

"I guess it's that same synchronicity. *2112* happened to be the summer of *Star Wars*, and *Moving Pictures* happened to be at the right time too. New wave came along, and that killed a lot of bands. Just like the late '60s killed a lot of bands from the early '60s, an awful lot of bands that we started out with in the mid- to early '70s did not survive that attrition. Because the only word is adapt — or perish. We were light on our feet because we had no preconceived notion of what we were supposed to be. We were not a hard-core rock ballad band or something, and our hair was subject to change — all of that.

"So many of the bands of the '70s, they were all what they seemed to be in the true sense. And if you take that away, what were they going to do? That's the trap they found themselves in. They couldn't pretend to be a punk band. Well we couldn't either, but we could pretend to play the music we loved. And that was why we could adapt through that time when so many other bands didn't. We did manage to tiptoe through all the changes of the '80s. We were very unfashionable, but maybe as a side note to this idea of us tiptoeing along the mainstream, the mainstream is what's fashionable and enough of that crept in to keep us and probably also a certain fringe audience entertained, people who were walking along the median of the mainstream, as it were."

Neil makes a good point here with his reflection on where the band exists relative to the mainstream. But it takes on different connotations depending on which arc in the trajectory we're looking at. At the time of *Moving Pictures*, Rush records were being bought by a teenaged male hard rock crowd. But as Neil articulated, that demographic was joining the band on the edge of the mainstream, with Geddy, Alex and Neil politely prodding them to read more, care more about craft and get a little progressive in their lives. And if they aspired to be musicians themselves, well, the guys were enthusiastically offering up a clinic, showing kids not only where hard work will get you but also how purely fun it is to play "YYZ," "Limelight" and "Tom Sawyer."

CHAPTER 3

EXIT ... STAGE LEFT

"I think we recorded a fairly sterile live record."

Perhaps another marker of increased success for Rush and their suddenly solo-flying manager Ray was that in advance of their *Moving Pictures* campaign, they would set up at Wings Stadium in Kalamazoo, Michigan, for three nights to rehearse their bigger, broader show, before presenting it there on a fourth night. A month into the tour, the guys would return home to Toronto for a triumphant three-night stand at Maple Leaf Gardens. Directly after, the trucks would roll up Highway 401 for six hours to Montreal, where the show would be recorded for use on the band's second live album, *Exit ... Stage Left*, issued October 29, 1981. Also making the album would be material from the band's two nights in Glasgow, Scotland, June 10 and 11, 1980.

In between Glasgow, which was part of the *Permanent Waves* campaign, and the subsequent *Moving Pictures* tour, Rush would do a handful of isolated dates in September 1980 to limber up before entering the studio to work on *Moving Pictures*. These were U.S.

eastern seaboard shows supported by NWOBHM up-and-comers Saxon. Featured would be pre-LP versions of both "Limelight" and "Tom Sawyer," neither of which differ much from the eventual finished product, right down to Neil's fills.

The reason the material on the record reached back so far was that the band had been recording the *Permanent Waves* tour for use on a live album that was supposed to come out before *Moving Pictures*, something the guys often spoke about in interviews at the time, offering that it would comprise performances from Glasgow, Manchester, Newcastle and the Hammersmith Odeon in London, and musing about making a sort of rock documentary at the same time.

"Our first tour in America was supporting Rush," explains Saxon bassist Steve Dawson, offering fond memories of playing with Rush. "Fantastic, brilliant. I mean, can you imagine me, from a little town in England, opening up for Rush, with probably the greatest bass player who's ever lived, Geddy Lee? He came over when we were doing sound check. They had done their sound check and we were doing ours, and he just came over and talked bass, if you know what I mean. Because I was fascinated with his sound. Because he plays with his fingers like me. He doesn't play with a plectrum. He plays with his fingers, and I was amazed at the sound that he got. And I was asking him how he did it. And Neil was just a quiet guy, kept to himself, and the guitarist spent all the time in his dressing room making model aircraft [laughs]. So we basically didn't have a lot to do with the other guys, but Geddy was really friendly, a good guy. And in fact, we talked a lot about UFO, me and Geddy, because UFO supported Rush just before us, and so we were swapping Pete Way stories. You can pass a lot of time because there's an awful lot of stories."

There'd be some drama — although not Pete Way–related — in April of 1981, when Kim Mitchell blew up Max Webster, who had been supporting Rush across America until then. Into May, fellow Canucks FM would begin a long support slot as Rush finished off a full blanketing of the U.S.

Supporting on the band's final dates of the tour in early July '81 would be the Joe Perry Project, with the Aerosmith guitarist going solo after the implosion of "America's greatest rock 'n' roll band."

Keeper of sanity on the road, Howard Ungerleider, remembers this situation all too well. Rush, of course, opened for Aerosmith in the old days, and as Howard relates, "Aerosmith had a tour manager who was not a pleasant man. Aerosmith had six hundred lights and they let us use sixteen. We were not allowed to have dinner with the Aerosmith entourage. Whatever was left over, Rush was allowed to have. Our contract rider was modest; we asked for a case of Canadian beer, a deli tray and some water. And he came in one day, must've been the tour manager, and said, 'You're in the United States now; you're gonna drink American beer.' Then we're not allowed to have a sound check until the doors open. When the doors open and the crowd starts coming in, you can bring your equipment onstage and then they would turn the PA down halfway. This went on for seventy shows.

"Their just deserts came when Joe Perry left Aerosmith years later. He couldn't get a tour because there were no bands out. There was one band out on tour and that was Rush. Many agents came to Rush's manager and said, 'Listen, can Joe Perry get on the tour? You guys are out.' 'Sure, Joe Perry, sure.' And I went to Geddy and Geddy said, 'Whatever their contract rider says, I want you to double it.' And I said, 'Really?' 'Yeah, make sure he gets a sound check and PA, and I want you to just kill him with kindness.' I said, 'Geddy, are you sure?' And he says, 'I'm sure.' Because Geddy Lee's a class act.

"Three months go by, and I'm in the dressing room one day and Geddy says, 'Is Joe Perry here?' I go, 'Yeah, he's in his dressing room.' And he said, 'You want to go ask him if it's okay if I come by and say hi?' I said sure. So Joe says, 'Hey, sure, yeah, he can come by.' So Geddy and I come by, we go into Joe's room, and Geddy goes, 'Hey Joe, how's it going?' He goes, 'Great, man.' Geddy says, 'Are you getting a sound check every day?' He says, 'Oh yeah, it's great.' 'You got food and stuff?' He goes, 'Yeah, more than we asked for. It's really, really great.' And Geddy says, 'Are you enjoying yourself?' 'Yeah, for sure.' Geddy says, 'Good, that's great. Because I'd never want you to feel the way I felt when we were touring with Aerosmith, and I was opening for you.'

"We had other bands too who would turn the PA down, 'Screw that band from Canada.' People were paranoid, paying for the PA, paying for the lights. So that's the adversity I was privy to before we were headlining. A long and muddy trench. Seventy-four hundred concerts. Those are the things I dealt with on a daily basis."

But Howard remembers this campaign fondly, in terms of his development as a lighting director. "Yes, and the thing for me that really made it come alive was when I had the three wings over the band during the *Moving Pictures* tour. I just loved that I could use the truss as a box, although it wasn't square, it was circular. I could put it over the band and make it do things."

Rush's stage presentation by now featured back-projected film, pyro and dry ice in what was estimated to be a $40,000 show. The final tallies for the tour were cited as a gate of $4 million from 905,000 fans at seventy-nine shows. But the guys could afford the extra expense now, Alex explains. "When *Moving Pictures* came out that's when we could actually get ourselves out of debt. Also, we were offered to re-sign, renegotiate, redo our deal. That's when a lot of those sorts of worries were dispelled."

Tony Geranios, an important part of the crew since 1977 and credited in *Exit . . . Stage Left* as "guitar and synthesizer maintenance," remarks that Rush "always offered value for money. After the keyboards started becoming a prevailing part of the sound, it was tying Geddy to the keyboards quite a bit, and Alex to the pedals. And I think the concern was there wasn't enough action onstage. Because they felt they should be running around and rocking out. That's when the video became more of an important factor. And as time went on, things started to loosen up. Howard's lighting designs . . . I can't think of a tour where I wasn't just totally blown away by what he's been able to come up with. It's a full media production. You get the lasers, you get the lights, videos, music, and to me, that follows along with their philosophy."

Geranios draws an interesting analogy between the shows and the crafting of the records. "Each new tour always impressed me. The fact their level of playing was at one plane, but then their level of creating was like twenty percent higher, and it would always go that way from album to album. They would try to deliver something they hadn't delivered before, make a statement musically that they hadn't been able to, or hadn't considered before. Everything is always one step better. Their progression with their music is the same with the shows. Every show has its own magical portion or addition to it, but all of them are of a caliber where the enjoyment factor is there."

But that doesn't mean things always ran smoothly. "We had some trying times with the keyboard stuff and also with the rear-screen projector," continues Geranios. "I remember one of the earlier shows, after we'd gotten a thirty-five-millimeter projector. Lee Tenner was the projectionist at the time. And we were setting up scaffolding, and I guess the people we'd been working with made a mistake, and the projector fell twenty feet off the scaffolding onto the floor. That was pretty horrendous."

Then there was that time back on the *Hemispheres* tour, on March 27, 1979, when Rush was supported by April Wine.

"Yes, we had like a week, week-and-a-half break, and we were gonna start up again in Salt Lake City. And I was having a lot of grounding problems, things going on with the Oberheim. So I sent it off to Oberheim, and they were gonna ship it back to me, but in Salt Lake City. We get in a day before the show actually starts. That's how everyone always worked, to make sure the crew was there the day before the show so there's no mix-up.

"I called up Oberheim and they said, 'Yeah, we shipped it out.' And he gave me a shipping number, and I called asking about it, and they said they didn't have it. A whole day goes by, and next day, day of the show, I'm calling again and saying, 'I can't find this thing; nobody has a record of it.' And Oberheim said, 'We'll get back to you.' And about an hour later they called me and said, 'Well, it's still sitting on the shipping dock. At the airport. The case is too big to go into any of the doorways for the planes that we fly into Salt Lake City. Look, we can put it on a truck and get it to you in eight hours.' And by this time, it's eleven, twelve in the morning.

"So I called up my contact there, good guy, never about the dollars, just really a great business person. So he told me there was one guy they sent an Oberheim to, one guy in the Salt Lake City area that had one. I got the number from him, called him up, got his roommate. And I said, 'I need this keyboard for tonight; will we be able to rent it?' 'Oh yeah, hundred bucks.' 'Well, fine.'

"About twenty minutes later, I get a call, 'Could you make that two hundred bucks? I just talked to my guy. He wants two hundred dollars.' 'Two hundred dollars, you get a pass, here, fine.' So we get this thing in, during sound check, still haven't met the guy who actually owns it. His roommate brought it down because the guy was at work. I'm going over with Geddy how to get the sounds and make everything work because we don't have the interface. So we get something to where it's useful, to get away with it for the night, everything will be fine.

"So we're in the beginning of the show, and I'm on the other side of the stage, on Alex's side, which is where I always preside for the most part. The guy who owned the keyboard started coming up on Geddy's side of the stage. He's walking up, and at the time, National Sound was doing our sound, and there was a guy named Dave Berman. Dave looked at this guy coming up and goes, 'Where's your pass?' 'In my pocket.' 'Put your pass on. You can't be up here without your pass.' 'I can do whatever I want.' And he took another couple of steps. Dave popped him right in the fucking face, split his lip. So as the security is carrying him off, several people around there are hearing, 'But that's my keyboard onstage' [laughs]. We got sued over that."

Off the road for the summer, Rush set up at Le Studio to go through what Neil estimates was fifty reels of two-inch tape. The producing credit would go to Terry Brown as well, with engineering by Paul Northfield. One bonus from the idyllic summer retreat was the writing and recording of "Subdivisions," soon to be the centerpiece of the band's next album.

Says Terry, "We had recorded in a number of different cities, and we'd have to sift through it all and find all the right takes and make sure we weren't shortchanging tunes. I think that record's just fine. We had a great time, did a lot of traveling, met some really great people, recorded with great recording trucks using good technology, and then we spent some weeks putting it together and mixing all the right songs and getting the continuity right."

Exit . . . Stage Left was issued as a double album in a gatefold sleeve. Hugh's clever cover art featured a character or element from every studio album on either the front or the wraparound to the back. Guys in overalls are "moving a picture" that depicts the *Caress of Steel* cover art. Both the naked man and the suited man from *Hemispheres* are represented, plus the young royal from *A Farewell to Kings*. There is a flying owl, and a road case features the logo from the debut. Way at the back we see the Starman and pentagram from *2112*.

On the front, model Paula Turnbull from *Permanent Waves*, standing stage left, pulls back the curtain, peering at the packed house waiting for the start of the show. Hugh recalls that Turnbull, now a famed model in Europe, was incensed that there was no trailer for her. The photo shoot was conducted at the Winter Garden Theatre, at that point unused but now revived, just around the corner from Massey Hall in Toronto (although the live crowd is from a Buffalo show). Hugh wanted to get the band on the front cover saying goodnight and exiting stage left, but after attempting the shot at about fifteen shows, he had to admit defeat.

As for the title, "Exit stage left!" is what Hanna-Barbera's pink cartoon cougar, Snagglepuss, says when he gets in trouble. The band even wanted to put Snagglepuss's tail on the cover but were hampered by the legalities of the idea.

All told, there are three amusing similarities to the packaging of the first Rush live album: (1) both have *stage* in the title; (2) both feature an empty stage; and (3) both were shot in Toronto, at locations about a minute's walk away from each other.

Interesting wrinkles to what is a pretty predictable record — both in the playing and in the track list — include the waltz music intro to "Jacob's Ladder" (actually a snippet of a big band piece called "Ebb Tide") and the huge crowd sing-along on "Closer to the Heart." The guys acknowledge this magic moment by crediting the Glaswegian Chorus — this one is from Scotland, along with "Jacob's Ladder," "A Passage to Bangkok" and "Beneath, Between & Behind," the latter two being the only songs from records previous to *All the World's a Stage*. The four Glasgow performances comprised all of side two of the original four sides of vinyl. Also of particular interest is Alex's classical guitar piece, "Broon's Bane" (Broon is Terry Brown's nickname), Geddy's Yiddish "vocals" in "La Villa Strangiato" and Neil's gratuitous bells in "A Passage to Bangkok." Neil's drum solo was inserted into "YYZ," where it would stay for two tours.

Exit . . . Stage Left was certified platinum, reaching #10 on the Billboard charts, #6 in the U.K. and #7 in Canada. A video version, much shorter than the album, was issued the following year.

Remarked Geddy of the record: "That one was an attempt to kind of overexaggerate how perfect you could make a live album. There was a lot of meddling with the tapes and trying to make sure we had the best performances. We also made a conscious effort to pull down the audience a bit and emphasize the music. In the end, I think we recorded a fairly sterile live record. So yes, that would entail the most tinkering of any of the live albums. We played around with making sure things were in time, snipping bits of time here and there. It turned into a bit of a nightmare of mixing and perfecting. And that was, as with *All the World's a Stage*, most of us being involved, although I think Neil tuned out pretty early in the process."

"We did a lot of recording on *Exit . . . Stage Left*," confirms Paul Northfield. "They did a lot of repairs on that record because their first live album had been so raw, and they were so uncomfortable with it. They went to the complete opposite extreme on *Exit . . . Stage Left*. Apart from any drums, they replaced almost everything — vocals, guitars, a huge amount, in order to have more perfection. Which actually makes it more of a hybrid; it's like a live bed track album with a lot of overdubs on it."

Neil, to his credit, admitted in the press, enthusiastically and without apology, to the odd repair. At the time, he saw it as a virtue and of course in one manner it is — you want to have a good record. Interestingly, all three of the guys have professed an animosity toward live albums, Neil, at the time, even going so far as to say he didn't think Rush would be making any more of them.

Indeed, there's a "stuffiness" and a "corporateness" to *Exit . . . Stage Left*. Call it the sophomore jinx or the curse of the second gig. Despite the band's initial discomfort with their first live album, fans gravitated to the rawness and realness of *All the World's a Stage*. *Priest . . . Live!*, *Extraterrestrial Live*, *Yesshows*, *Three Sides Live*, *Life/ Live*, *Worldwide Live* . . . it would be hard to find fans who think any of these bloated hockey barn productions possess the magic of the first live album from any of these bands. And then we get into the CD age and the idea of double albums and single albums and gatefolds is replaced by just "long" live albums, and the magic is gone. Most heritage acts — Rush egregiously included — started replacing the making of studio albums with more and more live albums. And then there's the themed set lists, playing one old record in its entirety, along with trying to figure out which is the official release, the DVD or the triple CD? And what do we do when the track lists differ? (Even *Exit . . . Stage Left* dropped "A Passage to Bangkok" from its original CD issue.) Decades down the line and blown vocal chords later, all of this pollution and dilution of the catalogue tend to strengthen in potency the talisman-like nature of an *All the World's a Stage*.

Exit . . . Stage Left would mark the end of the road for Ian Grandy as part of the crew, there since the basement jam days.

"I think they were mutually sick of me, and I was ready to go home," says Ian. "We had our second child, who was two months old, and my wife was like, 'I need you to be at home in the day.' And I really wasn't being treated very well at all. It's one of those things that you know you're getting the axe, and if you leave, you don't get any money. If you stay, you get some sort of settlement. In the last couple of months, it was the truck drivers who told me, 'You're gone at the end of the tour, you know. You're fired.' 'Yeah, thank you.' It's kind of disheartening. But it was the only time I was ever let go in my life, and I was quite happy to go. I was an accountant for twenty years after that, in construction. But yeah, we were going to Europe, and I hadn't even got my passport, because I knew I wasn't going."

As for why he was let go, Grandy says, "Well, it's my own fault, my own abuse of substances and all that. But when you're in that kind of position . . . I'll give you an example. They had something they sold, a promo thing, at the merchandise table, with all the roadies, except there were thirteen roadies and they only had twelve in the picture. I wasn't even on it, and the guys were going, 'You've been with the band the longest time. Like, you're not on this?!' And then Neil came to me, 'I just realized you're not on this. How can that fucking be?' Well, it's a little heartening. Especially when Neil is going, 'I'm so upset that this happened.' Like, I apologize to you.

"That seems to be that whole era," continues Ian, including *Signals* in his survey. "They got rid of me, they got rid of the sound company, they got rid of Terry. They really kind of cleaned themselves out. I don't think Alex was happy with *Signals*. That was my impression. He wanted to try something else. And what I've heard lately is, everybody is free to have Geddy's opinion. But after fifteen years, you know, what I've always told people is, 'The ninth time you're in Toledo, Ohio, the thrill is gone.' And I see their itinerary, and I'm going, Columbus, Cleveland, Pittsburgh . . . oh my God, how many times can you play there? I was ready to go. And no hard feelings, I went home, and I haven't been back in thirty-three, thirty-four years. I don't come and hang around."

CHAPTER 4

SIGNALS

"More was what we were after."

A s the band grew in stature and their second live album was produced, Rush began to apply their extra time to expand and think about what came next. What was to become *Signals* got a bit of a jump start amidst the "sessions" for the live album, taking place at Le Studio — of course, with a live album the band is not typically involved; however, much meddling took place to create *Exit . . . Stage Left* at that gorgeous recording studio in the wilderness, while Neil along with Tony and Skip from the road crew worked on something called "Tough Break," which was never released. It was here that the band themselves cooked up "Subdivisions."

Late October through the end of December saw the band include "Subdivisions" in their set and work from pieces of music during sound check, in particular "Chemistry," as they played Europe supported by Girlschool, followed by the southeastern U.S. supported by Riot.

"Everybody was great," recalls Riot guitarist Rick Ventura. "I actually remember Sandy filling in for Neil Peart during a sound check [laughs], because Neil wasn't there yet. And I remember Geddy checking us out when we opened for them at the Nassau Coliseum. A few times, actually, he would listen to us at sound check, and I'd think, wow, that's Geddy out there listening to us — interesting."

Adds Riot manager Steve Loeb: "Scorpions were cool, AC/DC were drinking already at breakfast and Blackmore made everyone clear the corridors when he was on the way to the stage. The coolest band was by far Rush — not a single issue. You want full sound and lights? You got it. That did not go down with anyone else."

"While we were on tour with Saxon, they offered us the Rush *Moving Pictures* tour in the States, and it was like a dream come true," says Riot leader Mark Reale, sadly no longer with us. "So we came back from the English tour, I think we did two quick weeks with the reunited Grand Funk Railroad, and then we hooked up with Rush, which was amazing, the best. It was just us and Rush, and every night, I think we played for almost an hour in sold-out arenas."

In late '81, Geddy lets his long hair down and indulges to a considerable extent his sense of humor, appearing on the Bob & Doug McKenzie comedy album, *The Great White North*. Bob and Doug are two typical Canadian "hosers," played by Rick Moranis and Dave Thomas, in the popular SCTV skit that went whatever constituted "viral" in the early 1980s. Dave is Ian Thomas's brother, Ian being part of the Anthem Records family, and Geddy went to elementary school with Rick. The album came out on Anthem and was a hit, going gold in the States and triple platinum in Canada, with sales of over 350,000 copies. Geddy sings (and speaks) on the musical track "Take Off," which is a novelty rave at radio, along with the duo's take on "The Twelve Days of Christmas." Geddy brought his whole family down to the session, which he says only took about an hour.

During this period, Rush again did well at the Junos, with nominations for Group of the Year, Album of the Year for both *Moving Pictures* and *Exit . . . Stage Left*, and Recording Engineer of the Year, and a win for Best Album Graphics for *Moving Pictures* (*Exit . . . Stage Left* was also nominated for Best Album Graphics, and *The Great White North* won Best Comedy Album). There was also a hit Rush Laserium show at the planetarium in Seattle, and *Exit . . . Stage Left* was broadcast on TV with FM simulcasts.

The band got some much-needed time off in early 1982. A one-month writing session at the Grange in the Muskoka Lake region led to two weeks of dates in early April, with Krokus and Riggs supporting. The late spring and summer sessions would birth *Signals*, but three months of recording didn't prove enough to get the album's synthesizer/guitar balance down, and the guys had to stay overtime, which cut into additional planned family time in July.

"I was learning the keyboards at that time," begins Geddy, modest about a path he had been on now for five years. "So that was kind of my thrust. I think I was actually taking piano lessons at that time too, to try to get more adept. I was fascinated with the electronic side of music and trying to integrate that into our sound, in a way that would give us more melody, you know, bring more emotion to a song, by the addition of a new texture. Suddenly a new melodic part could give the song more impact, more resonance. We always joked about wanting to be the world's smallest symphony orchestra. That was a way of trying to make that dream come true. Quite simply it was 'more.' More was what we were after.

"Those decisions seem like huge decisions when you talk about them in retrospect," says Geddy, on the increased use of keyboards. "But when you are doing them, they don't seem like such a big deal. We had these new synths and they were giving us noises and new textures. And anything that brought something new into the music usually spurred writing. And so we were mixing the live album at Le Studio, and we were bored out of our minds, and we had this Oberheim, and we started jamming. We had this new toy, and we used the new toy! We came up with the song 'Subdivisions,' and it kind of set the tone for the record.

"And, yeah, it ended up being quite a different thing, but it didn't feel like it was going to be at the time. It just felt fresh. Looking back, it is quite a departure, but I think that's the way it always is with us. We don't really have this big conference where we say, 'Look, change now!' We just kind of slip into something that seems new and fun to do, and we do it, and before we know it, it's over and it was 'Wow, they really changed.' But from the inside, it doesn't really change like that."

"I don't recall feeling we had to move away from something," adds Alex, echoing Ged's expressed spirit of exploration. "It was more moving into something, always looking for — from my point of view — a new effect or a new way of playing chords. I was experimenting and searching for things, not for some need to leave something behind but just to go somewhere else. Bringing the keyboards in, like this big Oberheim, was a cool new thing. And these chords sounded great and the synth sounds were very cool and there were other synths that were coming along. They were all fresh, cool things you wanted to base your writing around."

"It felt like we were doing something that was edgier," agrees Geddy. "We've always been guilty of being drawn to technology, like a moth to a flame. New gear comes by and it's like, 'Oh, we can get a new noise out of that, we can make a new sound, that'll be something fresh.' It's looking for that new thing to bring into our sound. And I think we all had a shared interest in it, but I guess I was the guy making the noises, so it would be fair to say I was pushing that direction. I started writing on the thing, just for fun, saying, 'Hey, what do you think of this?' And then we would take it from there and all get behind it. Everyone has their input, but because I was the 'keyboardist,' I guess it came from my banging around on it."

Again, a lot of this was inspired not just by having new toys but also by what exciting new music was happening around the guys, always enthusiastic first adopters, in the traditional sense, with technology, or with records by other bands. But of course first adopters also often share the teething pains, and so much of what they ingest and then push back out can be seen as fleeting and trendy. Bands could be flavor of the month, especially as far as the U.K. music papers were concerned. Syndrums and LinnDrums could make records unlistenable forever. Rush would enjoy some of the accolades for making music at the frontier, but they would also suffer some of the consequences, accused of jumping on trends, both in hairstyle and snare style.

"We always did listen to a lot of other bands," continues Geddy. "We always tried to keep our ear to the ground, always listened to what was happening. And around that time there was a huge synth movement, starting in England, with Ultravox. All of those bands that we liked were bringing fresh noises into rock music. So we were like, 'Me too; I want that too. Let's try that.'"

Curiously, Geddy uses the word *always*, but looking at the records from *Fly by Night* through to *Moving Pictures*, and indeed interviews with the guys through that period, one doesn't really see Rush picking up much influence from contemporary music. At the very beginning, it's about their '60s heroes, but after that, and even now, they don't really rattle off names of bands. You never hear the guys talk about Deep Purple, Judas Priest, Angel, Thin Lizzy, Queen, Styx, or even the latest Yes, Jethro Tull or Genesis albums around this time. If anything, on a substantive basis, one wonders if they were picking up more from Max Webster, FM and Pat Travers than anything else laterally career-wise or stylistically in their wheelhouse. Were they inspired by King Crimson? Gentle Giant? Rainbow? Peter Gabriel on his exalted solo tear? Punk came out, and they ran the other way, sniping about the unprofessionalism of punk bands, fueling further fire and ire with the U.K. press (and then if politics came up, double whammy). But there were all sorts of interesting keyboard developments along the way, across that list of '70s bands. Much of the early development seems to have come from Terry Watkinson.

And as for Geddy, it seems to be more about monastic communion with the gear itself, until he heard the new wave bands. "*Farewell to Kings* to *Hemispheres* even; those are all monophonic keyboards — single lines. String lines, melody lines added here and there, the line in 'Xanadu,' or white noise sounds and textures. Once you had the polyphonic world, if you can actually play it like a piano, it brought a whole other range of sounds into Rush music. And also a whole range of problems because, suddenly, here were these big block chords, or what musicians refer to as pads, soaking up the sound spectrum. And suddenly that forced Alex to take a different attitude toward the kinds of parts he was playing."

"There were many things I liked about the direction," says Alex, about moving into heavier use of the keyboard. "It looked like it was going in a good place, very modern and exciting. I did have my frustrations sonically — competing with the density of keyboards. Especially when you start layering them. They occupy the same frequencies. They are quite thick, and as a result of that, I went for a cleaner sound, trying to work around it. It was challenging but real rewarding most of the time. I thought it made it sound unique. And certainly, onstage, having these keyboards playing and as an accompaniment made for a much fuller sound. Plus it made us look really cool, with pedals and keys and playing bass and guitars."

Both Geddy and Alex have a point. *Signals* would not sound like Soft Cell or Human League because the keys being played were akin to rhythm guitar parts. That meant if Alex played straight rhythm guitar, the two would cancel out, or sound like some sort of odd double tracking of indiscernible sounds. This made Lifeson explore new territory, which on one hand was exciting. On the other, a little devil on his shoulder was telling him he was out of a job.

It's no different from how Fast Eddie had to adjust in Motörhead. If Lemmy was covering more of what was traditionally rhythm guitar territory, then Clarke could either address the dropout of proper bass or colorize up top. As it turned out, the band would sacrifice traditional bass sounds and frequencies, and Clarke would play a lot of higher-up two-string chords augmented by other screechy licks. Rush would get more "keyboardy" as the '80s wore on, and Alex would instead become a pinger and chimer — his solution to a problem he shared with Fast Eddie Clarke.

"Again, this all seemed very natural at the time we were doing it," reflects Ged. "We were all excited about it. I would bang up this chord progression and Alex would find a part that would fit with it, and away we would go. And before you know it, we've created a kind of four-piece sound from a three-piece sound. It felt like a natural evolution, but it was probably, to our fans, quite a dramatic shift. And it wasn't without its frustrations. There were times that Alex would be frustrated he had to move out of the way a little bit sonically to accommodate this pad sound. But his attitude was 'Well, it's new, it's fresh,' and he was all for it. Otherwise we wouldn't do it.

"We did change the way we approached songwriting. You've got lyrics, and normally it would be guitar, bass and lyrics and we would hash something out. And now it's guitar, bass, lyrics, keys — hey! As soon as I go over to the keys, there's no bass line that works in the same way, right? There's this pad progression, and now it's figuring out a guitar piece to go with it. Or Alex figures out a guitar piece that we loved, and then I tried to accompany it on the keyboards. It creates a different kind of music and a different kind of sound for the band."

Geddy admits the shift in style was a bit of an adjustment for him as well. "When we started rehearsing for the tour, I got frustrated because I couldn't play my bass anymore. I had to play these blocks of keyboards, and then the bass parts would end up being very rudimentary bass pedal parts. So suddenly I went from being a bassist to being kind of a lousy keyboardist [laughs] playing these booming bass pedal parts. And Alex turned into more of a soloist over top of all this stuff, and that's the way the songs were structured. So there were some adjustment problems for me live. It was the beginning of kind of a wrestling match.

"For the next few albums, we kept experimenting with how to balance new technology, new sounds, with still being a three-piece rock band. That was really the experiment over that whole period, right up into *Counterparts* — looking for that balance of Rush sounding like Rush, Rush being a rock band, Alex having the freedom to play the kind of guitar chords he wants to play, and yet use this beautiful idea to bring all kinds of externality into the sound. There is orchestration suddenly, there are all these harmonies, all these harmonic possibilities we never had before. And as a writer I found that super exciting! There was so much more music in our music as a result of it. But it came out at a price, and it came out as an argument, as to how to make everything we want happen at the same time. It was tough."

"It was very challenging," agrees Alex. "I wouldn't say it felt organic. I really had to think about what I was trying to do and where I was trying to steer the guitar. And it certainly wasn't like that for every song. There were some songs that were more difficult than others. But generally, it worked well, I thought. And also during this period, I used the chorus sound a lot, which is a wavy sort of sound, and that tends to take a little bit of the articulation out of the guitar sound. When you combine that with dense keyboard sounds that are sort of doing this same swirly thing, it makes for a difficult placement of the guitar. Whereas the straight guitar sound cuts through more easily."

As for Neil, he found the baking and making of *Signals* arduous too. "That was a very long process when keyboards came in. We needed to expand our sound palette or get another member. And by then we already had such good chemistry among the three of us that it didn't feel right to add someone else, so it became a DIY situation, with all of us trying to expand that palette.

"And keyboards, of course in the Minimoog era and with Taurus pedals, it was pretty primitive, with limited possibilities. But as they got polyphonic, there came more possibilities. I'm very much less of a 'less is more' and more of a 'more is better' kind of person. So I was always very excited about every growth that came along. And that's true for me as a drummer too. As more possibilities came along in sampling and electronic drums and all that, it was exciting and irresistible.

"That applies to the whole band too, as each new development came along. Some things, like the guitar synthesizer, died an unlamented death. But around *Signals* or so, keyboard sounds became bigger and took up more space. And then all through the

'80s, we started working with Peter Collins and Andy Richards on keyboards, and those guys had a million ideas and a million giant sounds. That's when Alex started feeling the squeeze, really.

"Sonically, I think *Signals* is the one he complains of, but there was always something going on," continues Neil, reminding us of the joyous heavy guitar on *Signals*. "Because Geddy was always busy with keyboards, sometimes Alex and I would be the rhythm section, and we would communicate about how our parts would intermingle. That was a really good phase to go through, just for that reason."

Any tensions with Alex and his role would be dealt with by this three-man team, but Rush's relationship with its "fourth member," Terry Brown, would come to the end after *Signals*. Not so much as friends — the guys were too sensible and Canadian not to be able to manage that — but Terry stepped down as their producer. It really was down to creative differences, and the knife would cut both ways.

"It was becoming a major thing, the electronics," explains Terry. "Lots of keyboards, electronic drums. I mean, Neil had the double kit not long after that, and that was something I didn't really get a handle on. It just didn't do it for me. Reading Bill Bruford's biography, he gets into that whole thing too, how technology was sort of driving everything at that point. And it was problematic — interesting, but problematic. It didn't appeal to me, the whole MIDI keyboard thing, that sort of upper technology in keyboards and electronic drums, sequencing, pedals. And it is becoming a very complicated issue, certainly for the band, to get those elements onstage working properly and doing shows night after night."

However, Terry doesn't recall Alex struggling much at being sidelined by the tech. "I didn't feel at the time it was a problem for Alex. It wasn't until I read about it afterward; at the time we never had that discussion. I don't know if he kept quiet about it; he might have had an internal struggle. Maybe he didn't feel the guitars were taking a predominant enough role, but I could cite many instances since then when I felt more strongly about how the guitars sounded. Looking back, it was just the tip of the iceberg."

Paul Northfield figures there was a significant shift in the dynamics of the band at that time, especially when it came to Terry Brown. "*Moving Pictures* became so successful that they probably had much greater confidence when they went in. They had been touring incessantly. I think they had done two hundred shows in a year on *Moving Pictures* and had been Billboard #1 or something like that. They had been on overdrive, solidly, ever since the release of *Moving Pictures*.

"And when they came into the studio, Terry had taken the time to be with his family and just take a break from the intensity of making records all the time. I think he needed time to get up to speed and get back in tune with the whole process. I don't think they had so much patience for that. Because they were like, 'Okay, we want decisions, we need what you think, we need to do this, we need to do that.' That was where I first sensed a departure between their ideas of what they each wanted to do. Previously they had never been that way.

"At this point the band were feeling their own strength and vision," continues Paul, "and their success was an affirmation of what they wanted to do. Terry was not in the same headspace as them, and so consequently there was tension. Frequently they wanted a clear, concise, 'Okay, we need to do this' or 'Okay, why? What's wrong with that take? Be specific.' And sometimes Terry would be not as specific as they wanted. But we got through it.

"So the tensions and the difficulties in making *Signals* were there, although it was an evolution. They were with Terry for a very long time, and they were very loyal guys, to a fault. To their own detriment they would be loyal to people, and I think they were suddenly starting to be in a situation where they wanted to branch out and be challenged. Their relationship with Terry had reached a point where they knew what he was going to say before he said it, and that was no longer what they were looking for."

Diving into the technology, Paul says, "As the arrangements got more textured, particularly in the '80s, keyboard sounds drove the interesting kind of creativity in the music scene. We went through a whole period where everybody was waiting for the next keyboard. Whether it was an Oberheim, a Prophet, a PPG, a Fairlight, the Jupiter 8 — all these new sonic textures coming in that nobody had heard before. They were fascinating and interesting, and so suddenly the guys, all of them together, went, 'We love this stuff, we want that to be part of the palette.'

"And so then it fell to Geddy, who had a love/hate relationship with it. It was exciting sonically but it became more complicated. There was a lot more to think about. How are you gonna play full chordal parts and not play bass? If you're using both hands on the keyboard, you can't play bass anymore. And a lot of stuff ended up being written with cool riffs and cool sounds on keyboards. Suddenly you realize that half the songs for the record have been written using keyboards, not guitar."

Through all that, indeed, the band persevered and eventually got a record made. *Signals* would arrive in stores September 9, 1982, wrapped in another austere, classy cover that placed Rush farther away from their heavy metal roots than ever: a pastel greenish-grey frame surrounding a Deborah Samuel photo of a Dalmatian sniffing a fire hydrant. Samuel took the shot on a piece of Astroturf on the roof atop her studio, with a fire hydrant rented from the city and painted bright red. To get the dog to sniff, she put dog biscuits underneath the hydrant. Hugh had only the title of the album to work with and was stymied about what to do with it, deciding at the end to inject into the concept a sense of humor very much adjacent to the band's. The back cover is a tribute to flagship song "Subdivisions." Featured is a fictional map with subdivisions centered around Warren Cromartie Secondary School. Cromartie was a Montreal Expo, a nod to Geddy's love of baseball.

Noted Alex on the baseball connection, speaking with Ted Veneman of *Harmonix*: "There's a bar called The Commons. It's in an old hotel in Morin Heights and it is really the only bar in town. It's a crazy raging place and in the number of years we've recorded up there, we've gotten to know the people who work at the bar. They have a girls' softball team, so when we got up there, they challenged us to a game. Everybody got baseball gloves — we got all set up for this game. We had a bit of field practice and we played them a game and we beat them. Then the guys' team offered to play us. All of a sudden, we got a little too busy. So it started there and then when we were doing the credits, we thought let's put in everybody's position from that game, and that's exactly what we did. And Warren Cromartie, oddly enough, was really into the band and through some friends in Montreal called and asked if we'd mind much if he came up to the studio while we were recording. So he came up and we met him. He was really into the band and we were really into the Expos. Geddy's a baseball nut and he was well aware of Warren. He's a pretty good drummer. Neil, of course, is a great influence. He came out on the road with us for a few days in Chicago and St. Louis and we've become good friends."

Signals opens with a whoosh of foreboding post-punk synthesizers, dark, Mancunian, perhaps toward Magazine or Joy Division. Notes Alex: "That keyboard has a very distinctive sound. When you hear those chords being played, you know it's that song right away. It's very recognizable. Catchy. It's hooky." In response, Geddy cracks, "Hooks is for fish."

As it progresses, "Subdivisions" brightens, darkens, brightens and then darkens again, yet always remains propulsive and oppressive, as Neil tells the timeless story of restless teen alienation. At the same time, Peart derides the conformity of suburban living and how it magnifies the politics of what goes on in high school. Like a good writer, he offers hope, specifically in an escape to the adjacent city. For all those Rush fans in small towns and medium-sized cities painted across the rust belt — Rush's home away from home — glamorous urban escape might be a longer bus trip away, but the message is the same. Universal.

Alex could definitely relate. "I remember living as a teenager in the suburbs. The glamour of going downtown on a Friday night, hanging around with much older people, being part of the scene that we weren't really a part of. All of the insecurities of being a teenager in the suburbs, school, all of that stuff. I can very clearly relate to it. Lyrically it was one of those songs that, when I read it, there was an immediate connection. There's a lot of work that gets done on lyrics, obviously, in Rush. But every so often we get presented with a set of lyrics that really nails it, and that was one of those songs."

"Absolutely, it was all about where we came from, and what we escaped," seconds Geddy. "That's the strength of the song, and what gives it enduring resonance for so many people in so many different countries. There are so many people who came out of the suburbs and know that feeling, know what that kind of cultural wasteland looks like and smells like, and that song really hit it for them. It wasn't the first song of Neil's that resonated with me. Being the guy who sings his lyrics, there's a lot of stuff before that time I could get behind. But it was a shift, because it was the first one that spoke more directly about where we all come from. And for that reason it is quite different. It's a song about alienation. When you are a teenager growing up, wherever you're growing up, you are experiencing some sort of alienation. You can't relate to anybody; you can't relate to the world around you. And I think in 'Subdivisions' it's very specific: cause and effect. Living in a bland, uninspiring environment is something to rebel against. And I think a lot of people can identify with those same feelings, that enclosed feeling of being trapped in a bland environment."

And fans can immerse themselves in this song and know they are experiencing the same yearning together, across state lines.

"I think it makes them feel better that they aren't the only ones who have that feeling," Geddy continues. "It's validation: I feel like this. It happens to me when I listen to music. When there's something that rings true to my life, you bond with that song. And obviously I came from a suburb, so when we're singing about that, we're not making it up. We lived it and we're talking about it. It has an authentic resonance. But it took some time for us to realize that song was kind of a touchstone for a lot of people."

"Every generation has that," adds Lifeson. "The Who with 'My Generation' and 'Teenage Wasteland,' the whole grunge decade. You become the carriers of the banner, I guess, and everybody kind of relates to you."

On the musical front, Neil explains that "Alex and I are the rhythm section in a lot of the parts of that song; that was a great role for us to play when Geddy's doing those keyboard parts. That's the first song where Alex and I locked in. When he's playing the rhythm, it's basically a bass part, and the bass pedals take the bass frequencies. But he's playing his guitar part, following the drums. So the two of us interlocked as a rhythm section that we hadn't been able to do before. Little things like that can carry you through. You learn from them. So often with specific songs I can trace a lineage: okay, we tried that experiment there and the next time we took it this way and it got a little better, and this time we really made it work."

Geddy recalls a dustup with Terry on the recording of the song. "He wanted to get a particular vocal sound, to play around with the mic, with the compression on it, and he had me in the studio singing it over and over and over and over again. And I just remember thinking this is not good for my performance, in the end, because by the time he has the sound that he wants, I'm going to be burned out on the song and need a break. Or my voice will be burned out. It was just a way of doing things that I didn't necessarily agree with, and there were a few different conceptual discussions, where we didn't see eye to eye. And it started increasing, happening more regularly. It wasn't a bad vibe thing, more a conflict of ideas. Those things happen in close quarters. If you are passionate about your ideas, you're going to insist on them a little bit. And if you get shot down, so be it. But everybody has to be all on board. We either all agree or we don't agree. And if we don't agree, we move on, try something else."

"I do remember this being a bit of a bone of contention," seconds Terry. "In 'Subdivisions' there's a vocal sound in there. And instead of doing it all in post — in other words, instead of waiting until I had the performance — I put Ged through about two hours of setup so that when we did the vocal, it sounded the way it sounds on the record, as he sang it. He wasn't very happy about that. I wanted to create the vibe in the chorus, and Geddy was like, 'Well, why don't you just do it later? Because I don't want to stand here and sing over and over again.'

"And I kept saying, 'Well, just bear with me, because we're really close; it's going to pay off in the end. It's an important thing.' I thought it was important to sing how he does there, as opposed to just singing a dry vocal, for instance, with a bigger reverb on it or whatever. So yeah, that was an issue. I'm glad we went through it, because it's an important part of that song; it gives it a color that is important, and I didn't want to be experimenting later. I wanted it to sound like a high school hall. So we did it. He put himself through it and it paid off — it's a great chorus. I would probably create that in post now, but whether it would have the same drama to it is something that could be debated for many hours.

"But we did that with a lot of different things," continues Terry. "Wah-wah or the delays on the guitar. Like, solos would have the right delay, and if wah was needed, it would be there. We wouldn't add it later, and sort of make something with something else. It was made the way it was supposed to be. Which I think is very, very important. When you are trying to create dynamics and flow in a solo or a vocal part, you need to be hearing what it is you are singing with, especially if there are dramatic effects on it. And I think that's very dramatic, the chorus in 'Subdivisions.'"

Terry is referring here to Geddy's dovetailed sort of response to the robotic, lower-voiced "Subdivisions," which is a great hook and a memorable part of a memorable song. This had widely been credited to Toronto broadcast personality Mark Dailey, whom folks around the metro area always mimicked because of his super bassy "City TV — everywhere" tagline. In fact, it is Neil who says this part.

Other than this vocal issue, Terry was on board with the prominent role keyboards played. This wasn't always the case, but in this song, no problem. "It's built around a keyboard riff, but it worked because I made sure. I love guitars and I love drums. So drums, bass and guitars were the forefront for me. And the fact that keyboards took up a lot of space on that record was something I had no control over. But it works for that tune. Without it, it wouldn't work.

"But later on, if the keyboards did take on a big role, sometimes the guitars slip back. And if you listen to all their records, you'll notice there's a difference in the perspective from one to another. I love 'Subdivisions' though. I remember driving down Kingston Road one day, in some beat-up old Toyota, and it came on and it sounded incredible. It still jumps out of the speakers — it's a very exciting tune."

"Well, you know, hindsight is twenty-twenty," laughs Alex, on whether he was happy with his role in the song. "I remember when we were mixing 'Subdivisions,' I kept pushing the faders up on the guitars. Because throughout the whole mix, it sounded low to me. But that was the nature of the way that song was developed. And that song sort of announces itself out in the choruses and bridges and takes on a different shift from all the instruments. But at the time, I found it difficult."

"It was hard for him," says Geddy, in support. "He had been the lead, rhythm. All the texture created came from Alex's guitar, and all of a sudden there is this other guy in the room, this electronic synth guy, filling up a lot of those roles. So he had to continually redefine his approach. It put him in a tough spot, and he always rose to the occasion. Sometimes after the record was finished, he would feel a little, 'Well, I don't know if I really got the sound that I like,' as a guitarist. So it was a constant comparison to the past, kind of his desire to have a super sound. When you're making records, you're always looking for that super sound; you're always looking for that album that sounds better than anything you've ever done. The nature of our collaboration is to adjust.

"Because you go in with an idea of what you think a Rush album should be. I have my Rush album sound in my head,

Alex has his Rush album sound and Neil has the same thing. And when you bring it to the table and you start listening to everybody's idea, you have to shift. There's compromise, there's adaptation, and you end up with something that none of us expected. Because you can't possibly know what is being thrown at you by the guys in the room, and a producer. It's constantly changing. The reason Rush works is that we allow ourselves that moment to adapt to someone's idea. I know it's a corny comparison, but in sports, say you're a batter. You come onto the scene and you're hitting everything, and then the pitcher adjusts to you and you have to adjust back. And it's kind of the same thing we go through with each other. We constantly are allowing each other latitude, and then we have to react to those new ideas and let that new adjustment take us to wherever we're going to go."

Baseball is never far from Geddy's mind. The band credits on the inner sleeve of *Signals* list Alex as first base, Neil as third base and Geddy as pitcher, which is a bit telling, as Geddy had been increasingly calling the shots across these records, becoming essentially co-producer as time went on. Other positions on the field are littered throughout the remaining credits, with Terry taking left field.

"I recall being totally into it, as we all were," continues Alex, who goes on to make a curious point. "But what would happen was there would be a one album delayed reaction. You know, you get into making a record, and like with *Signals*, you make the record — we were all on board, we loved it, we finished it, we're proud of it. Time goes by, you tour it, things start bugging you about it and you save those things that got to you until the next record. And if you go to the next record, and you smell it's going in the same direction, that's where you butt heads. You go, 'In retrospect, I wasn't happy about that particular thing. I don't want to go there.' And over the course of those synth-period records, it became increasingly an issue at the start of our writing sessions. What role were the synths going to play? And eventually they took a smaller and smaller role, as we found ourselves kind of drowning inside the possibilities."

"Yeah, it did kind of get like that," says Geddy, who says eventually it all became formulaic. "It just became the same suffocating feeling we had when we were doing those really long pieces. It was like, 'This has become a formula. This is wrong and it's got to stop.' And that's when we started looking for more inventive ways of using keys. Eventually we said, 'Hey, it's time to get rid of them.' So they slowly came into our lives, they swallowed us and then they slowly departed. And now they are always there if we need that noise, that sound, that melody, but I think we're happy going back to a three-piece world."

Adds Paul Northfield on this conundrum: "I do remember very specifically that on 'Subdivisions' it was hard work getting the guitar to sit. Because the whole of 'Subdivisions' is driven by a keyboard part, and so the role of the guitar is a supporting role, not the fundamental role. That was obviously a difficult one for Alex, because it's like, 'Okay, how do I fit around this huge keyboard sound?' It was kind of like hunting for a type of guitar part that would fit against the keyboard part, and I think that is something he never had to deal with before. If you took out the keyboard and tried to do that song with guitar, would it be that song? I remember us all struggling, and me too, in making suggestions about the way to approach a guitar part that might sit well and have a serious presence on the song, and at the same time allowing that keyboard part to be what it was."

And what did the team come up with? Well, Alex is in there pretty much constantly, but two things: he is mixed low, and it's almost as if his parts are reacting to the synth parts, in meek deference to them. Sometimes he is in direct back-and-forth dialogue with them and sometimes he is strumming behind them. It's a moot point, but in response to the hypothetical Paul conjures, if you took away the synth part and raised the faders on the guitar, "Subdivisions" kind of *would* be the same song. There are myriad ways to turn the song into a straight guitar/bass/drums configuration, as there are with any synthesizer-dominated song. But indeed, in the case of this one, Alex is already all over it, just not particularly loud — or inventive. One assumes the idea was to leave the inventing cap at home on this one and let the synthesizers ring out.

Next comes "The Analog Kid," which represents a joyous expression of not only guitars but also guitar riff, perhaps an example of the kind of correction Alex talks about, with respect to the album needing more Lifeson. It's only come chorus time that Geddy performs a synth wash of the listener's brain. Otherwise it's a wall of guitars, as applied to a fast-paced yet very melodic rocker. Through the first two tracks on *Signals*, it becomes apparent the band had found a plush blend of all their sounds, from sympathetic guitars through simple synths, down into gnarly enough yet not off-putting bass on top of smooth drums . . . there's something creamy about *Signals* that makes even *Moving Pictures* — much vaunted and digital — sound like a demo. This might be the first and the last time every texture and frequency on a Rush album meshed with sonorous tranquility.

Neil's lyric for "The Analog Kid" feels like a seamless continuation of the story laid out for us in "Subdivisions," with a boy lying in the grass and dreaming about possibility. There's even a love interest, with "The fawn-eyed girl with sun-browned legs" written as a tribute to a girl Neil met at fifteen while on family vacation in Ohio and subsequently wrote letters to the rest of the summer.

"It's kind of that postadolescent period you go through," explained Neil, during the album's radio premiere group interview, "where everything but where you are seems to be larger than life. Whether you're in the suburbs or a city or a small town, whatever, it all seems to be so gray, whereas when you talk about faraway places or think about London, England, or Los Angeles or New York, these places seem to be totally removed from your experience and they seem to be literally larger than life, such romantic things. And it's basically a picture of that vision, you know, of being in what you're used to and dreaming about what you're not used to."

Neil admits the nice turn of phrase in this one, "too many hands on my time," was inspired by the Styx song "Too Much Time on My Hands," inescapable on the radio in 1981.

Musically, "The Analog Kid" is comfortable terrain for Rush, and Neil gets that. "Certainly, our fans get impatient when we're doing anything other than just 'rock.' I even understand all of them as a music fan, because you tend to grow and develop yourself that way in your appreciation. I never listened to lyrics when I was a kid — until I started writing them and took an interest in the craft and became sensitive. But it was guitars and drums, you know? That's what I responded to as a teenager. I'm generous about this deliberately because I understand all the viewpoints and appreciate them all — and of course welcome them all. Anyone who likes our music, it's wonderful, and for those who don't, it's wonderful too. We made it as good as we could, and that's a work ethic I ascribe to."

Asked by Greg Quill from *Music Express* about how his lyrics match up to the music, Neil says, "Many of the rhythm shifts and style changes the songs go through are actually built into the lyrics in some way. Other times we're deliberately perverse. In 'The Analog Kid,' for example, Geddy and I were talking about possible musical treatments. When you read the lyrics, you're right, it would have made a lovely ballad or a medium tempo soft rock piece. We said, all right, that's what the lyrics suggest — let's not do it that way. Let's take an entirely different point of view, using two diametrically opposed dynamic approaches — hard rock for the verses and something really watery, almost angelic for the choruses, cut off the thrust of the song and back-pedal."

Next up is "Chemistry," which could have been called "Signals." In any event, it serves as the album's title track conceptually. Alex has called this one a true collaboration both musically and lyrically. In terms of the music, the band cooked this up during sound checks as a bit of an experiment where each member threw in a musical signature. Neil came up with the rhythms heard in the choruses, Geddy the synth washes in the bridge and Alex the jagged chords heard in the verse. Lyrically, Geddy and Alex had some phrases they sent Neil's way, with Peart arranging them and adding to them, creating a song about actual chemistry and less knowable forms of chemistry like personal relationships, music and the paranormal.

Closing side one of the original vinyl is "Digital Man," which might serve as Rush's best expression of their love for what the Police were doing. Not only are the verses and choruses conceivable as Police-style reggae, but even the driving 4/4 rock parts, with Alex's jazzy, rainy guitar, sound like the Police in heavy rock mode. Plus there's a jammy instrumental break that evokes images of "Walking on the Moon." If we didn't get that this was progressive reggae but reggae all the same, Geddy sings of Zion, Babylon and tropical isles.

This track was worked on at both the *Exit . . . Stage Left* repair sessions and at the Grange in Muskoka, where Neil penned lyrics by the fire (this was March in Canada — still winter) and Geddy and Alex configured the music in the barn, which had been set up for jamming. Terry needed convincing about this one because of its obvious reggae influence.

Notes Paul, "The band always — and Geddy particularly — was happy to be influenced by people they liked. And for the fans, that's something they appreciated and sometimes they didn't. But from day one, where they used to be heavily influenced by Zeppelin, and then later, everything from the Police to Frankie Goes to Hollywood — they were quite happy to try to integrate it into what they did. At the time when the Police were really big, the guys loved them, and it's obviously in there on *Signals*, on 'Digital Man' and 'New World Man,' where they sound not that much like normal Rush at all. But when they liked something, they would allow it to influence them and see where it took them. At the same time, you have to be objective to get the best stuff. You want to introduce ideas from other people, but then you have to make them your own and arrive at a place where you go, 'Yes, this is good not just because it's different and I'm bored, but good because it actually is a powerful statement, meaningful.'"

"That was the mishmash approach to trying to take diverse influences and make them work together," noted Neil at the radio premiere. "It starts out basically as a hard rock trio, then goes into a ska or reggae style of rhythmic approach, then it has sort of a modern European contemporary approach to the sequencer chorus and then goes right back down to a basic trio again for the instrumental section, and then builds up through the changes again. It's all very confused [laughs]."

"It's all very confusing to me too," seconds Ged. "We spent so much time on that, trying to get it to feel right. And for the longest time we had no faith in the song, and then suddenly it just blossomed. And now for me it's one of my favorite songs on the album. It just works great. It was a battle to get all these influences to feel natural somehow, to feel like they worked. It was like fighting the machines around you for days, and then eventually it just came together."

"Digital Man" features one of Neil's most obscure early lyrics — perhaps he's even writing a little new wavy, a little flippant. He's explained that it's essentially addressing what you'd think if you were a futuristic guy, or a "now" guy, on the cutting edge of current technology. It's a stretch though to say there's any thematic link to "Subdivisions" or "The Analog Kid," as the band has suggested. This one's closer to the oblique character portrait in "Tom Sawyer" than anything else on *Signals*. In any event, Neil says his lyrics on *Signals* are about reality, real people, even going so far as to say they are nonfiction — it has been suggested the inspiration for this one is Peter Jensen, who engineered the digital mastering of the *Moving Pictures* album.

Geddy put a finer point on the Jensen connection, telling Jim Ladd, "The song came out of a little bit of personal comedy. We had the title way before we had a concept. There was a guy we hired, I think it was on *Moving Pictures*, to bring all this digital equipment so that we could master the album digitally, and he was sort of a 'strange' example of modern man, without going into too much detail. We were sitting around talking, and Le Studio had gotten their own digital equipment, so there was really no need to hire our digital man this time.

"And we were trying to figure out beds, you know, bed assignments, how many guys in the crew we could take to the house near Le Studio, because the situation is you live right on the premises. So somebody came out with the phrase, 'Well, I guess we won't need a bed for the digital man' and everybody went [snaps his fingers] 'Fantastic!' So we wrote it down and Neil developed a whole concept about the transience of modern man in the society we're living in. That spurred the tune and the feel for the tune, but it represents technology getting to a certain point, the ease that one can float from one part of society to another, and one part of the world to another, the communications race and the whole situation."

As for the reference to Zion, Geddy explains to Jim that "Zion is two states of mind really. There's the Zion of the Rastafarians, which is really the one I guess we're talking about; it's supposed to be the homeland and the ideal. The Rastafarians are always trying to get back to Zion; they try to mold their lifestyle where they originally feel they come from. In that particular chorus, I think it's sort of a perplexing situation with our digital man. Because here's a guy working with modern technology and being as modern as you can possibly be, and yet he's thinking about these simple soulful places like Zion. 'Lover's wings to fly on:' it's, don't carry me away too much on these computer bits; leave something for my soul. There's these digital men and women running around the world totally being trained and they're like, 'Yeah, I am the digital guy; I'm hip to this thing and I know the whole rap, and I have to inform everybody else.'"

The angular and electric reggae continues onto side two of *Signals* with "The Weapon," designated Part II of "Fear." The song stems from a drum machine pattern cooked up by Geddy and his friend Oscar, which Neil then had to learn on regular drums.

As Neil told Greg Quill of *Music Express* at the time, "Nowadays, lyrics seem to come first, simply because they establish a framework or a mood. Sometimes the other guys come in with lots of musical ideas that don't have a place 'til the song is written. An interesting exercise in juxtaposition is 'The Weapon.' I had these really doomy, black images in there and Geddy had written a lot of the musical sections for it at home, as a sort of electro-beat, modern dance exercise. We weren't sure that we'd ever use it.

"Now, because Geddy has to sing the words, a lot comes down to decisions he and I make. He persisted with his idea that we should approach the treatment again from a really abstract point of view, juxtaposing his electronic dance music with the dark, doom-laden lyric of mine, and making it work somehow. And I think we did. I'm really glad it took the brooding, heavy quality away from the lyrics. 'The Weapon' is part of a three-piece I've been working on, called 'Fear.' It has to do with the way fear is used as a psychological weapon against us all. To bring it down to mere words, I'm dealing here with religion and religiously controlled government, not necessarily with war or the nuclear arms race."

Next is "New World Man," which as an advance single had fans up in arms more so than "Subdivisions." The jarring clash with past Rush values was not so much the reggae lilt or Alex's benign Andy Summers guitar lines, but rather the sequenced synth part, which is almost comical in its nerdy new waveness. The song was designated Project 3:57 because that was the amount of time deemed necessary in order for the band to have a full album's worth of material. It was written and recorded nearly spontaneously, in two days to be precise, which Neil figures might be a Rush record.

Explains Geddy: "That was something that started to happen early on. We always felt there was one more song we could put on a record. It started way back with *2112*. 'Twilight Zone' we threw on at the last minute. We wrote it in the studio, recorded it, all over a matter of two days. And that became a tradition for us that we kind of looked forward to. What's going to be the last-minute song on this record? Because so much of our stuff is rehearsed, planned out, it was nice to have something on each record that was off the cuff. 'Vital Signs' was like that too, as was 'New World Man.'"

"'New World Man' would be the one I was thinking, hey, this sounds a lot like the Police," figures Terry. "Deep down inside, my thoughts were 'Why are we doing this?' The Police are doing it so well themselves; why are we doing it? But we pursued it, and we made it unique enough that it has some interesting parts. And lyrically it has some substance. I've grown to love it over the years, but at the time it was a hard one for me to get my head around. It just seemed an odd way to go. I'm not really a big reggae fan, so that also affected the way I thought about it. If the band said to me, 'We need some kind of influence; what do you think we should do?' reggae wouldn't be what I would have suggested.

"But it was a very commercial tune. I saw that, and I worked hard to make sure we put all the elements in and it sounded the way it should in order to come across as a commercial song. I don't know if it was consciously commercial or subconsciously commercial. Invariably we would go in with a set number of tunes, and I would see the commercial aspect in a tune, like 'The Spirit of Radio,' which really wasn't commercial, but it turned out it had so much energy and just jumped out at radio that it worked. But I'm sure if I took that into an A&R department at that time, from a different band, they would probably tell me to go home and rethink my career."

Lyrically, Neil's idea was to knit together some of the themes from the rest of the album, but more than anything, the character seems like an amalgamation of "The Analog Kid," "Digital Man" and "Tom Sawyer." For his part, Geddy associates it with "Tom Sawyer" and "Circumstances," figuring the unifying concept of all three is Neil's interest in change.

The song reached #1 on the Canadian charts, staying there for two weeks in October of '82. In the U.K. it got to #42 and in the U.S. it hit #21, becoming and remaining the band's only Top 40 single in the States. The song sensibly went into the band's live set. But shockingly, moving forward, despite its being the band's only U.S. Top 40 hit, between the years of 1986 and the retirement of the band in 2015, "New World Man" would be performed on one tour and one tour only, the campaign in support of *Vapor Trails*.

"Losing It" is the only so-called ballad on *Signals*, and the band's first since "Different Strings," if that could be called a ballad. Featuring a regal, renaissance waltz pattern and an *A Farewell to Kings* vibe, the song looks at two professionals losing their skills from age, a writer and a dancer. For the latter, Neil took some measure of inspiration from the Shirley MacLaine movie *The Turning Point*. The writer sounds very much like Ernest Hemingway, and indeed the final lyric is "The bell tolls for thee."

Asked by Jim Ladd about this song and whether he fears "losing it" from growing old, Geddy says, "I don't know if it's necessarily by age, but of course I think anybody who considers themselves to be even a little bit creative has a fear that that'll all suddenly be gone one day. I don't think about it too much. I hope I don't wake up one day and I'm, like, a cookie, 'I can't do anything but lie there!'

"I think it's a fear that exists; to some artists it's a devastating fear. After they finish a record, it's like 'Oh God, will I ever be able to do this again?' I used to feel like that. After I wrote a song I thought was good I'd never think I could write a song I thought was good again. But you get more confidence in your ability. And the longer I'm in the business, I realize I'm getting a little loonier and I have a sort of lunatic confidence in myself. So I figure, 'Okay, yeah, put me in any sort of situation and I'll do it.' I'm happy as long as I have something to do. As long as I have an album to work on or a song to write or a gig to do, that keeps me happy. I guess there's a little bit of fear of growing old and not being able to do those things. I'd say it exists. I think it probably does in most musicians or in most people."

Neil has indicated that a second layer to this tale posits whether ignorance is bliss when it comes to great talent. In other words, which is more tragic — never having mastery at a craft, or having it and then losing it?

Wrote Neil in the *Signals* tour program: "Like the verse sections for 'The Analog Kid,' the main theme for this song came from Alex's holiday exercises (we all did our homework!). We worked out the verses and choruses while we were in rehearsal and made a skeletal demo of it with just keyboards and drums, then put it away until we got to the studio. We had talked for a while about getting Ben Mink to play electric violin somewhere on this album, and this seemed like the perfect track. Once we got into the studio, we developed the jazzy solo section, recorded the basic track and gave Ben a call. Fortunately, he was able to get away from his group, FM, for a couple of days and bring his unique instrument up to play his heart out for us . . . We worked him hard, squeezed him dry and threw him away. He just stood there in front of the console, taking it and giving it, fueled by occasional sips from a bottle of C.C. Not only the monumentally fantastic solo did we demand, but we had him multiple-tracking an entire string section as well. That'll teach him to be our friend!"

Mink remembers what it was like working with Geddy for the first time. Ben would be deeply involved in Geddy's solo album, *My Favorite Headache*. "It was the first time I'd worked with him," recalls Mink, meaning Geddy. "FM was touring on the *Moving Pictures* tour with Rush and that's where I met Geddy. We became fast friends, and then when they were working on the next record, he said, 'You know, I think we'd really love to have the violin. Would you be into doing that?' They sent me a cassette, which was the method of sending in those days, and then I went to Montreal, Morin Heights, and spent a day or two tracking and just having a blast. Just a wonderful experience.

"Neil was there, Alex was there, and while Geddy was doing his keyboards and vocal parts, we were in the other room forming a wedding band. So everyone was there all the time, where Alex was the violinist and I was the guitar player, and Neil played 'Wipe Out.' We put together a whole set of like ten tunes. It was the Ziv Orchestra, in honor of Zivojinovic, which is Alex's last name. They're fantastic people, really, and as a producer and as a musician, it makes your job so much easier when you've got people who can really play — the real thing. And then you unfortunately get used to dealing with people who are that talented, and when you meet mere mortals again, then it's a lot more work."

"He's a wonderful player," says Terry about Mink, "and he has a very strong sound. What we did was, we had a spot for him to play, and asked him to develop some parts, which he did. Then we sifted through it — the usual stuff — and got the right take of it, the definitive take. His personality comes out in his playing."

"Losing It" wasn't played live until the R40 tour of 2015, Rush's very last go-round. Mink joined them for the world live debut of the song, in hometown Toronto, and on one other occasion live. The other three of the five times total the song was played, the violin duties were handled by Jonathan Dinklage.

"Countdown" closes *Signals* with surging sinister synth sounds similar to the ones that opened the album eight songs back. Alex is hitting spare chords amidst helicopter sounds, and Neil systematically arrives at a rhythm, his drums sounding gorgeous. There might be a reason for this. After calling "Countdown" "the troubled child," Neil, standing in the ruins of Le Studio, said, "I remember we moved the drums from here over to that side of the room because we couldn't get it to feel right. And it was the last track we were trying to get for that album, and just nothing was working. We changed all the drumheads to a different kind. Any coach knows, right? We just had to keep trying different things, so there was a lot of heartbreak and tensions. And playing a song a hundred times over again, it hurts after a while. Any time you have a collaboration, there's gonna be disagreements. But overall, it's such a rich memory for me."

After the continual build through and over the top of the first verse, we're into a bit of post-punk, followed by heavy prog — a bit of everything we've heard across this provocative and well-assembled record. As a bonus, late in the sequence, there's even something of a true synth solo, where Geddy plays on a Minimoog. Notes Terry, "I remember getting extremely involved in 'Countdown,' and trying to make that as realistic as possible so it had some value to it, not just the intro but the whole song."

Neil curiously thought the song "didn't work," but lauds the first attempt at writing a song that is essentially a short documentary.

The track is inspired by a trip the band took to Cape Kennedy in Florida (specifically Red Sector A, the VIP area, hence that song title on *Grace Under Pressure*) to watch the liftoff of the space shuttle *Columbia* on April 12, 1981. This would be the record's third and last single, and its video would be memorable for its NASA-authorized space footage. Suitably, Neil spoke of the album in general as the first that was pointedly about real, ordinary people, their dreams, their ideals, their environments. Astronauts are arguably beyond normal people, but they too began as the boy watching the sky in "The Analog Kid" or the teen on "Subdivisions" or, possibly, along the way, something of a digital man. Neil dedicated the song to two such people, astronauts John Young and Robert Crippen, and the rest of the folks at NASA who treated the band to a "truly once-in-a-lifetime experience."

"It was an experience that none of us will ever forget," Alex told *Hit Parader*. "We had been invited down to the Cape to witness the launch through some people who work at our record label. When we got there, we met a man named Gerry Griffin, who works for NASA, and he was incredibly informative and entertaining. He spent hours taking us on a VIP tour of the facility and telling us stories about some of the launches they've had over the years. We all felt like little kids listening to the stuff he was telling us. It was like we were in a dream.

"As it happened, we almost didn't get to see the launch. We had flown into Florida right after a show in Nashville, with another gig in Dallas the next day. The day of the launch there was a computer malfunction which postponed the launch for a day. Well, we had waited until the last possible minute to leave the Cape and make our plane to Dallas. We were so late, in fact, that our limo driver had to actually drive the car onto the runway in order to get us there in time. We made it to Dallas all right, but we hired a private plane to take us back to the Cape the next day — we weren't gonna take any chances. Luckily, everything else went fairly smooth, and we saw the launch the next day. It was absolutely one of the most incredible moments of my life."

As Howard explains, "We ran into Gerry Griffin, who was the director of NASA, because we let his children into a show once. And he was so grateful that he had phoned up the band and said, 'I'm inviting all of you to come to the launchpad and watch the takeoff of a space shuttle.' Which was really cool. We stood around it and it was a *Close Encounters*-type vibe. We're all standing in the dark watching. We were the closest you can get to the launching pad, which was three miles. We were in front of Walter Cronkite. They were behind us, and we were standing up front with all the heavy brass. We eventually watched it lift off, and that was one of those really great life experiences — standing there and just watching it take off while it rips the sky open. It inspired the song 'Countdown.' Every night we were on tour we had that song, and we would launch that shuttle from the stage."

The band was able to get some footage from NASA that they put into both their stage show and the production video for "Countdown."

"NASA was incredibly cooperative with us," says Alex. "They were willing to give us these special films, which the public never has access to. NASA has cameras located on the launch towers, on the engines — practically everywhere. Most people are only able to see what's on TV. Normally those other tapes are reserved only for administration officials and scientists. But through the help of Mr. Griffin we were able to procure some of those films and incorporate them into a video. It really adds to the presentation."

Neil sums up the overall experience of recording *Signals*, not focusing on the hardship of it, but indicating he was pleased with the result. "Oh, we changed hugely through the '80s in a wonderful way, and *Signals* was a very happy album because we came off the success of *Moving Pictures* very confident. We really branched out broadly on that album, all over the place, stylistically, rhythmically, melodically, arrangement-wise — we were growing hugely through that time."

Pretty quickly, because of the two strong singles, plus the "Countdown" video, and in no small part due to spillover from *Moving Pictures*, *Signals* went platinum in the States, reaching #10 on the Billboard album charts, but also #1 in Canada and #3 in the U.K. *Signals* came a year and a half after *Moving Pictures*, and the band had issued a double live album in between. It would be another year and a half until we saw the next studio record, and shockingly, Terry Brown wouldn't be its producer.

"There was a lot of success coming out of England with keyboard bands and pink hair and that sort of stuff, but I just wasn't into it," says Terry. "And I didn't really understand it well enough, so I didn't have the expertise and the chops to be able to say, 'Let's do this; this is great.' Because I didn't like the electronic drums. That didn't go down very well. So we said let's take a little break from each other. Well, unfortunately the break's been way too long. But it was needed. I mean, if you think about it, it's rare for people to work together for that long a period in any case — we did ten albums together over a period of about seven years. It was a pretty creative period, so I'm happy with it.

"But basically, that was the end of my tenure with them. I don't think it's rocket science. I wasn't there anymore. They wanted to do something else, and they've done it for the last ten albums. And that's great. We reached a point where a change was necessary, and it certainly wasn't going to be with Geddy, Alex or Neil. The only other change would be me. As Neil put it, it's like boyfriend and girlfriend — they need a break from each other — and who knows if we'll get back together and do something in the future? Well, he didn't live up to that part of the bargain, but we did split up. But yeah, it was time for a change. I had other things I wanted to do, and I didn't really want to do an electronic band, which is where I thought it was going."

"In a genuine way, honestly," is how Neil characterized Rush's break with Terry. "We had such an important formative series of projects with Terry that were all mutually satisfying and fun. We were brothers. To the point where you would make that fourth member of the band analogy. But that of course meant we started to think like him. And I remember *Signals*, when the three of us were away working on the songs and arrangements, we could always say, 'Well, Broon will tell us to cut that part.' We could already think what he was going to say, and sometimes we would make that change, anticipating it. And we had that same thing subsequently with Peter Collins — we did a few albums together — that we could think what he would.

"And the same thing with writers and editors. I've learned from them all, and I notice when I'm writing my own work, I would think, 'Well, Paul would tell me to do this; I know he will, so I'll just do it.' But that's dangerous when you're trying to progress and learn. A relationship has to grow. We had only ever worked with him, so naturally we were curious to see what someone else might bring to us, might take us different ways, as many people have over the years, right up to Nick Rasculinecz, who kicked us into different directions and urged us out of our habits and out of ourselves and many other things. That's been a cyclical pattern that has happened with a lot of people, and not just with Terry. And it really was genuine. We just knew, 'If not then, never,' and we have to do this."

The rending and ending were accomplished with a pretty impressive level of maturity and diplomacy — the main summit took place on the tour bus after a show in Miami — but that seems to be a given in the Rush camp. Loyalties run deep and for years and years, and when there's a split, it's always accomplished with civility and tact.

Neil says the band's time with Terry was "a remarkable, magical thing. Because we grew up together, we evolved together, in the largest sense. And you know, we did get out of hand in all those ways that bands err to, but we didn't stay there. We would scold each other, in a way, or chide each other, a gentle tease. 'Don't act like a rock star, okay?' And the others of us were sensible enough to go, 'Oh, I don't want to be that person.'

"Self-correcting again. It is very much the dynamics of this band to grow together that way. I've never tried to deny there were frictions or disagreements. It's how they're handled. That's the ultimate point that maybe we can teach. If only we would all explode on each other, but honestly, that has never happened and it won't, no matter how serious our disagreements will be. We'll find a commonality.

"And I like that better than compromise, because none of us should compromise. But we can find common ground from the three extremes that we all are. We are sometimes opposite each other, but in a way that does allow us mutual respect — the magic word. It's about not responding with rage to anyone's criticism or suggestion. But that does happen! We've all seen in the behind-the-scenes footage somebody going completely disproportionately out of their minds over a tiny bit of criticism. A band can't survive with that kind of thing.

"But you can survive: you tell someone what you like about the thing, but, 'Maybe it seems like you're trying to go for . . .' Here's an example of a dynamic that will work. You will hear some music and they'll say, 'I can see what you're trying to go for here, and I like that, but it's maybe too much of that. This riff shouldn't repeat too many times.' It's all a disagreement, now that I think about it. We always disagree — but it's in a productive way.

"When I bring lyrics to Geddy and he has to set them to music, he'll go, 'Well, I really love these two lines.' Okay, what a great way to start — he loves them! Start from a position of strength and security, so he's already made me feel good, and then he says, 'Well, I can see what you're going for; I don't like those too much, but if I can add two more like that . . .' And I'm already there: 'Yes, I wish that could happen.' I want him to like them. And I want them to be made.

"So it's all positive — all of that. It is essentially disagreement, but lyrics are not a script. It's not the Ten Commandments; it's just a bunch of ideas. And for Geddy to like any of them is great, and if the two of them put it to music, that's fantastic. And I don't compromise anything at all. If anything, I end up with more than I ever had. That's the other part of it. It raises the game by saying, 'Yes, those two lines could be better.' And then I make them better, and the whole thing is better than if mine had been a dictate, a mandate. 'Take these lyrics and don't change a word.' Who would suffer? Me.

"Desire must be the underlying factor," continues Neil, on making the art and the personality work over a long period of time. "And that little word, that contains a multitude of continual satisfaction, continual stimulation, the enjoyment of working together — and not feeling compromised by it. I feel like I do my best work with those two guys. So why would I not want to, you know?

"I like the three-piece balance, honestly, because we always noticed that it was hard to have factions. In the early days, I was in bands that had five members, and it would always be three against two. You would break up into teams like that. It's pretty hard to do that in a three-piece. We would have two against one, and the one has to decide, okay, do I really want to be isolated, all by myself? It's not me and my pal against those guys. When you're isolated by the other two guys being mad at you, that's not a nice feeling. I have to think that's part of it. If the other two guys think you're wrong, maybe you are. That's a whole different dynamic. And it takes maturity and circumspection to make that work. But there has never been any extreme isolation like that. When I bring up these things, I hope you understand they are tiny little issues, little ripples in the stream as we went along. But there was always contention. Working together is always about disagreement."

Paul Northfield was also there, watching the creative fissure form between the band and their unofficial fourth member, Terry, in real time. "I was caught in the middle sometimes because I could see their frustrations and the fact they wanted very clear and precise direction. Sometimes when they weren't sure themselves, they wanted a clear 'Okay, we're going to do this.' And I think Terry wasn't able at that time to give them the kinds of answers they were looking for. At the end of the day, there was tension making that record, there's no question about it. It felt, in some ways, that they'd grown apart. I did have a feeling it would be the last record they were going to do with Terry. But you don't know. Things could've changed just as easily."

The Professor, May 10, 1980, at the Palladium, New York, NY.

May 11, 1980, at the Palladium, New York; this was the last of a four-night stand.

Geddy with blue Rickenbacker, Madison Square Garden, New York City, May 18, 1981.

Alex and his classic *Moving Pictures* tour look, same Madison Square Garden show as left.

Another shot of Neil from May 10, 1980, at the Palladium.

Neil, Maple Leaf Gardens, November 17, 1982. Support on the night was Vancouver post-punk band the Payolas, featuring future production legend Bob Rock.

Geddy, Providence Civic Center, Providence, RI, December 5, 1982. Support act was Irish blues rocker Rory Gallagher.

Alex and his leather pants, same Providence show as left.

Geddy and a good look for him, Sporthalle, Böblingen, West Germany, May 6, 1983. Support on the night was Nazareth, who Rush supported in 1974 and 1975.

Alex: singer! Same show as left.

Ads for *Moving Pictures*, *Exit . . . Stage Left* and *Signals*.

Full band shot from Sporthalle, Böblingen, West Germany,
May 6, 1983.

RUSH

WEMBLEY ARENA

KENNEDY STREET ENTERPRISES
PRESENT

RUSH
IN CONCERT

Friday, 20th May, 1983
at 7.30 p.m.

UPPER TIER SOUTH
£5.00

TO BE RETAINED   See conditions on back

MAY
20
1983

ENTER AT
SOUTH DOOR
ENTRANCE

53
ROW

E
SEAT
★**32**

NEW WORLD
TOUR 1982-83

ALL AREA

GRACE UNDER PRESSURE

ON MERCURY RECORDS AND CASSETTES

RUSH GRACE UNDER PRESSURE

THE RUSH TRADITION CONTINUES WITH
"GRACE UNDER PRESSURE."
A MASTERFUL COLLECTION OF 8 NEW CLASSICS
ON AN ALBUM THAT SETS A NEW STANDARD OF ROCK.

RUSH

TOTAL ACCESS

GRACE UNDER
PRESSURE

WORLD TOUR
1984-85

WELCOME
TO THE
Rush 1984
"Grace under pressure"
– tour –
as we all know, toronto is ☆RUSH'S☆
hometown.....
Geddy Lee   Alex Lifeson   Neil Peart
invite you, their most loyal fans to be
– a part of –
the videotaping of their show!!!
you have the **3D** glasses,
you'll know when to wear them,
Smile! you'll be in everyone's
livingroom!

★ STAR JAM ★

NEIL PEART
STYLE

RUSH
EXIT... STAGE LEFT

RCA
SelectaVision
VideoDiscs

STEREO

RUSH!
(AT ONLY £4.49 IT'S BOUND TO GO FAST)

RUSH • GRACE UNDER PRESSURE **£4.49**	THE CURE • THE TOP **£4.49**
ROGER WATERS • THE PROS AND CONS OF HITCH HIKING **£4.49**	OMD • JUNK CULTURE **£4.49**

John Menzies

For people who appreciate music... and money.

With
**NEAL SCHON
STEVE SMITH
T. LAVITZ
NEIL PERT**
Produced by
RONNIE MONTROSE
PJ 88004

THIS IS SERIOUS
**Neil
Peart
No:1**
1985 Modern Drummer Readers Poll Results

VOTED NO. 1 ROCK DRUMMER

VOTED NO. 1 MULTI PERCUSSIONIST

VOTED NO. 1 RECORDED PERFORMANCE
(RUSH – Grace Under Pressure)

Zildjian
THE ONLY ■ SERIOUS CHOICE

- IN CONCERT -
R U S H
30PM WED OCT 03 1984

NO REFUNDS/EXCHANGES

Geddy with his hands full in Germany.

Richfield Coliseum, Richfield, Ohio, July 5, 1984. Support on the night was Gary Moore.

Echoing Neil's statement, Geddy also says, "We got to the point where we could kind of predict what he was going to say before he said it. His comments, although always true to his own sensibility and always honest, were comments we kind of knew were coming. And at that point, we looked at each other and said, 'Are we learning as much as we can be learning?' We were hungry to learn new technology, new ways to record. We were really into new input. And we had the feeling it wasn't going to happen unless we made a change. There were a couple other incidents during the recording of that record that came from us being more confident about what we were doing and having a bigger say in our own production. It's like father/child arguments. What we wanted to do was maybe different from his way of doing things — it was a natural outgrowing."

"We were all about change," seconds Alex. "That's what we lived on. We just came to a point where we really wanted to work with other people, just to experience it. Not with one other person, but with many other people. We grew up and it was now time to go out in the world and learn the next stage. And that meant leaving the relationship we had with Terry. So he came out on the road with us for a few days, and we traveled, and we just talked about how we were feeling, and we were very open about the whole new direction we were going in. He was a grown-up, a professional and he was like a brother, and so he understood where we were at and where we wanted to go. Like any kind of breakup, it's a little bit sad, but at the same time it was very exciting and liberating for us. I knew we needed to do it, and it was unfortunate that this was a person we had learned so much from and who had given us so many of his hours, invested in us, and you know, we had a lot of fun with. But it was just time to move on."

"He taught us a lot about structuring our music and taking a visual approach to sound," muses Geddy. "And that's one of the key lessons, in my life, as a person who makes records, to take that visual approach. It was kind of a painting you were doing, using the sounds as colors, how to balance them and all of that. He was a very progressive thinker, always up for an experiment, always up for something new. But we were hungry for a different opinion, but he was a big brother to us in a lot of ways, so it was difficult. And we do have fun together, with whomever we're working with. I mean, you've only got one life; you may as well enjoy it while you're working."

Ray says he had nothing to do with the decision. "No, those decisions never come from outside. They're always inside. We talk constantly about what we're going to do next, and we talked about the frustration some of us had making that record, and we just felt we were moving in a new direction. We had new technology and we wanted a fresh approach. We all agreed; there was no arm-twisting."

On Terry having been informed, Geddy says, "I think he was surprised. I don't remember the meeting so clearly, but my feeling is that he was surprised, and a little disappointed, that we chose to do that. But he totally understood. At least that's the face he painted for us. He's a good guy; he's not going to sit there and make us feel bad about it. He's a really good person. Even if he thought it was a terrible idea, he wouldn't make us feel bad about it. That's just the kind of person he is."

"Of course he was disappointed," adds Alex. "We had quite a long and active relationship. He came in in the very beginning. He was with us on the first record, and we put in a lot of miles together."

"He lived a couple blocks from me at that time too," says Geddy. "So we saw a lot of each other socially. So of course, it was difficult. You don't want those things to change. But at the end of the day, the music is first, and we've always put it first. Almost always [laughs]."

Reflects Terry, "I *was* surprised because I felt we would work this little glitch out. Because we always had. Plus we'd made a successful record. It wasn't like we made a dog. It came out, it had legs, did great business. Because it was a great combination of creative ideas; the chemistry was good between the four of us — really good. And I think when they moved on and did *Grace Under Pressure*, that became very apparent. But, you know, that's easy to say in retrospect.

"But so much water has passed under the bridge since then. I think it's been more emotional since then, to be honest with you. Just seeing what has been going on with their career: the recordings and how much I liked and disliked some of them and felt they may have not really made the right decisions in terms of recording. But again, that's the way I feel, looking at it from my standpoint. They are obviously satisfied with them, and they are the ones who have to pay the bills. But I enjoyed working with them so much — of course it would be nice to have done the next record and the next record. But I did a really nice body of work with them — that's enough. I'm satisfied. There have been times where I thought I should've been there to rectify a few wrongs, but again, it's so subjective."

With each new album, Geddy was taking more and more interest in the production of the records. Post-*Signals*, he got involved with a Toronto new wave band called Boys Brigade and produced their lone album, a self-titled record issued in 1983. He had also produced the third and last Wireless album, 1980's *No Static*. Howard Ungerleider had signed a management deal with Boys Brigade, which was then shifted over to SRO. This was not ideal for the band: the session dragged on for six months because

Geddy of course had to tour *Signals* — as well as figure out how to quit smoking, which he managed to do during this period.

"Yeah, I'm shooting my mouth off more and more every record," laughs Geddy, on his interest in the production side of things. "I was a student of production. I loved records, I listen to a lot of music, I wanted to make records, I wanted to be a producer at that time too. And so I was increasingly vocal throughout those years. Though we all were. I mean, we all had production ideas. We were all interested to a different degree. Alex was more interested in the whole engineering side of things. He loved to have his hands on the board. And I was into production ideas and different ways of recording songs, different song structures.

"For me it was hard to know what the role of a producer was. And in a way, because we had had Terry, we were a little spoiled by a guy who was an engineer and a producer and kind of collaborated with us. And it wasn't until he left the scene that we got the real education of what the fuck a producer does, because everybody has a different idea of what a producer is. You talk to a lot of musicians and they think the producer's an engineer. Well, that's not a producer to me. A producer is a guy who has his mind on the song — at all times — the structure of it, the performance, the thrust of the song, the resonance of the song. He has the song's best interest in mind at all times. Not the way the bass sounds or the drum sounds — that can be part of it too, but to me that's between musicians and the engineer — the producer oversees that. But I didn't know that at the time, and the journey from Terry Brown to the next record was a long and nightmarish one. And through that journey I learned a lot — we all did — about the role of producer. More from talking to thirty different producers than from making any one particular song.

"We were getting more confident. We had more ideas and we wanted to play with them," continues Ged. "For me, it comes from being a writer. The production thing is a natural extension of the writing of the song. Because when you start writing the song, you hear it in your head a particular way and you want to make it match. You want the actual recording to match that picture in your head. It can never do that without killing someone along the way, but it is something you strive for. That's how you start. And I think that's why I got interested in production. Around that time, I started working with a couple other bands, doing side projects, helping them with producing and learning the job of producing, which is a tough and thankless one [laughs]."

Geddy and Alex both agree that as a type, Terry was an engineer/producer, with Geddy saying, "What the frustration of *Signals* led us to believe, in a way, is that we want to have someone who is a producer/producer — a different background. That being said, Paul Northfield was starting to engineer for us, and Terry had stepped behind the console and became that producer/producer. But I think we still viewed him as an engineer/producer."

It must be said that many "producer/producers" are just lazy producers who can't engineer, or can't be bothered to engineer anymore, having apparently outgrown it (after having outgrown tape-op and tea boy). In other words, it's too flattering to call most of them a producer/producer — producer is far enough as far as titles go, with the caution that half of them don't produce anything but vague suggestions and cocaine debts. Indeed, Rush were "spoiled," as Geddy says, with Terry, this so-called engineer/producer. That's not to say the guys were wrong about Terry's sudden lack of genius ideas, but a solid engineer/producer is about as valuable a commodity as many bands are likely to see in their lifetimes.

"Maybe I was too pushy," reflects Geddy, about his growing role during *Signals*. "I'm sure I was feeling more confident. At the end of the day, when you're in a band, you are possessive of your stuff, your sound. But we've never had an atmosphere when we worked when ideas aren't welcome. Whoever is in the room, they have an idea, hey, speak up. We've always considered ourselves pretty open and democratic about that. But yeah, I was having more and more ideas, and over the next few years I got fairly possessed with production. And some of my ideas Terry didn't necessarily agree with. We had our moments where we would disagree about the end result or how to get the end result. And that happens in the studio. It wasn't the first time, and it won't be the last. You owe it to yourself to express your ideas. It's part of the process. Sometimes it's going to be argued about. Otherwise everyone is just being too damn polite. I would rather the right idea come out than everyone be polite and make a shitty record."

The *Signals* tour kicked off in early September of 1982, with old friend Rory Gallagher supporting most dates through to the end of the year. Picking up in mid-February, support came from Golden Earring, the veteran Dutchmen enjoying their first U.S. hit record since 1973's *Moontan* with *Cut*, courtesy of smash single "Twilight Zone." Onto March, Rush had with them the Jon Butcher Axis. April featured three Canadian dates where Rush did their part to support baby Canadian bands, featuring Harlequin in Quebec City and the Tenants at two Montreal dates. The tour ended in England in late May, after a few German dates supported by early mentors Nazareth. *Signals* is when Neil started to cart along a bicycle for the first time, his recreational plans getting more elaborate over the years, culminating famously in the incorporation of motorcycling into his routine.

"By that time we were really trying to develop rear-screen projection stuff," recalls Alex of the tours in the early '80s. "Eventually we had two projectors going, and synching them up was a nightmare — a lot of problems. Staging of course changed with every tour. Lighting changed, as the instruments themselves changed. Also there were the different levels that Howard would use in bringing the audience into it more, using surround sound as well.

"The Three Stooges thing we used, I think on three different tours," confirms Alex, who goes on to address the subject of Rush's obvious sense of humor, which is in full force at any given Rush show (although more and more as the films got more elaborate). "I think our humor is that goofy, dry sort of humor, typically Canadian; I guess a cross between Monty Python and something American. But when we're making a record, whether it's a musical thing or some piece of artwork, or some goofy thing, almost always, in the end, we take a step back and say, 'You know what? That will be funny for the next two weeks, but in five years, it's probably not going to be very funny.'

"We've always tended to be a little more serious about the presentation and what goes on the record. But within the band itself, when we're around each other, we spend eighty percent of the time just laughing and goofing around and cutting each other up. Like kids. Because in a lot of ways, we're just those kids that got together to start this band. I haven't really had to grow up. You know, I hang around with younger people; I have my whole life. I've never had to be really serious about those kinds of life things. I take my responsibilities seriously, but you know what I mean."

But improving themselves personally was still always part of the mix. "We would do stuff on the road, just challenge ourselves in another way," says Alex. "On the *Signals* tour we took the Berlitz French course on the road, and we would have different instructors in every city we went to. We had our books, and we'd sit on the bus and speak French to each other and all of that. And sadly, because you don't use it all the time, I'm very rusty with it, I think. We probably all are — but boy, we were doing pretty good. It's just another way of taking what can be dead time and being a little more constructive with it.

"Geddy and I have played tennis for the last twenty-five years at least, on the road. That was the big sport for us. And about ten years ago I started playing golf. Geddy loves going to art galleries. We go to movies." Neil, true to his tenacity, stuck with the French lessons for two tours (after all, he did have a house in Quebec), while Alex and Geddy bowed out after one, Geddy's interest somewhat lingering because he had a son taking French immersion in school.

Explains Howard, on the evolution of the show at this point: "What got bigger for the band was their following. We did three nights in Chicago. That was sort of unheard of back then. When you start doing multiple evenings, you know, three nights in New York or Chicago, two nights in L.A., you know success is strong. And I loved it. I wore so many hats back then — tour manager, lighting designer, travel agent, tour coordinator — I was able to grow the show economically with the band without stressing the budget, making them look great at the same time as delivering a quality show for medium dollars, where everyone was happy. What I like to do is custom-design lighting rigs. So every tour I did with Rush there was always a new lighting system."

The *Signals* campaign — dubbed the New World Tour — was of reasonable length, not exactly brief, but not out of control either. This was deliberate and began a trend that would continue, in concert with the band's growing priorities outside of rock 'n' roll.

"We're all having these experiences in different ways," explains Geddy, "these discussions at home, and I don't know how it got broached. Usually Neil is the one who pushes for time off before anyone else, although that changed. But at some point, we said look, we can't be one of these bands who try to conquer the world.

We just cannot do everything that is offered to us, as heartbreaking as that is to management. Our manager was crying. We can't stay on the road all the time. Let's count our blessings, but let's do it in a way that is productive and is helpful and try to satisfy our fans the best we can. But we can't go everywhere; otherwise there will be no time left for us. You'll have marriages that are falling apart. The cracks were already showing. We've got to go home and heal stuff.

"I guess we were just turning into grown-ups. And a lot of musicians don't do that. They choose not to do that, and somehow, they make it work. I wish I knew how to do it. Maybe they bribe them, I don't know. We couldn't do it that way. There's something about our middle-class values. We were having families, and we had marriages that were in crisis and we had to do the right thing. I've been justifying that to our fans for a thousand years. 'When are you going to come to this country?' 'When are you coming to England?' You know, it's a choice you make. You can be the most successful band in the world, or you can be a pretty successful band and have a life outside of it. We were trying to do that, trying to be parents to our children, trying to be husbands to our wives.

"There's no doubt in my mind we would've crashed — or we would have fought our way out of it," figures Geddy. "If we hadn't made that decision, I'm almost one hundred percent convinced the band would have gone down the drain. Because our marriages would've failed, and we would've suddenly become different people, living in a different way, and the pressure would not have been equal. Because the three of us were not going to start suddenly feeling differently at the same time. I mean, who knows? It's hard to say, but my gut tells me it was a thing we had to do to survive. What I used to say to our manager is, 'It's better than breaking up, right? One tour every other year is better than no tours ever.' Yeah, go get his side of the story. It'll all be his idea. 'I thought they were working too hard.' Don't believe a word he says."

CHAPTER 5

GRACE UNDER PRESSURE

*"There was a two- or three-week period where it
wasn't above minus thirty-five."*

With the MTV age well under way, and futuristic music and fashion all the erudite rage, Rush seemed to have made a well-timed shift into preppy adulthood, haircuts included. Over the course of one and a half albums (side one of *Moving Pictures* and all of *Signals*), they managed to bring a sound they invented and owned alone into the mainstream (partly because no one else would have it) through the application of a blinding paint job.

The band was conspicuous and eyebrow raising, in retrospect, operating completely alone with their zig to every other '70s band's heavy metal zag. But then, Rush is weird. It comes back to this idea that Rush is intellectually curious, searching for the new so bravely that their legacy is of little regard — for the band, that was then, this is now.

"Yeah, we were aware of Metallica," muses Geddy. "I remember the first time Metallica played in Toronto. My friends from

New York told me they were coming here, and I went to see them and I loved them. And they were outrageous. And progressive in their own way, right? Progressive metal, in a sense."

Metallica first played Toronto on January 19, 1985, at the Concert Hall, a large, civilized venue that Geddy could have navigated with ease.

"But we're not a band that plans anything too far in the future," continues Ged, "and to me, that's the beauty of being in this band. We really don't know what we're going to do until we sit down and do it. Sometimes you get together and your writing is softer, or maybe we've been listening to something different and you're intrigued by it or the lyrics don't suit speed metal. So you go in a direction that the moment dictates. That's the really amazing thing about the creative process, just allowing the moment to be what it is. So Alex, Neil, myself, at that point in time, sound like this and think musically like this. That's what Rush records are, for me. Sometimes they don't adhere to the genre and that's just the way it is. There's nothing we can do about it. It's just like the newscaster says, 'On this day in 1982 . . .' That's what we were all about. That's a reflection of our creative thinking at that moment."

And yet, as Terry accurately points out, there were still plenty of guitars on *Signals*, and surprise, there would still be plenty of guitars on the band's next album, the difficult-to-birth *Grace Under Pressure*. In a subtle way on this album, Rush were still Rush, the aggregate of all their records dating back to 1974. Seeing Rush live at this time wasn't that different from how it was in the '70s. Put another way, chuck Rush on a bill with any of the bands they came up with and it's still a rock 'n' roll show start to finish, only Rush would have a few extra, very no-nonsense and clear sounds cutting through the typical din created by guitar, bass and drums careening off the concrete.

As strange as the existence of this platinum act playing progressive metal with a new wave edge was the parallel existence of a band celebrating Peter Gabriel–era Genesis; Marillion and Rush would come together for a five-night stand in New York City in late September of '83, shows done in isolation between records.

"I remember it being a great gig," recalls Geddy. "Somebody just suggested it would be a great venue to play, and sometimes you just want to change the way you do things. And we thought, 'Wow, that's neat.' I mean, for us to do that kind of venue was really cool, especially because it ended up being more than just a couple of shows. It's just nice to change things up, plus we needed to warm up a bit for the recording of *Grace*."

Interestingly, press at the time had Alex and Geddy eager to get to work on solo albums once the current trek was over, with Neil set to work on a book of poetry and openly musing about writing some fiction.

"We toured with Rush a few times," recalls Marillion guitarist Steve Rothery. "What happened was we came over in 1983 and supported them at the Radio City Music Hall, the famous place in New York, five nights. It was before *Grace Under Pressure*. And that was hard work; it was like being thrown to the lions every night. But we did it, and then we came back and supported them in 1986 and 1987, about twelve or fifteen shows with them across the States and Canada. They kept to themselves a little bit. We probably chatted most to Alex, of the three of them, but they all seemed very nice."

At these Radio City shows, the band tried out early versions of "Kid Gloves," "Red Sector A" and "The Body Electric," products of the August writing sessions the guys conducted at a Horseshoe Valley lodge retreat near Barrie, Ontario, an hour north of Toronto. Then it was back to Le Studio at Morin Heights. The scramble for a producer ended when the guys settled on Peter

Henderson. During the short U.K. jaunt at the tail end of the *Signals* tour, the band checked out Steve Lillywhite and Trevor Horn of Yes fame. Lillywhite agreed to the job but then backed out to work with Simple Minds. Henderson was not the band's first choice and they made the decision quickly — a bad omen that was soon chilled on the rocks of the frigid Canadian winter. It was a grinding toil to make Rush's tenth album presentable.

"*Signals* was a turning point," begins Alex, "the last record we did with Terry Brown, and we felt the need to move on and see what it was like to work with other people. We had planned to make *Grace Under Pressure* with Steve Lillywhite, and he agreed to do the record. We met with him and everything was fine. And then in the eleventh hour his manager called and said, 'I'm really sorry but Steve's not available anymore.' And it was devastating because we were all set, we'd been writing, we were really looking forward to it.

"Producers back then were booked months and months and months in advance for projects. So we went to the B-list to see who was available, and Peter Henderson had done a lot of great engineering work, so we decided to go with him. It was a very difficult record to make with Peter. He was a great engineer and a lot of fun to be around but a little indecisive when it came to making some important decisions.

"And we didn't want to make those sorts of production decisions when we were recording the record," continues Alex. "We wanted to concentrate on playing and what we were doing. In the four months it took us to make that record, we had one day off, the first Saturday, and the rest of the time we worked like crazy. We were in Quebec at Le Studio and that winter was particularly cold. It hit minus forty-five for about three days, and there was a two- or three-week period where it wasn't above minus thirty-five. It was really, really cold, and it was hard work. That record was a really tough record to make. But we got through it, and we continued with that whole idea of working with other people."

While dealing with a notorious Quebec winter and a less-than-ideal relationship with their producer, the guys were wrestling with technology, even more than they had with *Signals*.

"Technology was driving the change," explains Paul Northfield, with respect to the obvious evolution in the Rush sound unfolding before him. "Everybody was enamored with the challenge and the possibilities of technology. It gave you a whole new palette to work with. Things like Frankie Goes to Hollywood, Trevor Horn's productions . . . there were some extraordinary records being made then that were groundbreaking sonically and arrangement-wise. And I think that any band like Rush who are interested in being creative, primarily, as opposed to just playing the thing they did well, they were always pushing, always looking for new things.

"So the technology itself sort of tended to dictate that and drive it. I was only peripherally involved in *Grace Under Pressure*. It was done at Le Studio, and I was the chief engineer at the studio at the time, and they had discussed with me about working on the new record. But that was after they had gone through trying to change producers. Steve Lillywhite had pulled out on them at the last minute, and so they were scrambling. I think their ultimate choice of producer was one out of pure convenience.

"They discussed me being involved in the production of the record — I remember, because they flew me to Toronto — but I know specifically Alex wanted to work with somebody he didn't know. He wanted something completely different. He worked with Terry for ten years or more and was looking forward to the challenge of working with somebody who had a completely different point of view. And that led them to Peter Henderson.

I think in retrospect, they would've liked to work with Steve Lillywhite, or somebody like Trevor Horn."

"This was a big move, leaving our security of Terry Brown behind and stepping out into the world," Geddy says of the search for the new producer. As to why he thought Steve Lillywhite would have been a good match for Rush, he figures, "He had a great affinity for guitar music, and yet he had a fresh, modern approach. The music that was coming out of England was something we were listening to a lot, and we felt he was in that new wave of young producers from England who were really exciting. We met him when we were on tour there, kinda said all the right things and we started to gel. He just seemed like a challenging, interesting guy to work with. We were impressed with the Big Country stuff he'd just worked on, and the XTC stuff really had an original sound. He had a great live drum sound. I know from a sonic point of view, that appealed to us. It was just something raw, yet technologically hip, that we liked about him."

"There was a great energy about all the records he worked on," says Alex, "sonically as well as coming from the music itself. All that music from England wasn't great, but there was something that had a rock base in his work, but very modern at the same time. I remember when we met with him in Birmingham, we were all very, very fired up. And he hung out for a couple of days with us, and we were just starting to get comfortable."

And then, sighs Geddy, "He got an offer to work with Simple Minds and he blew us off, basically. And we thought that was incredibly ungentlemanly, unprofessional. We had always worked with very good guys who said something and did it. It was the first time we worked with somebody where obviously his word didn't mean much. I think it was always his dream to work with Simple Minds, so even though he made a commitment to us, he blew us off.

"We were shocked, actually. We were already in preproduction, we were halfway through writing material, and we had a date in mind, and this guy totally fucked us over. And we thought, 'Okay, what are we going to do now?' We're supposed to make a record, our first record with a new producer in our entire career, and halfway through the writing, the guy disappears. Panic set in. And people are throwing us names — one after the other and the other, and most people were already booked at that time. You can't just pick up the phone and get the best producers in the world. 'What, you're busy?!' It was a bad situation. Anyone else we were interested in working with was already spoken for, as they should be.

"We wanted somebody interesting, somebody who had something interesting to contribute," continues Geddy. "An interesting take on things. And we started this long, torturous interview process. We were at this rehearsal place outside of Toronto. Hidden Valley, kind of a ski resort in the off-season. We set up our gear there, and we lived in a lodge, and we rehearsed in the ski area, and one after another, producers flew in to meet with us. It was quite something. We played them some of the stuff we were working on, we listened to their comments and talked among ourselves and analyzed it. It was weird.

"The plus side was, we were hearing about all kinds of ways of recording, all kinds of ideas for making records. Different opinions on our music. We almost worked with Rupert Hine at that time. He couldn't make it happen, schedule-wise, so that was another disappointment, because we always admired his work. And then Peter Henderson walked in; he'd done those Supertramp records that we really liked a lot, and he had come up with the school . . . the Geoff Emerick school of engineering, Air Studios, Beatles, the Beatles world, the Beatles training center for young engineers. He had some great things to say, so in the end, we were quite up against it, and we said okay.

"I guess it was time to get co-production because he was an engineer/producer," says Geddy of Henderson. "He wasn't a guy we were ultimately after; he wanted to engineer everything himself. And he's a very good engineer. Very different from anyone we ever worked with in the past."

Which wasn't going to be good enough, says Alex. "His heart was in the engineering. And when it came time to make certain decisions about where a song was going, or suggesting something that could spark something else, he wasn't always available for that. There was much more pressure on us to come up with the ideas for the best arrangement of the song. We needed someone who sparked us. We didn't want someone who works for us but someone who could present inspiration. Just that little spark that takes you to a little place that everybody wants to go."

"This was more out of desperation," I think, says Paul Northfield on the band's ultimate hiring of Peter Henderson. "Not that he was a desperate choice — he was somebody who seemed to fit the bill, had the experience they were looking for and who was different. I think they were a bit shocked at the process of working with Peter. There was a lot of second-guessing in the recording process that they hadn't been used to. They were looking for a decision maker, somebody who would challenge them, and I don't think Peter Henderson gave them that. He was a well-respected engineer, but I don't think his abilities as a producer were the kinds of things they were looking for. That was quite frustrating."

About the process of mixing the record with Henderson, Paul comments, "I remember it being extraordinarily long, whereas in the past, when I'd been working with Terry, our mixes would rarely take a day — one day per mix, and some mixes would be quicker than that. I think that was the first time they'd been in a situation where they were mixing a record and they spent four days mixing one song. That was a new era of experimenting with lots of different options, and they found that very difficult. It wore them out, that record. Geddy knew that when they finished the record and he said goodbye to Peter, he wouldn't be seeing Peter again. Because the process of making that record had been torturous."

"We accepted that we were settling in a way and he was not the kind of producer we had started out looking for," says Geddy. "And, Peter, good guy, really hard worker, let me tell you. He'll sit behind the console, forever ['too long,' interjects Alex]. But not a leader for us. Not someone who could help us learn the things we wanted to learn. He was the kind of producer that didn't really know what he liked until he heard it, and he had a really difficult time explaining to us what he thought we should do.

"And this was devastating for us. Because we were like, 'Holy shit, after all this, we're producing ourselves, basically.' We had to produce him to produce us. We would finish a take and say, 'Hey, Pete, how was that take?' And he would say, 'I don't know; do you want to compare?' 'Well, you're in there, you just heard it.' So we would go in and listen to it, and he would look at us and say, 'Well, what do you think?' That's how it went. It meant a very long, very difficult recording session."

The session lasted four months and began to take a personal toll on the guys. Geddy says the session "almost cost me my marriage because I became so obsessed with the production of that album that the few days I was able to go home, I would be sitting with my wife and I couldn't leave it behind."

It was a tough session among the members of the band as well. "It was intense; we argued," says Geddy. "I think one of the very few times we ever didn't really get along was on that session. So here we are, all good guys, trying to make this record together, thirty-five below zero, dead of winter, at Le Studio, forever, it seemed, just going on and on. We just bitched at each other. It wasn't the work. We were united in our frustration of making the record, so when it came to work, we did the work. We didn't fight about it. We had songs and ideas, but on the fiftieth day or something, you would have too much vodka and you would just be bitchy with each other, you know? You crack up a little bit. We stopped having fun.

"And even with the mixes, we would do a mix, and we would do like forty verses of the song or something ridiculous, and we knew we had to listen through them again and find the version we liked, and it was just not the way to make a record. It was hard, but it was a good lesson to learn: leaving Terry and having to deal with that. I think we made a good record, but it really cost a piece of us to make it."

"There are some great songs on that record," agrees Alex, "and the record sounds really good. It definitely stands out among all our albums."

"But it was like, okay, this is the world without Terry and it's not very gentlemanly," laughs Geddy. "But live and learn. And I think that terrible experience taught us more about how to make records than any good experience can teach you. You learn from the bad stuff, unfortunately."

Yet neither Geddy nor Alex regretted the choice to change producers overall. "I don't think so," says Alex, when asked if they regretted the decision to let Terry go. "We may have said, 'What did we do?' But it was just a comment on the moment. I think we were committed."

"We were way beyond that," agrees Geddy. "We were up to here with making records. We were a bit kind of nuts, frankly. It was a real ballbuster. And I remember afterward taking the record to have it mastered with Bob Ludwig, getting there and putting on 'Red Sector A' and realizing the mix didn't have any bass pedals. For some reason I had left — or we had left — the bass pedals off that song. When it's tough, believe me, it's tough to the bitter end."

But the record indeed got finished, emerging from hibernation on April 12, 1984, wrapped in a layer of rime frost, namely Hugh Syme's chilling and impersonal cover art, a little sci-fi, a little apocalyptic, definitely freeze-dried. Punning on the spiffy title, Hugh also included the image of an egg in a C-clamp. For a band photo, Rush enlisted elite Canadian legend Yousuf Karsh, who conducted a studio group shot to be used on the back.

As Alex told Geoff Barton, "We were all sitting around in Horseshoe Valley, writing new material, and we were discussing what to do about the LP sleeve. I said to Neil, 'Why don't we go for a real nice black-and-white portrait on the back? We've never really done anything like that before.' Geddy immediately latched onto the idea and said, 'Yeah, why don't we get Karsh?!' Everyone's reaction was positive, but we didn't think we had a chance. We thought, well, we can try, but he didn't strike us as being the kind of photographer likely to do this sort of thing. But he did! I don't know if you've seen any of Karsh's books, but basically, he's a photographer of Hollywood actors and royalty and just about everyone in between. Looking at it, you can see that Karsh's pictures are very honest. They're not flattering in any way. Everybody in the band looks a little older, a little rougher. But I think that's good. It's definitely not a rock 'n' roll picture, but it's a very true, realistic picture of the three of us. Plus there's the inherent power that you get with a black-and-white photograph. It's quite emotional."

As with the three previous records, *Grace Under Pressure* opens with the track lined up by Rush Inc. for maximum commercial impact, "Distant Early Warning," which got a fancy-pants video to push it into households who want their MTV. But the song is of an interesting construct, ambling in on a reggae vibe so light that Neil is hitting rim shots. Things don't stay that way however, because turning the song borderline anthemic is a big chorus, made even more impactful by a preceding full-throttle prog intro. Not a lot of synthesizer-borne provocation to this one, but that leaves room in the mix for the band to provoke through a Police vibe, Alex doing Andy Summers as well as the Fixx and INXS.

"That's when I started the skinny tie collection, in the '80s," chuckles Neil, setting the scene through the record's matching visuals, on display in the video for this song. Neil in fact started wearing skinny ties back in the *Permanent Waves* era, but in this video, it's Alex who dons one. "We tried to outdo each other for the silliest skinny tie every night and wore ties with bowling shirts and all that. It was fun. After all, fashion is supposed to be fun. We were still young, so it was not any effort. We didn't have to hire an image consultant to tell us how to dress for the '70s or the '80s or the '90s, and after that we were beyond fashion as one should be at a certain age. It was an honest reflection. We didn't have to try to stay relevant or write songs for people younger than us or write down at any time. We were always writing about our concerns, and our audience members have always been able to stay with those same concerns."

When asked about the album themes, Neil says, "*Grace Under Pressure* was not just about metaphysical things; it was about my friends, people who were having trouble. The key line in 'Distant Early Warning' is 'You sometimes drive me crazy, but I worry about you.' That's the ultimate expression of compassion. And I used a William Faulkner title in that too, *Absalom, Absalom!* It's the story from the bible where King David allowed his son to die, and the plea is 'Would God I had died for thee.' The ultimate expression of compassion. When I found out what that meant it gave me chills — still does really — the 'Absalom, Absalom' thing — because what greater gift, to lay down your life? All of us have probably felt that in our lives to love someone that much. That to me was the highest expression I could think of for the compassion that song was trying to express.

"When those things became part of the writing, it was at a very humanistic level. Yes, I've been through writing science fiction fables and fantasy tales and all that, but that was for fun, you know? A lot of it was for fun. When I read more and lived more, I really — as far as I was concerned — became a student of human nature. And all those songs are about people. I would see people doing things and I would remember them. I'd read an interview with a battlefield photographer, and he had started as a young man going into the field thinking that if he could just get the right photograph it would change things. People would see war and people would see desperation and human brutality and then they would change. Well, I had that same illusion about songs. I thought if I could just get the song right, people would see, and they would change. So if I could write about hypocrisy, and if I could write about the mistreatment of each other and misunderstandings of ourselves and all that . . . that's what I was trying to get to. Certainly, from *Moving Pictures* onwards, I was trying to find big metaphors for small things instead of small metaphors for big things."

Big metaphors for small things: that's a good clue to help us decipher the considerably inscrutable "Distant Early Warning" lyrics. The big metaphor here — and the imagery, set props and machinery — comes from the Cold War, something certainly on the minds of everybody in the early '80s. Here, it's a metaphor for personal relationships, the gulf between people (see also "Different Strings" and "Entre Nous"). Underscoring this is the chorus. The way Neil has arranged the words makes it sound like it's the world that drives him crazy with worry, or conversely, it's an unnamed intimate in his life or a universal intimate that might exist for anyone out there in the real world. There's no bigger metaphor than the world and there's no more smaller "thing" than what goes on between two people we're unaware of across the coffee shop.

This song too, seems to build on the likes of "New World Man" and "Digital Man," more specifically the chorus of the former and the verses of the latter. And one can't help but notice an influence from the Police. I once asked Stewart Copeland if the debt has been acknowledged. "Effusively!" he laughed. "We are good friends. And they are so fucking Canadian, those guys. And they don't mind all the early jabs I used to hurl in their general direction, which once again was all about the hairdos, not about their musicality. I just saw all three of them a month ago over at Neil's place. And how we did laugh together, I tell ya. But Neil never fails to mention the, you know, debt of inspiration. But they're so Canadian — that's how they do it. You know what I'm talking about."

"There is always something interesting," says Geddy about the Police catalogue. "Like the way they used rhythm, the way they structured songs, his attitude of the drums — really interesting. Or the way that Sting would emote. He would multi-track his voice in a particular way and create this really cool sound. Those are the kinds of things that resonate with another musician. We didn't want to sound like the Police, but you can draw from all these bands that are doing good things. Sometimes it's a singer of a kind of music that is very divorced from your kind of music. But I hear something that singer does, whether it's a male or female: 'Oh, that's really cool the way she just used her voice. I can learn something from that.' These things influence you. You just add them to your stew, to your repertoire, to your toolbox, whatever you want to call it, and they inspire you."

Adds Alex, "You don't really want to hear something and copy it. Like Geddy said, where it's coming from is what inspires you when you hear that band. You know, the Edge, I love the way he was using delays. He wasn't the first guy to do that, but he was very effective in the way he incorporated it as part of his style of playing. And the same with the Police. Andy is an amazing guitar player, really crisp sound, and yet there was power in his playing, the way he played his chords, the way he struck them, the counter-rhythms he would play. That was very influential and inspiring."

But in terms of figuring out how to fit guitar into what was suddenly a four-instrument band, Alex says that was all his doing. "This was purely about the application in our band, how I wanted to address that. I didn't really search somewhere else to hear how somebody else did it. We were unique. But there are so many components, other than just the guitar and the keyboards. There is Geddy's bass playing, which is very active, at that time. And his vocals, and lyrically, the number of words, and Neil's energetic playing. There are a lot of complicated things in the soup."

"The thing you look for is not the thing you already know how to do," adds Geddy, sagely. "I wasn't listening to a lot of metal or prog rock bands. Because you kind of know how to do that. You're listening for things you don't know. You want something fresh. You are searching for those ideas that have not occurred to you, that you can apply to your own style and sound. That make you a better musician."

Geddy admits he doesn't quite know where, after all this fearless exploration and exploitation, Rush ended up fitting in the '80s. "We've never had that conversation," he says. "Ever. I don't think we've ever used the words, 'Are we relevant? Is this relevant?' No, we do what feels right and we try to keep it natural and not think of those things. It's too big — no thinking allowed. It's too big to think about. You can't think outside yourself and be inside at the same time; I don't think it works. So we come up with a sound or a song or an idea we like and one thing sparks another. Every record is like a journey that is unknown until it's finished. We don't really know what we're doing until we finish doing it. And then we look at it and go, 'Wow, that worked out.' And that's a time capsule; that's this period of time. And I love that about us. We don't know what the hell we're going to do until we're in the business of doing it, until we are in there working and writing and it's about the moment. That's a very satisfying thing for a writer or musician — it's a nice way to live."

As on *Signals*, track two is a fast-paced rocker, only the business of the song is somber, commemorating the death of Le Studio staffer Robbie Whelan, who died in a car crash near Le Studio in May of '83 while working on Asia's second album, *Alpha*. Whelan was thirty-one years old and left behind a wife, Carla.

"Robbie was the assistant engineer here," reflects Neil, walking through Le Studio years later. "He was a part of all the volleyball games, and the song I wrote, 'Afterimage,' is about him. I mention the footprints on the lawn. You know, that was us playing volleyball at the other end of this lake, until the sun would come up. And then, you know, the usual musician's hours — sleep 'til noon and get up and go back to work. And then we would take a break at dinnertime; we'd play a few games too, right up to when the snow would fall. We'd be shoveling off our volleyball court because it was such a necessary output and exercise."

Adds Geddy, "'Afterimage' was a very personal song and was really about the loss of a friend. So I think we took extra care to make sure it was very heartfelt and that recording went well."

As Alex told Jas Obrecht of *Guitar Player*, "'Afterimage' is a story about a dear friend of ours who was killed in a car accident. We wanted to celebrate his life, but there is a sadness to the music, and the guitar solo is a translation of that. I think about him every time we play that song. He worked at Le Studio, so we were right there where he was. We turned the lights down a bit, and I was emotional and excited. I don't know how many times my eyes got all teary going into that solo when we were running it down. Halfway through, I'd get so fired up that I would go out of time, so we'd rewind it to the front, and I'd go [in sobbing voice], 'Okay, let's try it again.'"

Indeed, one can hear the emotion in the playing of all three guys, Neil hitting hard, Geddy articulating on bass and Alex playing almost punk rock-angry with his chords. Of interest, once the original driving verse where this straight-line magic happens is over, we never hear this arrangement again. Many moons later there is another verse proper, but Alex has switched to muted Andy Summers–like picking. All told, "Afterimage" is quite a progressive metal song, with lots of oddly stacked parts and two verses that are different from one another and separated by so much. Perhaps due to the pain of it, the song was performed on the ensuing tour, after which it was never heard again.

"Red Sector A" opens with more chimey guitar from Alex, set to Neil playing his best Stewart Copeland–busy hi-hat, both attentive to a bubbly sequencer pattern. But the melody is dark, as is the lyric.

As Neil explained to Jim Ladd, "I read a first-person account of someone who had survived the whole system of trains and work camps and Dachau and all of that — she was a young girl, like thirteen years old, when she was sent and lived in it for a few years. And then first-person accounts from other people who came out at the end of it, always glad to be alive, which was the essence of grace. Grace under pressure is that. These people never gave up the strong will to survive, through the utmost horror and total physical privations of all kinds. They just never, ever wanted to be the ones who were shot, you know? They were always the unlucky ones, which was an important thing that I wanted to bring out.

"And also, I learned from the first-person nonfiction accounts I read that these people would keep their little rituals of their religion. If it was supposed to be a fasting day, even if they were starving to death, they would turn down their little bit of bread and their little bit of gruel, because this was a fasting day. They had to hold onto something, some essence of normality; you know, that was important. And that moved me. That's intense.

"I wanted to give it more of a timeless atmosphere too, because it's happened, of course, in more than one time and by more than one race of people. It happened in this very country in which we sit. You know, the British did it, no one can set themselves above that. Slavery involved how many countless countries in terms of the commerce of it all — people shipping them around like animals. No one can set themselves above that in a racial or nationalistic way. So I wanted to take it out of being specific and just describe the circumstances and try to look at the way people responded to it.

"Another really important and, to me, really moving image that I got from a lot of these accounts was that at the end of it, these people of course had been totally isolated from the rest of the world, from their families, from any news at all. And they, in cases that I read, believed they were the last people surviving. You know, the people liberating them and themselves were the only surviving people in the world. It sounds a bit melodramatic to put into a song, I realize, but it's true. So I didn't feel like I needed to avoid it as being overdramatic because I heard of it and read of it in more than one account."

Particularly poignant of course is that Geddy sings Neil's words, Geddy's parents having been Holocaust survivors.

Closing side one is "The Enemy Within," which is the closest Rush would ever get to ska. After explaining to Jim Ladd the concept of the Fear Trilogy (this is part one; we'd already gotten the subsequent parts with "Witch Hunt" and "The Weapon"), Peart says that "eventually I got my thinking straightened out and the images that I wanted to use and collected them all up and it came out. 'The Enemy Within' was more difficult because I wanted to look at how it affects me, but it was about more than me. I don't like to be introspective as a rule. I think I'm gonna set that down as my first rule: 'Never be introspective!' But I wanted to, and at the same time I wanted to write about myself in a universal kind of way; I want to find things in myself that I think apply."

The expensive but tacky sci-fi production video created for this song echoed the messaging of the "Distant Early Warning" clip, namely that Rush was a futuristic, cutting-edge band. Despite actively attempting to drive viewers away, with its darkness, close cropping, jerky editing and intentional blurriness, this video was picked as the first ever to be played on MuchMusic, Canada's version of MTV, when it launched August 31, 1984. Unsurprisingly, MuchMusic would become a boon to Canada's long-running and undisputed biggest rock band. In turn, Rush enthusiastically got involved in made-for-TV video clips, a synergistic pursuit with all the film footage they would craft for their stage presentation. In fact, at this time, Geddy had mused that the band wanted to make a video for every song on the album.

"The Body Electric" also got the same kind of dystopian treatment, Orwellian even; it was certainly sci-fi, with more focus on story than its brethren clips. It makes sense given the lyrics, and the music makes sense given the lyrics too, the guys turning in a robotic, mechanized sound collage.

"We started getting obsessed with rhythm around that period," says Geddy, who makes a good point — with *Grace* and the records moving forward, for all the debate over keyboards, there's just as much weirdness going on rhythmically. "Especially Neil and I. And even in Alex's playing. Alex is one of the great rhythm guitar players on planet Earth, and rhythm guitar players don't get their due at all. But yeah, we were trying to make our music rock and groove, you know? And that's not easy. Especially for white Canadians.

"So you could say that in one sense, our influence early was classical, adventure-influenced rock, and now we were trying to take rock and complexity and make it groove. And that was like a new toy for us that we were bringing into the music. We were progressing and trying to become better musicians, and that always pushes the writing. And where our writing fails from time to time, it's because we pay too much attention to our needs as players. Sometimes the player part of it dictates what you're writing and what you need to do as a player, and that's the end result. So I guess what I'm saying is there's lots of reasons that fans have turned away from us at certain points in our career, and there's nothing we can do about that."

This one was based on an old *Twilight Zone* episode from 1962 called "I Sing the Body Electric" but more so is a basic story about oppression, "2112" for robots, as it were, with the protagonist trying to break free from hardwired patterns. At the start, one might say it's the story of the album cover, but by the end, an intriguing narrative is implied. It asks what happens to its consciousness when a machine pulls the plug on itself. Since 1001001 is the ASCII code for I, it's as if while the bytes break to bits, through the haze the android is hoping to retain some sense of self.

"With 'The Body Electric' solo, I got frustrated and crazy," Alex told *Guitar Player*. "I couldn't find a direction for it; I tried this and tried that. I'd work on something for a few hours and then go, 'That's bullshit. This is the same stuff that I've done a million times before.' I'd put the guitar down and go out and watch the hockey game or whatever, trying to get some kind of inspiration. I went back in and thought, 'Screw this. I'll go wild.' And all of a sudden everybody turns around and goes, 'Hey, yeah! What was that?' We played the tape back and thought it was pretty funny. That's what sparks it: you hear something that's crazy and funny. It was more of my personality, and it just went from there. After that, it took about forty minutes to do the whole solo. There's a wang bar in that solo. I use it a lot now — too much. I'm noticing lately that my left hand is becoming much lazier. My vibrato is something that I worked on for a long time, and it's gotten really lazy. It's much easier to reach back and use the bar, and it's such a nice vibrato. It's down-and-up rather than the up-and-back vibrato that you get with your hand."

"Kid Gloves" is one of Rush's irresistible hooky melodic rockers, and inspiringly guitary, with Alex double tracking a Telecaster against a Gibson, the ultimate schoolyard brawl when it comes to axes. A jagged 5/8 verse gives way to rewarding pre-chorus and chorus all with minimal synths.

"It was difficult to get a starting point on that one," reflects Alex concerning the song's disorienting guitar solo, speaking with Andrew MacNaughtan, one of the band's key photographers, now sadly passed. "The way I usually write solos is I'll throw around different ideas, and I'll keep playing until I lock onto something. And then I'll keep that and then try something else and start fitting the bits together and then go back and redo the whole thing. That's basically what happened with that solo. I remember it taking a very long time. I spent close to two and a half days working on it. It's funny, you know, you can spend hours and hours trying to get just a direction and a starting point. Once you have one, the solo may take ten or twenty minutes. The solo on 'Kid Gloves' ended up taking about forty-five minutes once I had locked in on a direction. Then everything just fell into place."

"Red Lenses" is alternately jazzy and post-punk, with Alex obtuse and texturizing and Neil being both tribal and electro. Lyrically, this one touches upon troubles in the news, the song perhaps serving as a microcosm or summary piece for an album that in general has Neil reacting to the swift and shifting world around him.

"There's a quote by a French novelist," reflects Neil, "maybe Flaubert, that what a novel should be is a mirror, just moving down the road, a traveling mirror. And I like that for a band too, as maybe a traveling pair of headphones picking up what's going on around you and reflecting it. In so many ways, 1983 was a very tense year in the current events of the time, and the band was in upheaval. We were having trouble getting a co-producer we wanted to work with, and we were going through stylistic changes.

"The Soviets shot down that Korean Airlines flight that year, and a lot of my friends were having trouble with work or with relationships. It was just like an angst year, and that so comes out in the music. At the time it wasn't one of our most popular records by any means, but people that like it really like it. And I totally understand why. Because if your life was like that at that time, it's the soundtrack of your life right then.

"And again, it's so heartfelt — all that angst is in the music. It can be felt there. Sometimes it's addressed overtly like in

'Distant Early Warning' or in 'Red Lenses,' but other times it's just part of the tension in the music. Those underlying things, like the anger in '2112,' they communicate. So yeah, I do like that. I compared it once to being like a satellite dish actually moving down the road. Maybe that's more apt for our times. Because we were there during the video age, and later we were there when rock rediscovered guitars in 1990 with Guns N' Roses and Soundgarden and Pearl Jam, where before that, guitars had been relegated to the petrified forest of wilderness."

It's hard not to think about King Crimson when confronted with the oddball "Red Lenses." Neil was a Bruford fan, and Bill went through his own radical modernization process. Heck, so did King Crimson as a whole, fittingly, from an album called *Red* to the "red album" of the red, blue and yellow period of the early '80s. In fact, Alex has a lot in common with Adrian Belew on that record — 1981's *Discipline* — and Geddy's vocal here possesses some of the conversational experimentation on that record, also courtesy of Adrian.

"Electronic drums are a bitch," laughs Geddy, on another aspect of the track. "But you know, Neil still played a lot of his natural drums. I can't remember how much on that album he featured the electronic. But we were just starting to move into that area. Peter was great at recording all that stuff. He really knew how to record, and really had a different attitude about compression, which I think made a big difference on the way that album sounds. From a technical point of view, it was everything we wanted. It was just what it took to get it.

"But they're not really drums!" Lee says of the electronic sound. "They're a percolator version of . . . I mean, you've got the drummer of the century in there. You've got a motherfucker of a drummer, and he makes his real drums sound so incredible. And to hear him on electronic drums is a bit of a letdown. But he has the gall to use it as a completely different instrument, which is to his credit. He's created a symphony of sounds. He uses the electronics and the real. But in the early days, it was fun for him to play electric drums, just as it was fun for me to play synths. So it was something he needed to experiment with. We got them sounding great, but they are a lot of work. It was the same thing when I first started playing synths. You first plug them in and they sound terrible. You've got to really work with them. Because at first, they all sound zizzy. So he was going through growing pains with electric drums and I was going through growing pains with synthesizers — it was just wrestling a new technology."

Claustrophobic *Grace Under Pressure* album closer "Between the Wheels" was the first song the band came up with during their writing sessions, followed by "Afterimage" and "Kid Gloves." Alternately brooding and hopeful musically (compare with Max Webster's "Cry Out for Your Life"), there's very little hope in the newsreel lyrics. Here Neil reverses the device of "Distant Early Warning" and uses a small metaphor for something big, wheels for wars and the idea of historic cycle.

"This album doesn't seem to have any ballads," noticed Alex, speaking with Andrew MacNaughtan. "Yeah, you're right. There's no acoustic guitar on it either. I think it just happened that way. I suppose we were in an angry period, musically and lyrically. We were getting the *Globe and Mail* delivered at our rehearsal lodge up in Horseshoe Valley every morning. The whole thing with the Korean Airlines happening and the breakdown of the nuclear arms talks. It was one thing after another. I think it really influenced Neil's writing, in the respect that it came out angry. I think the music mirrors that anger, as 'Between the Wheels' is a very oppressive, strong song. I don't think a ballad had a place on this album.

"There is a lot going on right now that you can be angry about, even be concerned about. Neil is just becoming more of an observer. I think his lyrics are asking some very important questions, rather than telling a story. In that way his writing has changed, and it's become more condensed. He's getting more value from his words. Music is a very personal thing. It can be whatever you want it to be. If people accept it, that's great. If they don't, no big deal. If you are lucky to be successful at it in financial terms, great, but there is other success as well — writing a good song. That is what comes first. I don't think the topic you write about really matters. If you want to make a political statement, it's your music, go ahead; it always occurs in folk music. But if you want to sing about how brown your carpet is, then that's fine too. I don't think there are many parameters for what you can write about."

As the record comes to a close, we really get a sense of the solid, sensible sound Rush achieved here, most notably in terms of the synths as set against the guitars, "Between the Wheels" illustrating this point particularly impressively. *Signals* was superlative as well, but a little warmer, more woodsy analog. Here the synths cut more, as do the guitars, and with occasional electronic drum whacks, it's a whole new world. But there's ample bass and treble despite so many characteristically midrange frequencies pressed at us.

"We were trying to refine the attitude of the guitar/synthy band," figures Geddy. "We wanted to be that Rush of *Signals*, but with more three-piece rock firmly in place. More aggressive, more true to Alex's tone, bring his tone back in a bigger and richer way but at the same time trade off between that and using a synthesizer sound. That was what we were after. We kind of achieved it. I think there are some great songs on that record — 'Between the

Wheels' and 'Distant Early Warning'; I think those are real successes, when we look back. We had our moments on the record, that's for sure."

"I was much happier with the character of the guitar sound," agrees Alex. "It was closer to what I had in my head. You've got a vision in your head and you can see it clearly, and you strive to get the sound to match what you have in your head, and very seldom do you ever get to it. I remember feeling much better about the edginess of the guitar sound on that record in its relationship with the keyboards. We were using keyboards too that had a brighter character to the sounds, and it put it up in a different range and made it more of an effect rather than an integral part of the musicality of the song. The guitar could play its role."

It was the same general setup for Alex as last time, however. He says, "Yeah, I'm still using the Hentor, the Strats with the humbuckers and the Flapsocaster. No, no changes really; I was always on the lookout for new gear, you know, effects that came along." Note here Alex is talking about a Hentor Sportscaster, rechristened as the Porkflapsocaster.

Geddy says it was common for Alex to get into spats with engineers. "The battle with him and engineers was not to use the pedals," he says.

"Yeah, they always want to put them on after," chuckles Alex. "The argument was . . . that's my sound, that's the way I hear it." What Alex means is that he wants to control his effects up front, from his pedal board. "That's how I like it. I don't want to add it after. Ged made a comment about engineers once, something like, 'I wish I could just fucking cut all their heads off.' Something like that."

"You can't live with them, you can't kill them," says Geddy. "He had that argument with every engineer we've ever made a record with. Spurred on by me. But Peter was a hell of an engineer. I mean, that record was really well recorded, when I think back. He had a great instinct for sound and a really good base in sound. So the record does sound strong, and that's a credit to him. He was a terrific engineer. And he was a good guy, but . . ."

Despite Rush continuing to poke, prod and provoke their fan base, *Grace Under Pressure* reached platinum in the U.S., same showing as *Signals*. The album rose to a #10 placement on the Billboard charts, #5 in the U.K. and #4 in Canada. Four complicated videos were released from the record as the band put the effort in to keep in the face of the MTV generation, hard-selling a sound that was no longer particularly adjacent to old-school heavy metal, and yet not new wave enough to cross over into Duran Duran, Simple Minds or A Flock of Seagulls terrain, let alone compete with the Cars, Huey Lewis, Michael Jackson, Bruce Springsteen or Prince.

The *Grace Under Pressure* tour kicked off May 7, 1984, in Albuquerque, New Mexico, Gary Moore supporting for a couple of months, followed by the likes of the Pat Travers Band and Fastway. Championing the Canucks, Rush also shared stages with Red Rider and Helix. Late in the sequence, Y&T replaced Fastway, who had supported all through October. All told, pairing with these acts sent a particular message — the guys still wanted borderline heavy metal bands getting their fans all riled up. June 1984 had the band doing a rare festival date, the Texxas Jam, alongside 38 Special, Ozzy Osbourne, Bryan Adams and Gary Moore, who was in the midst of his long run with the band. There were no European shows this time, but Rush managed to get to both Japan and Hawaii for the first time.

"We had a terrible situation in Japan," recalls Ged. "After our show, I think we had a day off in Osaka, and we had done the traditional Japanese bathhouse and massage. We were very relaxed and we were sitting in the hotel bar having a few

drinks with our road crew, and we heard some terrible shout-
ing. Neil was ensconced in this argument with this Japanese
man who was insisting on beating his wife in public. And Neil
of course was trying to get him to cool down. And the harder
he tried to get him to cool down, the harder he was hitting
his wife. And of course, we all came out there full of whiskey
and anger and tried to break it up. But the hotel security staff
was treating us like we were wrong, like we were interfering in
a personal squabble, to the point where we were being carted
away. I guess apparently this Japanese fellow was a Yakuza
member or something. Anyway, they did not appreciate us
trying to help the woman. When last we saw her, she was laid
out on the floor. It was pretty ugly."

"Actually, we only went once, and I don't think we slept the
whole time there," laughs Alex, when asked his impression of
Japan. "It was only four dates. It was so unique; the audience was
unlike anything we'd ever played for, so programmed. They all
jumped up and clapped at the same time like crazy, then sat down
and didn't move. When they left the venue, there was not a shred
of paper or anything on the floor, extremely neat. They have that
light system at the Budokan; it's like a streetlight, where if it's
green, you can have fun and cheer, if it's amber, sit down in your
seat. If it's red, the concert stops and everybody goes home. And
they would stand up in groups. You would have six people stand
up and cheer and go crazy; they would all be wearing orange
sweatshirts. Then this group over here with green sweatshirts
would stand up and cheer, then sit down. It was the most bizarre
thing. And then Hawaii, Hawaii was a riot. We had such a great
time. It was just an extension of the whole crazy tour. We got
there, and I think we had a couple of days off, and then we had
the show there. It was just like any American show."

But there's a reason, says Alex, that Rush didn't become a true world band, the likes of Iron Maiden or Deep Purple — loaded up with so much technology, it came down to pure economics.

"I guess we had played four shows in Japan, you know, generally two small venues and two larger venues, and even the larger venues were small by North American standards. There were a lot of people there, and there was an interest from the record company to have us come and see how it would go. And really, it went very, very well. But at the end of the day, I don't think we felt like we were breaking new ground there, or it was a new territory to conquer or that we were going to make a lot of money. Because we obviously lost a lot of money playing four shows.

"But at the same time we wanted to experience Japan," continues Lifeson. "We wanted to see what it was like. We went to China on that trip as well and Hong Kong. We made it a bit of an adventure and ended up doing a couple shows in Hawaii as well. It was a worthwhile experience. We had a great time, but it was hard to justify doing it again under those conditions. We get asked every tour, 'When are you coming to Japan?' whenever we do interviews or with fans. And it's always difficult to say. It's very difficult as you get older and you play less shows on a tour to get everywhere you can. I mean we really, really concentrate on North America, particularly America. If we were doing 150 shows a year, yeah sure, okay, we'll play anywhere. But if we're only doing about sixty shows a year, it's tough to get everywhere.

"But we had a wonderful experience there. We never adjusted our clock. It was impossible. So we were waking up at four o'clock in the morning and we'd have to wait, and we'd have breakfast and we'd start sightseeing at six o'clock when no one was around and the cities were just waking up. It was really cool because it was a very different perspective. And there you go onstage at six so you're done by eight, eight thirty, and then of course it's sake and sushi for the rest of the night."

CHAPTER 6

POWER WINDOWS

"First of all, Geddy, your voice."

N ow that Van Halen had joined Rush wholesale in endors-
ing keyboards — "Jump" would help turn *1984* diamond, for
sales of over ten million copies — it was proven that even the
coolest of heshers smoking cigarettes behind the backstop could
explore their inner New Romantic. Of course it all started with
Led Zeppelin's *In Through the Out Door*, and then quietly for a
while there, it was Rush tinkering in the lab, validated along the
way by both Yes and Genesis, both plugging into the improbable
and finding success despite their respective radical rethinks.

In 1985, Geddy, Alex and Neil would take modernism in the
extreme, celebrating the success of bands like Tears for Fears,
the Cure, Sting, Eurythmics, Talking Heads and a suddenly
electronic Kate Bush, with their *Power Windows* album, a
shocking step further into technology and time stamp.

When asked, Neil stood by the controversial era about
to ensue, one marked by a pairing of the 1985 record and its

follow-up, *Hold Your Fire*, noting of *Power Windows*, "That's one I particularly really like. If you try to divorce yourself from musician to fan, I think as a fan, I would particularly like those records, just because they are such a feast to listen to: so much texture and so much variety and rhythmic exploration. To me they remain very satisfying pieces of work to listen to. So I think that's about the highest tribute I can give it: they are something that I would like as a fan.

"*Hold Your Fire* is somehow a little more introvert in mood, musically and lyrically, as much as they tend to feed on each other," continues Peart. "That definitely strikes me now, just thinking about it. *Power Windows* is more dynamic and more extrovert, while *Hold Your Fire* is more textural and introvert. But I like them equally in their two moods. *Power Windows* really hangs together well as a whole body of work, I think, the way it's shaped. Running order is something we've always spent a lot of time and debate on. And I think it's a great running order on this; from top to bottom I think it's a really good performance."

As far as the technology goes, "those two albums were very much embroiled in all that. We were working with Peter Collins, who was equally ambitious as a producer and arranger and song designer in a lot of ways. And we were working with a keyboard player, Andy Richards, in England at that time, who was king of the flourishes and the dramatic moments.

"We were a different band, and to stop work with someone like Terry Brown wasn't a reflection on him, or our relationship with him," continues Neil, on making the change. "It's just that you share a certain period of time and growth, and then we were restless for difference. It's not a question of better or superior ability or anything. So Peter Collins came along when we were much more interested in song arrangement, which is absolutely his forte. So he contributed to that element of our growth and was great to work with as a friend. But Terry Brown was too; for that period, we were very close, and he has a great personality and character in the studio. There's no comparison in any terms of good or bad. It's simply the people we were at the time. Like any relationship, I guess."

Peter came heartily recommended by Thin Lizzy's Gary Moore, who had been a Rush back-up act. Other than that, said Geddy at the time, Peter's credits, such as Musical Youth and Nik Kershaw, were quite obviously non-Rush-like. Add Blancmange and Tracey Ullman to that and the connection gets no clearer, which is the way Geddy wanted it. Why not have someone in who knows things we don't know? Conversely, why bother with someone who is primarily versed in skills we three have already brought to the room?

"*Power Windows* was a really important record to me, and I think a really important record to the band," adds Geddy, "because it was the final and essential blending of keyboards and guitar for Rush. What we had fucked around with and experimented with for years all came together in my view on *Power Windows*. It's one of my favorite albums because it has that combination of textural, really creative use of keyboards, and it's still a rock record. And Alex's guitar sounds big and fat and juicy, and that's what we wrestled with for *Signals* and *Grace Under Pressure*; you know, up until that point, those were all experiments. *Hold Your Fire* was the record that told me this whole four-piece was getting tired. There was a shift in the way we were writing on *Hold Your Fire*. That began the slow devolving of Rush. But I think *Power Windows* is a really important record in our career. If I were to pick those pinnacles, it would be *2112*, *Moving Pictures* and *Power Windows*."

Significantly, to get to this record that both Neil and Geddy hold in such high regard — although calling Alex's guitar "big and fat and juicy" makes me wonder if Geddy is mistaking Saxon's *Power & the Glory* for Rush's *Power Windows* — a strong modernist producer would be needed, one with radical non-rock opinions.

"I was working with an artist called Gary Moore who was opening up for Rush on their tour," begins that man, Peter Collins, who would begin a long and productive career-defining collaboration with Rush. "And I took my engineer from London with me. We went to L.A. and recorded a single with Gary called 'Empty Rooms.' The band had obviously heard the rendition of the song live before I got involved. And then they heard what I had done with the song afterward, and they were interviewing producers at the time. They obviously liked what I did with Gary's tune and invited me to come to see them play in Providence, Rhode Island."

Collins says as a pop producer he knew little about Rush. "I was just kind of dipping my toes in the water in terms of rock music. So I went out and bought some Rush records. I wasn't too keen on Geddy's voice and thought the records sounded horrible. So I thought, well, you know, I'll go and see what it's all about. So of course when I got to Providence, Rhode Island, it was a massive stadium of kids. You know what a Rush concert's like. I had no idea what to expect there. I was completely blown away.

"And then backstage I met them all for the first time and they asked me what I was doing. And there was an artist called Nik Kershaw that I was working with in England at the time, my first sort of successful album project, and I think they really liked Nik Kershaw. They asked me what would be the main issues I would address working with them. And I said, 'First of all, Geddy, your voice' because it was a very strange voice to me. One of my big strengths was producing vocals, so I wanted to get my hands on his vocals, as it were.

"And I said, 'The sound of your records, they sound terrible,'" continues Collins, admitting he was at this point fully immersed in the current sound of the '80s. "Trevor Horn was sort of the vanguard of that, the Frankie Goes to Hollywood sound, the Yes *90125* album, which were very high-tech. All the new equipment was coming in, the new digital reverbs, the new keyboards, the Fairlights, Synclaviers, all that stuff. And in England everybody was into those sorts of sounds. And so Rush's organic sound really didn't make much sense to me. It didn't sound relevant to my world. I was shooting from the hip when we met. I just said, 'I think your records could sound so much better.' So I wasn't flattering in the least. I mean, I was incredibly impressed with them as people, but, you know, I just told it like it was, and I got the gig."

There are various reasons why Collins might have appealed to the band. First, the Rush guys, now superstars, were likely being agreed with far too often, and a bit of pushback probably felt fresh. Second, they'd just been through a grind of an experience with a producer who was the complete opposite, not exactly a yes-man, but definitely lacking in strong opinions. Third, they were perennially hungry to move forward, and they were all quite on board with the new sounds, not to mention the latest fashions. Finally, as well, there was a little bit of another dynamic — arguably Canadian and sparingly admitted — the guys didn't want to embarrass themselves. Just like when they were teenagers, Rush wanted to hang with the cool crowd, and what's cooler than making the most futuristic music they could? This put them in the orbit of young people, not to mention an aesthetic that lined up with the ideals of MTV.

"They were not explicit, but they wanted a change in direction," continues Peter. "I wasn't that aware of the difficulties with *Grace Under Pressure* at the time of meeting them. I was just kind of cocky. I had a lot of hits in England, singles, and I felt I was at the top of my game. So I told them pretty much what I thought needed to happen, and they were very receptive to it. I think Rush, unlike say an AC/DC — AC/DC would make the same type of record over and over again, which their fans love and expect — Rush always try to develop into a new area, a new dimension, with every record they make. And I think I gave them the sort of ammunition to do that."

Perhaps as harbinger of what was to come, the writing and rehearsal sessions this time were conducted at Elora Sound Studio, northwest of Toronto, instead of a pure rural outpost. Granted, Peart scribbled his wisdoms in a farmhouse, and the twenty-four-track facility where Geddy and Alex sculpted music was fitted into a barn. Between writing and recording, the guys went on a short limbering-up tour in Florida, logging four shows and an onstage rehearsal session. Pre-LP versions of "The Big Money" and "Middletown Dreams" were performed at these shows. True to past patterning, they were similar to the final versions, no material changes necessary, although more so "The Big Money," as "Middletown Dreams" is less angular and sort of rocks out a bit more in this live rendition.

After their "spring training" trip, it was back to Elora for some more writing. The first fruit borne of their lingering live energy was "Emotion Detector," while Neil scored a breakthrough with both "Territories" and "Middletown Dreams." In Florida, on Peter's recommendation, the guys met with Australian engineer James "Jimbo" Barton. Liking what they heard, they hired him on for the upcoming project.

Peter Collins was given a clear picture of where the band wanted to go with him, in the form of a seven-song demo cooked up at Elora. These demos also show that the band was pretty clear on their direction, although, unsurprisingly, there are less electronics and more organic playing. Geddy is also still playing his Steinberger bass, resulting in a warmer sound than the one in the final product, which would make use of Peter's Wal bass, although Geddy would go back to the Steinberger for the tour. As well, Alex is more prevalent, and Neil is just going for it. Even Geddy throws in some extra licks — really, these are some pretty polished demos, and with a lot of chemistry to boot. Amusing, "The Big Money" is played faster on the demo than it is on *Power Windows*, like the earlier live version, and it's preceded by what sounds like typewriter sounds. There's also quite a different path taken for a bit there, after the solo section. The ending also hadn't quite been worked out.

Recording *Power Windows* was not a cheap affair. Venues like the Manor and Air Studios on Montserrat were utilized, as was Abbey Road Studios — five studios in all. Basic tracks were done over a five-week stay at the Manor, which is also where they availed themselves of Andy Richards, who helped with programming as well as the performance of some synthesizer parts.

"We were for the most part having a fantastic time at the Manor in Oxfordshire," recalls Peter. "You know, it was this big manor house belonging to Richard Branson from Virgin. When we arrived, there were these Irish wolfhounds at the gateways, and when we got in there, there was a big baronial dining hall with servants — it was a great time there. So I kind of remember the fun we had making that record, rather than any anxiety."

Into May, the band transitioned to Montserrat for guitar parts and lots of long hours of experimentation with amps and microphones.

Collins took a more hands-on approach to producing than did Henderson, one that was more in line with what Rush was looking for. Says Collins, "I like to think of myself as fairly decisive in the studio, hence they gave me the title of Mr. Big on

Power Windows. I do remember them saying they suffered from indecision at a production level on *Grace Under Pressure*, and they didn't want that, so I was quite happy to dive in and take charge. And when they really didn't like something, they spoke up, but they kind of went along with the direction I was pushing it in."

As for Peter's impression of the guys themselves, Peter draws an interesting comparison. "Coming from England and working with mostly young bands, young bands in England were kind of living hand to mouth and there was no real sense of camaraderie, and I never expected it. There was sort of 'we're sticking up for each other' but at a relatively superficial level. And when I met Rush it was the first time I'd experienced that kind of deep brotherhood among band members, where they actually, genuinely loved each other. Which was a most strange phenomenon for me to experience because my life in England with musicians was extremely superficial. They would fire somebody in an instant, whereas that kind of mature sense of being very, very comfortable with each other, knowing everybody's limitations and accepting and working and trying to keep everybody up, that was refreshing.

"And I accepted them as who they were, as good musicians who seemed to have a great connection with each other. *Power Windows* was a six-month project, and over the course of that album I got to know them much, much better and was able to fathom out some of the insecurities that existed between the three of them.

"Dealing with Geddy, I think he was looking for another bass sound," says Peter, addressing what some of those insecurities might be. "He had used the Ricky and used the Jazz, I guess. I had recently bought a Wal and that was the happening bass in England at the time, and I managed to persuade Geddy to switch to that. I don't think he was sure at first, but he loved it quickly, and I think he used it for a couple of albums. I had given him such a hard time about the vocals at our first meeting, so he was kind of curious to see how I was going to deal with that. Neil didn't have any insecurities — he knew exactly what he wanted to do with his drums; there was no issue there.

"And Alex, Alex's sound to me needed some attention. He had this board of pedals and switches — we found out during the course of that album there were a lot of electrical mismatches. So there was a lot of out-of-phase and bizarre stuff going on, which, as I look back, was probably good. But at that time, we had to try to work with that. There was some conflict between the engineer and Alex on that one, which also became quite difficult when we went to Montserrat to do guitar overdubs. The problem of his pedal board was compounded by the fact he had a very bad skin condition, which being in the Caribbean exacerbated, so his fingers were in pain while he was playing guitar. I think the band had a problem with his sound. I can't say that for sure, but the band was happy for me to dive in and get to the bottom of what may be the problem, electrically speaking, with his sound."

The mission was pop — English pop.

"Yes, modern pop music. And to do that I was using for references what I thought was good and trying to bring them into that world, the new recorded sound, the SSL compression. I don't know if they had worked on SSL boards, but using the bus compression on the drums and really making the whole thing pop. Their records up to that time had a very organic sound, and I didn't understand the term *organic* in those days. I've subsequently become Mr. Organic, but in those days, it was all about hyping the sound up. That's what made it exciting. You gave it a kind of unreal quality, and that's what I tried to do for them. And we used — as you can hear — a lot of reverbs, a lot of compressions, and I brought in Andy Richards to supplement the keyboards. I think we used orchestration for the first time, Anne Dudley on 'Manhattan Project.' Those were things that were natural for me to do to bring their sound into what I thought was contemporary."

Montserrat, poignantly, part of so many rock 'n' roll recording sessions and subsequent memories, no longer exists, having been wiped out by Hurricane Hugo in 1989.

"It was a wonderful atmosphere in Montserrat," muses Peter, adding to that memory bank. "We're in the Caribbean and we're all there to have a good time. We arrived and there was Desmond with the piña coladas waiting for us at the studio. You know, we'd start at noon, and there was this magnificent swimming pool. You look out the window of the control room and there was the ocean. It was just completely idyllic.

"Well, when we started doing the overdubs, Alex, as I say, had this skin condition which made it very difficult for him to play. So here we all are in paradise and Alex is struggling to actually play because it's so painful. There was not much we could do about that other than, you know, basically feel like we were torturing him, going through these guitar overdubs. It was difficult; I had a fixed view about what was good and what was not good based on my being an English producer. Some of the stuff, now as I look back, that he was trying to do, I understand why he was doing it, but at the time it didn't make any sense to me. So I was pushing him in certain directions he didn't want to go, as well as having problems with his fingers. The wall of sound concept was a little alien to me. Or not alien, because I had done sort of Phil Spector–type productions in England. But the guitar wall of sound, where it all became — to my ears at certain points — mush, I wanted to fix that and clear things up a bit. And then we got into issues with his pedal board."

Peter detected what was almost a sense of embarrassment from Alex concerning the predicament at Montserrat.

"Here we were in the Caribbean, having gotten the tracks fairly quickly. Everything had gone really, really smoothly, got some great tracks and the Andy Richards stuff had gone down well. And when it came to doing guitars in the Caribbean, with Alex's fingers swelling up and it taking as long and being as difficult as it was, you know, clearly Alex was embarrassed. He would have liked to zip through everything as painlessly as we had done up to that point. But the guitar is so paramount with a three-piece. I mean, everything counts, but particularly the guitars establishing all the melodic instrumental quality. The guitars are a lot of work to do and I think it was embarrassing for Alex, especially being the first time we had all worked together.

"We were extremely detailed about the parts," continues Peter, on the demands placed on Alex. "I'm a very parts-orientated guy, as is Geddy, and so we were exacting some very high standards in terms of establishing the parts and making sure they worked around the vocals properly. And as much as we had done in pre-production, there was still some parts to be established once the vocals were down. Also the way the solos got put together, I didn't know the process — and on *Power Windows*, I found out. Basically, Alex would just play solos, and Geddy would assemble them and then play them to Alex. The two of them would make adjustments, I would make my comments, and that's kind of how it went down. And getting used to that process means the producer stepping back and letting that happen and then seeing how that all worked. It might have been a bit stressful for Alex to be under that sort of microscope."

There were other setbacks as well, incidents that caused the making of *Power Windows* to be a long, drawn-out affair. "One of the early things that happened, coming back to the bass, Geddy liked the Wal bass and he played it and said, 'I think we should try new strings.' So his guitar tech took the strings off the Wal bass, and he cut them off rather than unwind them, the old strings. Put the new strings on, and Geddy said, 'No, I think I prefer the old strings.' Not a good moment. And Jack Secret, Geddy's guitar tech, when it came to do the first keyboard over-dub, plugged 220 volts into a 115 volt and blew the keyboard up."

Though Peter had stepped into a leadership role as producer, he appreciated Geddy's leadership qualities instead of entering into any sort of potential power struggle with him. "If you know Geddy, he's very concerned about every aspect of the band, from artwork, back projection, sounds of everything and how it's all put together. He's extremely interested in every aspect of Rush, and he's prepared to spend the time, and the other guys are happy to let him do it. And of course, he's incredibly articulate and is very helpful. He knows how to speak the language of producers and engineers and musicians, so dealing with him from a production standpoint is great. He's very analytical, logical and is prepared to experiment and go through all the options and sort of swill it around in his mouth and decide, hmm, that's the best way to go."

Power Windows, Rush's eleventh studio album, would be issued on October 14, 1985, preceded at radio by "The Big Money," put up for debate on September 26 of that year. For cover art, Hugh Syme would craft a technically meticulous realist painting, one that is featured prominently in the Rush offices. The inner sleeve features individual shots of the band by eminent Toronto pho-tographer Dimo Safari, who catches the guys in all their '80s preppy glory. Hugh's father had recently died, and he had felt that doing an ambitious cover would be therapeutic. And ambi-tious it was — Hugh and Dimo had to carefully stage the whole scene to get a photograph to work from, and so various rooms were scouted, as well as the vintage televisions and of course the boy on the cover, Neill Cunningham, who is described as a "junior stockbroker."

"It just came about," notes Neil on the album cover art. "In those days I would be writing a group of songs without a particular idea or concept in mind. And very often, as with both *Power Windows* and *Hold Your Fire*, a common thread emerged through the course of the writing. And I realized, of course, the common denominator here was power, different kinds of power. So it was a tongue-in-cheek kind of idea, power windows, looking out at power, simple as that. And then Hugh Syme, the art director, always has a quirky sense of humor, as with *Moving Pictures*, always wanting to twist it in a couple more directions if he can."

The messaging of the cover is pretty prescient given today's preoccupation with our cell phones. The boy seems somewhat perplexed about whether reality is on his various screens or outside his window, as he aims his remote control errantly and helplessly at the night. In the context of 1985, the message was a good one as well, given the power of TV in general and the power of MTV in particular, when it came to the music industry.

It makes sense that "The Big Money" would be the advance single, as well as the first song on the album, as it's a spirited, up-tempo song with more guitars than will be the case across the expanse of the album. Geddy and Neil also get to play energetically, with sparkly spark, most feverishly represented by the ensemble fireworks of the crescendo to close, one of Rush's famous "fake" endings.

Alex loves what Geddy does on this song, calling him "the funk master — that's the '80s, right there. It's interesting how he incorporates contemporary bass parts from that period. Also, I know this started with the bass pedals, but that also is a good example of the way we would approach playing the songs live. There's no bass guitar playing when the bass pedals are on. So he's playing the pedals and then the bass guitar replaces the bass pedals, when that part is over. And that was kind of a rule we had back then, that we wouldn't do something we couldn't do live. Very funky. And the tonality is quite different, but that was indicative of his tonal style of that period. He used the Wal and the Steinberger, and they have that kind of plunky sort of sound to them. Unlike the more recent stuff he does with the Fender Jazz bass, which is a deeper, rounder tone."

Notes Peter, "I seem to remember Alex saying, 'Well there's not much space for me with all those keyboards.' But, you know, there's fantastic guitar parts on there, which were present in the rehearsals, so they were always going to be there. At times it might have got a little bit too much, but I like to think we tapered it back. The intro on 'Big Money' was heavily keyboard orchestrated, and I think it's quite spectacular even today. And Alex, I can't really remember whether he dug that or not. To be honest with you, it was something of a democracy, and if two out of the three liked it, it usually went down."

On the evolution of "The Big Money" during the Florida concerts, Geddy says, "I remember 'Big Money' really improved after that. We got the right kind of rock-out attitude in certain parts of the song — when we played it, certain parts of the song got an instant cheer. And that kind of thing is a great confidence builder."

For the title of the song, Neil took inspiration from the 1936 Dos Passos novel of the same name. This was the second time Neil has referenced Dos Passos's U.S.A. trilogy, first time being "The Camera Eye." The song makes smart, rapid-fire observations about "big money," but there are some particularly amusing lines, most notably, "Sometimes building you a stairway — lock you underground" and "It's the fool on television getting paid to play the fool."

The profusion of keyboards made it necessary for much of the sound to be triggered by pedals when played live. In terms of the genesis of the parts, Geddy would take a first shot at programming, after which Andy Richards would take over and embellish, either through additional programming or performance.

The song was the subject of a full-on production video that uses live footage — Alex resplendent in a powder-blue suit, Neil with his rat-tail hairdo — and then-state-of-the-art computer animation. The band play on a lit-up Monopoly board with the words "Big Money" replacing "Monopoly"; behind is a pricey-looking cityscape. A car flies by with a "Mr Big" license plate, which is a reference to producer Peter Collins. Speaking of producers, the producer of this video is Geddy's brother, Allan, who has had a distinguished career in film and video through the years, with Rush and outside of the band. The model for Hugh's front cover painting, aforementioned Toronto youth Neill Cunningham, makes an appearance at the beginning peering through binoculars as he is painted on the back cover of the album, and then in later frames and sequences floating by.

"Grand Designs" (also a Dos Passos reference) finds Neil framing various aspects of nonconformity, championing substance over style, precious metal over "a ton of rock" and "swimming against the stream." Musically, this one's another example of the band's progressive reggae writing, near brisk enough to be called ska, with Alex doing the chordal stabs but little else.

Notes Peter, "With young bands in England, the guitar players didn't like keyboards, so I was used to that. It was to be expected from the guitar players. I didn't pay that much attention to it. Geddy and Neil for the most part liked what was going down, and if it was universally not liked, it was cut. I don't remember him being that upset about it, to be honest with you; I really don't."

Adds Neil, defending the keyboards, or at least acknowledging that they couldn't be ignored in 1985: "Yeah, those two records, those two tours, I think represent the apogee of that particular involvement in music and arranging. We were very ambitious as arrangers then. I was describing before how the course of study becomes your learning. You begin to play first, and then you learn how to write songs, then you're trying to learn how to arrange them and produce them. And the course of study almost goes that linear — for our band anyway. We started off concentrating on playing and then it became that progress of wanting to refine skills. Technology became more reliable; that's the thing. God, when we first started with sequencers in the early '80s, they were so unreliable. *Signals*, and even *Moving Pictures* had 'Vital Signs' on it, which was sequencer-based. That was something I had to hear onstage every night to be able to play to. And then into *Signals* and *Grace Under Pressure*, it was experimenting with all the early synthesizer advances and all the attendant frustrations and unreliability."

The end of this one is quite amusing. Neil found himself inspired to keep jamming along with the repeating sequencer line, so they kept a longer chunk of these endings upon endings. Then the band had to learn how to play these slight variants in sequence, so to speak, to pull off the song live. The achieved effect is similar to that of "The Big Money" and "Mystic Rhythms"; it's as if the band has chanced upon an outro that is rewarding enough to let linger.

The next track, "Manhattan Project," opens, appropriately, with military snare from Neil before becoming a bit of a ballad, Geddy singing softly over spare drums and synths. By the second verse, Alex creeps in with Police-style guitar, all deft build toward a powerful chorus where the nuclear bombs are detonated over Japan. At this point we hear what sounds like fretless bass licks. These were played by Andy Richards on a Roland JP-8000 and were sampled for live use, despite the challenge of getting them to sound right as samples.

There's a geometric organizing principle to Neil's lyric, which was crafted after Peart did a pile of research on the invention and detonation of the bombs over Hiroshima and Nagasaki that ended Word War II in terms of the Pacific, days before the end of the war globally. Neil recalls working on the song on a child-sized desk in the farmhouse up at Elora, during the writing and rehearsal sessions. The first verse begins with "Imagine a time," the second with "Imagine a man" (J. Robert Oppenheimer), the third with "Imagine a place" and the fourth once again with "Imagine a man," this time referring to Paul Tibbets, the pilot of the B-29 Superfortress *Enola Gay*, which dropped the first bomb, Little Boy, on Hiroshima.

As the band explained on the interview trail, thematically the songs on the window cluster around the concept of power. This one is about the power of science, while "The Big Money" is about the power of big business, "Emotion Detector" is about the power of relationships and "Grand Designs" is about the power of ideas.

"Creating the bomb was a very human event," noted Peart, speaking with eminent Canuck journo Keith Sharp. "It wasn't just a bunch of faceless potentates in the Pentagon ordering the destruction of millions of people; it was a bit more complicated than that. We're talking about America's top scientific brains getting this patriotic job to help the cause of freedom, democracy and the American way by building the bomb. They couldn't say no. If they did, they'd be branded as neo-Nazi and would have been ostracized, if not executed. Once they had the power, they had to use it for fear that if we chickened out, the enemy wouldn't. Where there's power, there's always the danger of misusing that power. Each song addresses both sides of the argument, but overall, I think this is a lot more positive than the message in *Grace Under Pressure*."

"Marathon," perhaps a metaphor for ambition and life but really, pretty directly about running a marathon, finds Rush again sort of redefining reggae, with bass, guitars and drums hinting at reggae tropes, while vocals and keys are just nu-Rush. At over six minutes, there are perhaps extraneous parts, a few extra sonic collages that could have been dropped. Though to be charitable, maybe they serve as apportioned soundtrack bits to various physiological stages experienced by the marathon runner.

As Alex explained to *Kerrang!*'s Mark Putterford, "We thought it was going to be a marathon at first because it's made up of so many parts and each part is so different. But oddly enough, we just went bang, bang, bang and flew through recordings. All the parts locked together like a big jigsaw puzzle and it was great. Whereas 'Emotion Detector' was the opposite — we thought it would be easy to do and we ended up having real problems. Again, this song deals with power — the power we have within us to push and drive ourselves towards the goals that we aim for. It's not an easy road; in fact it's always an uphill climb, but it depends on how much of our inner power we want to use to get us to the end of the road."

"I think this song is real close to Neil," continued Lifeson. "He took up cycling during the last tour. The biggest enemy you have on the road is boredom, and even though we love what we do, the routine of it all is tiring. And his goal was to hit a hundred miles on his bike every time we had a day off. He would take his bike out at six or seven in the morning and just disappear until six or seven at night. He has this drive within him which pushes him forward all the time, and 'Marathon' really concerns this aspect of his character."

The Chinese proverb "The journey of a thousand miles begins with one step" influenced Neil's thinking on this one as well; Peart also intimates that the song is about achieving goals through the process of sensible pacing.

There's both orchestra and choir on "Marathon." Likely an unintended spot of messaging, but one can imagine this runner succumbing to a heart attack and getting called up to heaven, endorphins cushioning the ride.

"Parts of that record we recorded at Abbey Road Studios, which was a huge thrill for us," says Geddy. "A lot of the orchestra were London Symphony players, and it was the big room in Abbey Road where so many big records had been recorded — that was the first time we used an orchestra in any of our songs, I believe, so that was a real treat. We all arrived at Abbey Road and we were like kids again, going through this famous place and sitting in that magnificent room. Of course, it was terribly disconcerting to see all these symphonic musicians, and in between takes they're fucking around, cutting things up. We're overhearing all these disparaging, typical comments. You know, you have this impression of symphonic musicians, and then you realize they're just musicians like us.

"But it was really a lot of fun. I was walking around taking photos. It was a pretty cool moment. We recorded a choir for 'Marathon,' and then we went to this church in another part of London where this really marvelous choir was singing, and it was a really great-sounding room. Peter wanted to record them in that room. Having been in a three-piece band who worked only with each other for so many years, it was gratifying to work with Peter, to suddenly start going to these really interesting nooks and crannies of London and working with these other musicians and arrangers. We worked with Anne Dudley on that record, a wonderful arranger. She used to be in Art of Noise and had worked a lot with Trevor Horn. It was a great experience to suddenly realize there's all these other talented people out there who can contribute to your music, not take away from it, just enhance it. It was a real awakening, in terms of production and arrangement, and as musicians."

"Territories," with its oriental musical overtones, today might have Rush accused of cultural appropriation. As the song progresses, this one has Alex hitting some big power chords, or at least as big as they get on this record — as elsewhere, with his pings and squalls, his guitar sounds strangled, gasping for air.

Having recently completed a bicycling trip in China, Neil told Keith Sharp that "Territories" was in fact inspired by an earlier trip. "The lifestyle in China is too different for us to comprehend. There was little I could parallel with our style of life. So I took a small image and translated it into a larger one. China calls itself the Middle Kingdom and sets itself apart from everyone else. That mentality translates across the world. For example, every country we've ever visited always claims to have the world's best beer. It's become an in-joke with us — we laugh every time somebody says it because we know everyone else says the same thing."

Elsewhere, Neil has explained, he found it amusing that the Chinese call themselves the Middle Kingdom: they are placing themselves above the rest of the people on Earth but not quite as high as those in heaven, an amusing twist on the concept of modesty. Peart's more recent trip to China, a little reward for having finished the album, found Neil joining about a dozen strangers — Canadians, Americans, Australians — to take his new hobby up a notch.

"We certainly got to see the negative side of China," Neil told Keith. "The overpopulation is a real problem, and the sanitation left a lot to be desired. Our leader came down with dysentery and had to be hospitalized in Peking. We all came down with varying degrees of dysentery, chest colds and head colds — there were so many germs floating around. The physical part of cycling was tough too. We cycled eighty miles one day, seventy miles the next, then we'd stay at small village hotels with no bathrooms. You'd arrive at the place all hot and dusty and you couldn't even take a shower. We were quite a novelty to the Chinese. They don't see us on TV. To them, Western culture consists of Richard Nixon, Coca-Cola, Wham! and Rambo. It's quite sad to think that those things represent us to the majority of Chinese people."

The amusing "better beer" in-joke, voiced with a bit of a raised eyebrow, serves as a metaphor for what the whole song is about — as does China. Using China as a stepping-off point, Peart is talking about the drawbacks of thinking in terms of territory. As for the drums, Neil put his snare aside and went tribal — rigidly. The title of the track was inspired by the New Territories area near Hong Kong, with Peart seeing the larger theme in that name as well as liking the sound of the word *territory* itself.

"Middletown Dreams" is another atmospheric and chimey near-ballad, with Neil using rim shot instead of whacked snare across the intro verse. Activity levels pick up and the song becomes yet another one of these origami-crafted high-tech reggaes where Geddy gets to cook a groove with his articulating Wal.

"I used the exact thing 'Territories' warns against as a device in 'Middletown,'" Neil told Nick Krewen of *Canadian Composer.* "I chose 'Middletown' because there is a Middletown in almost every state in the U.S. It comes from people identifying with a strong sense of neighborhood. It's a way of looking at the world with the eyeglass in reverse. I spent my days off cycling around the countryside in the U.S., looking at these little towns and getting a new appreciation of them. When you pass through them at fifteen miles per hour, you see them a little differently. So I was looking at these places and looking at the people in them — fantasizing, perhaps romanticizing, a little about their lives. I guess I was even getting a little literary in imagining the present, past and future of these men, women and children. There was that romantic way of looking at each small town.

"But also each of the characters in that song is drawn from real life or specific literary examples," continues Neil. "The first character was based on a writer called Sherwood Anderson. Late in his life, Anderson literally walked down the railroad tracks out of a small town and went to Chicago in the early 1900s to become a very important writer of his generation. That's an example of a middle-aged man who may have been perceived by his neighbors, and by an objective onlooker, to have sort of finished his life. He could have stagnated in his little town, but he wasn't finished in his own mind. He had this big dream, and it was never too late for him, so he walked off and he did it.

"The painter Paul Gauguin is another example of a person who, late in life, just walked out of his environment and went away. He too became important and influential. He is the influence for the woman character of the song. The second verse about the young boy wanting to run away and become a musician is a bit autobiographical. But it also reflects most of the successful musicians I know, many of whom came from very unlikely backgrounds. Most of them had this dream that other people secretly smiled at — or openly laughed at — and they just went out and made it happen."

Alex emphasized to Mark Putterford the fit of the song to the theme of power. "Yeah, the power of dreams and desires; wanting to get somewhere which isn't easy to get to. This was not an easy song to record. In a way, it was our dream to get the thing finished! For me personally, I was never happy with the guitar parts, and it took a number of rewrites before we actually got it together. But in the end, the number was very satisfying for me and it was well worth all the trouble."

Neil indulges his penchant for juvenile wordplay for the titling of "Emotion Detector," a straight personal relations/psychology-type song, very direct, with Peart nicely embedding the word *power*. This one, "Territories" and "Mystic Rhythms" all have a trace of that Chinese music tonality; however, come chorus time, the guys hit a home run, with the most emotional music on a record that is almost oppressively austere, hard and shiny, not to mention painfully faddish.

"There's always one song that you're terrified of doing," Alex opined, in a wide-ranging look at the album with *Guitar Player*'s Jas Obrecht back in 1986. "You think it's going to be really tough, and 'Marathon' was the one. We wrote it and thought, 'This song is going to be like pulling teeth once we get in the studio.' Of course, we get into the studio and it's a breeze. And a song like 'Emotion Detector,' which we thought would be a breeze, was the killer. It was very, very difficult to get the mood right.

"I'm still not really sold on that song. It never ended up sounding the way I had hoped it would. Half of 'Emotion Detector' was done in one pass. Actually, that song had a whole different solo that took quite a bit of work. We left it, went ahead with some other parts, lived with it for four or five days and Neil didn't feel quite right about it. He didn't think that it made the proper kind of statement to the song, so we reexamined it and I gave it another whirl. That was tough. It's one thing to rewrite a rhythm guitar part — you've got stuff to lock onto. But it was so hard to divorce what had been in my head as a solo for three months and come up with something that was a totally different feel. But I am satisfied with the results."

With respect to his approach to solos at the time in general, Alex explained, "I like to play about eight or ten tracks of solos, and then I get kicked out of the control room. Everybody sort of dives in. Geddy likes to really get into doing that. He and the engineer sit down, and Neil makes some suggestions. Of course the producer is there too, and they piece together a solo. I come back in after a couple of hours when they have something assembled, and if I like it, then we either stick with it or we keep that as a starting point and go for another whirl over some of the older tracks."

Power Windows closes strongly with the atmospheric and dramatic "Mystic Rhythms." Set to a hypnotic, pounding beat from Neil, stark keyboard stabs compete with a pensive and behaved Alex on a song that seems to aim at *Security*-era Peter Gabriel. Neil's lyric is surprisingly plain-spoken, which as we arrive at the end of the album, has turned out be a consistent trend throughout. The song was in fact issued as a single, getting to #21 on the subchart U.S. Mainstream Rock. The video for the track, produced by Jerry Casale of Devo, is a cornucopia stuffed with visual metaphors, an inundation for exploration and extrapolation for those who dare.

Geddy has indicated that pretty much everything on this song was "synthesized" in some way — in fact, Alex plays an Ovation acoustic guitar, not that an astute listen would reveal such a sound.

"This song deals with more of a cosmic power," Lifeson told Mark Putterford, "a power that we sit in frustration and look hopelessly at — like when we look up at the stars in the night sky and can't even formulate a concrete idea of how much power is there. It's such an unknown. It's an internal power which has always been there and will still be there long after we've come and gone."

"It was a struggle because he had loads of guitars and loads of options," recalls producer Peter Collins. "I do remember that. So, you know, we'd have to go through all the options, and it was a very time-consuming process. And of course, when you've got that many options, sometimes it becomes overwhelming and you kind of lose sight of where you're going. It was a struggle to keep focus with the guitars. 'Mystic Rhythms,' those parts were all sorted out in preproduction and it was just a question of getting the sounds right. But it was a struggle, and I think also Alex felt particularly bad because we were in a paradise island and here he was with his fingers in a bad way, going through all the options with guitars. Plus we're all getting used to each other; the dynamic between me as producer hadn't been established."

But in terms of butting heads with the guys, Collins says, "I was a bit of a coward. I let the engineer, Jimbo, deal with a lot of those sonic issues. You know, I'd just lean over to Jimbo, and say, 'This isn't right; get it sorted out,' and he would actually lead the charge. I'd be sort of smoking my cigar, waiting for them to get it sorted out. And I'd be the final arbiter in the producer's chair. I would make the decision."

But one wonders if it ever got to be the bridge too far, so to speak. Geddy calls "Mystic Rhythms" the most synthetic track on the record, but all seven of the others are only a shade less processed.

"They were excited and they were also concerned," admits Peter. "They were worried that a song like this was maybe going too far. But then too far was always good for them. To be honest with you, I didn't really care — that's what I was going to do. I had it in my mind: this is what needs to happen, and however I was going to cajole them, seduce them into going in that direction, that's what I was going to do. And you know, Geddy was initially very reluctant to have another keyboard player come in — that had never happened. And the only reason I wanted to do it was because Andy Richards played all the Frankie Goes to Hollywood stuff, worked on the Yes album and he really had the sort of sounds that made sense to me. And Geddy, God bless him, he said, 'You know, let's give it a shot, and if I don't like it, we won't use it.' But he ended up loving it, to such an extent that

Geddy created a cape for Andy, with a huge Star of David on the back, and he put it on sort of Rick Wakeman style.

"But I was thrilled with it when it was all done," continues Collins. "And then when it actually got some criticism from the hard-core Rush fans that prefer the old sound more, the more organic sound, I thought I'd overproduced it. They thought it was too slick, and then I thought more about what I'd done and determined to sort of back off some of those aspects on the next record — should I be asked to do the next record."

Peter had this tendency to fine-tune, but then as time went on, he underwent a deeper evolution. "Yes, it was only maybe ten years later that I spent more time in America and got more into American rock. Because don't forget I was coming from really a pure pop background — folk and pop in England — so I had no point of reference really. I didn't listen to a great deal of rock music. I listened to Yes and Zeppelin, and so I was more of a pop guy. So I thought this is nonsense. But certainly, now I really understand what they were saying. It would be hard for me to make a *Power Windows*–type record these days with my current sensibility. But at the time, I thought, 'These people are completely out of date, and they need to wake up.' I was young and foolish. But again, one of the reasons I think I got the gig was because I was so critical of their previous sound — it didn't make sense to me. So I achieved what I wanted to do on that record. And I think they were excited and thrilled by it all."

And look, *Power Windows* sold over a million copies in the U.S. — and very quickly, passing gold in December of '85, two months after release, and achieving platinum in January of 1986. Rush was still a powerhouse both on record and in concert halls, which was even less in question. On the charts, *Power Windows* was the third Rush album in a row to rise to a #10 placement on Billboard, hitting #2 in Canada, where the album also sold platinum.

The tour for the record was strictly a North American affair. Commencing in December of '85, the band tackled America, east to west, supported by Steve Morse. Into February and March of '86, they played a handful of Canadian dates close to home, supported by neo-proggers Marillion and FM. Marillion stayed on into the rust belt states, and then in April, the band took on Blue Öyster Cult as support, in a turning of the tables similar to what happened with Uriah Heep. The final few shows, in May of '86, saw incongruous support from the Fabulous Thunderbirds.

The band was facing new technological challenges but gamely conquering them — in fact, you'd have to say Rush were continuing to lead in this field. Maybe they weren't the most computerized band on the tour circuit, but in terms of a hybrid of modernity with a root identity as an old-school yet complicated power trio, there was no one with their hands quite as full as Rush in 1985.

As Alex explained to Jas Obrecht of *Guitar Player*, "It's no problem. We were a bit apprehensive. I mean, we wanted to stretch out on this record, but we didn't want to go too overboard. We've never been that kind of a group. We've always held the stage show as being very important and as we got into it, Peter suggested going a little bit further and further, adding more tracks to the record. We'd go a little more out on keyboards and sounds and effects. So when we started preparing for concert rehearsals, Geddy went in with Jim Burgess, a programmer in Toronto that we use for a lot of stuff, and he set it up so that we got a lot of the sequenced parts down on Emulator. They're constantly being programmed throughout the evening for the different songs. We put all the old synth sounds from the Oberheims and the Minimoogs onto the Emulator. We condensed the whole keyboard setup and made it a little more sophisticated. It's really not a problem to get all that stuff back on there. We just put them on a disk and call them up as we go through the song."

Alex says he's playing bass pedals too. "Yeah, I've been playing them for a long time. 'Subdivisions,' 'Spirit of Radio,' 'Manhattan Project,' 'Marathon' and 'Mystic Rhythms.' I would say on probably forty percent or fifty percent of the songs. But a lot of those times, Geddy's playing bass pedals at the same time, so it's not like it's taking over a bass guitar part in all instances. It sort of restricts where you end up onstage. I have a pretty vast array of things now with the Korg MIDI pedals, the Moog Taurus bass pedals and my effects devices. It covers just about a fifth of the stage. I think with this tour, Geddy's really got his hands full with a lot of parts. He's always complaining that he doesn't have enough time to play bass anymore, which is really his first instrument. Through the years, he's been forced into playing keyboards, doing that whole end of it."

But the band would retain their proud tradition of not augmenting the presentation with a fourth set of hands. "We talked about that a long time ago and decided that rather than disrupt the chemistry between the three of us, we would just learn other instruments on our own. And the world of synthesizers is very fast paced; it's constantly changing. It's amazing what you can do with your big toe; you can have incredible string sounds, all kinds of sounds. No limit to it now."

"My first relation to it is: What kind of drum set did I have?" says Neil, who was playing his red Tamas with a Slingerland snare. "That's an important touchstone. And of course we were embroiled in a lot of music technology at that time. So the live performance was a challenge, a real undertaking. We were still trying to juggle expanding our sound so much, with Geddy taking on so many keyboards and both of them triggering so many keyboard events with feet and hands.

"And I was getting into sampling at that time too, so that was a time of particular ferment and experimentation in technological ways. When the Who first started performing *Who's Next* and Keith Moon had to play the tapes of 'Baba O'Riley' and 'Won't Get Fooled Again,' and they were trying to work at the forefront of technology at the time, it was difficult and frustrating. *Quadrophenia* was largely sabotaged by trying to do too much with tapes and all that. That's in the '70s. Go ten years later when sampling and MIDI became available. Because it's available, of course, we wanted to use it. It made possible so much. But in the context of live performance particularly, we became nervously dependent on technology, where we would have to hear certain sequences and triggering going on to stay in synch with each other."

Neil knew the album was going to be a difficult one to get across in the acoustic crudity of hockey barns, but the challenge had to be met. "We had to reproduce that," he explains. "I guess that's part of the personal onus for us. We really felt the challenge of wanting to reproduce what was on the record. Yes, we could have played just a stripped-down version, but for me, using sampling is a good example. I always like to use things I could physically play. So every sound was the result of a hit or kick; there was an organic relationship there — that to me was kind of a point of honor."

Six months in total, playing half of every month, the *Power Windows* tour represented a clear indication that the band was asserting their independence against the Solar Federation. Geddy, Alex and Neil were hacking out time for themselves so they could become proper family men, but they were also becoming increasingly multidimensional, not just musicians dabbling in hobbies. They wanted to become, each in their own modest way, Renaissance men of sorts.

"It would've been in the middle '80s when that started to happen because they were getting older and they had kids and whatnot," explains manager Danniels. "We would've gotten down to sixty, sixty-five, seventy shows on a few tours. When the *Roll the Bones* album came out, we went back up closer to the one hundred twenty mark, and consequently it was a bigger record than we had had in a while. But they always loved being onstage. There is a point in your life where you don't love the travel as much. You love the camaraderie, you love everything about it, except for travel, and you start to miss being at home. I've watched that happen with them — I saw it. I don't think it's any different from what happens to athletes, who sometimes retire sooner than they would've. If you only stayed at home and played the home games, they would last five years longer. But that's not how the business works. And for a musician, there are three home games in the whole season, not half the season."

But no question, the insanity of the schedule, both recording and touring, for the first ten years is what got the band to where they were. "Yes, they had a fabulous work ethic, and it was the key to their success. Had they not toured like that, I don't think we would've been able to do this for this long and had this kind of foundation. They really grew into their career and played these places over and over again."

On the subject of having the discussion about scaling back, Ray says, "Understand, one of the things that has kept this band together for so long is that if any one of the three of them has a real issue, it's taken very seriously. And there's never been an issue that was more important than the band itself or the three of them getting along. When it comes to touring, Neil is the one who enjoys it the least. Alex is the easiest. If I could book a two-hundred-city tour, Alex would probably kill himself doing it, but he would make the effort. He just likes being out there.

And Geddy, it's a perfect combination because he's right in the middle. Geddy likes to do it, not perhaps as much as Alex, but he likes to do it. He likes to find that middle number that is the right number so it's not missing too much but not burning both ends of the candle at the same time."

But in the same way lawyers have roles, Ray says, "It was always my job to convince Neil to do more, and to give him reasons to do more. I mean, I would sit and talk with him, and I don't want to look like a British band coming to America doing thirty-five dates. It's not that profitable. You have to look at the size of the cities you're missing. So over the years I learned to try to encourage him to do more, and to give him the best of what I had. I would try very, very hard to make sure we played as many markets as we could, and that anyone in America — other than if they were living in Hawaii or Alaska — could get to a show if they made the effort.

"You can't have your biggest record over and over again, unless you're a pop act," reflects Ray, on the state of the band at this juncture. "And then when that stops, it crashes. And I think we all resigned ourselves to the fact that *Moving Pictures* was going to be the big record. And in their minds, they tried to make interesting records, and records they thought were better. But when you look back ten years later, you go, 'How the hell are we going to do better than that?' I think their goal was to make really, really good records, and what happened happened. And in my world, as long as I had fifty or sixty shows, and could get to Europe once in a while, I could keep the momentum going."

And the record labels — Mercury in the U.S. and mainland Europe, Vertigo in the U.K. and Sony in Japan — had to resign themselves to the fact that the band wasn't going to promote themselves in the flesh as hard as they had.

"Always, always," muses Danniels. "The labels eventually realized — and they're not fools — your biggest records, you get one hundred twenty shows, and your not so big records, you do sixty shows, and it becomes obvious what one of the key ingredients is. So of course, the label wants you to do twice as many shows as you are doing. My goal was to work with it and to make sure we were a national attraction in America, and not regional. We would still go and play Nashville. We would play gigs in the southern U.S. And the theory would be, you play Nashville so people in Memphis — or from three or four other cities — could get to you. And to play Nashville wouldn't certainly be the most profitable day. You'd be leaving money on the table in other places you could've gotten too. You know, three shows in the Carolinas are not exactly the most profitable dates for Rush. But there are a lot of people who live there — you've got fans and you want to get to them."

"That was a gradual thing, a hard-learned lesson," reflects Geddy. "You only learn those things when your life is falling apart, and you realize you've just spent too much time away. And I would say from '85 on, we started learning those lessons. That's when we stopped playing outside of America so much. After the Japanese tour, we just started pulling back the reins, cutting our American tour dates, making sure we instituted a policy where if we were out for three weeks, we would come home for ten days afterwards. We started playing fewer American cities; we stopped playing Europe every tour. We would play every other tour, or three tours, and eventually we kind of ignored Europe.

"So that was the beginning. We just all made a more concerted effort to take time away from the band and pay attention to our families and kids and all that stuff. At that point, we were still traveling by bus. You can get the nicest bus in the world, but it's still a bus, and it's very hard on your system to do the gig, get on the bus, drive for four hundred miles, get up in the middle of the night and go into your hotel room and finish sleeping. It lends itself to a lot of abuse, because you're so bored on the damn bus. You drink more than you should, you smoke more than you should, all that stuff. It's a tough environment and I think it's one that contributes to a lot of physical deterioration.

"It looked like, if we let this thing keep going, there were any number of countries we could expand to. And it's like, do we have the time? Can we afford this in our lives, to be a band twelve months a year? We realized we couldn't do that. That's when we said, 'Look, we're not here to dominate the world. We are thankful we've had this much success. Let's just step back a bit, take stock of our lives at this point and try to bring some reasonable attitude to living.'"

Providence Civic Center, Providence, RI, November 7, 1984. This show was rescheduled from September 25. Support act was Y&T.

Lost in thought in Lovecraft country.

At Buffalo's Memorial Auditorium, July 12, 1984. This show, rescheduled from July 7, feautured as support fellow Canucks Red Rider.

Memorial Auditorium, Buffalo, NY, February 27, 1986. Support came from U.K. progressive rock revivalists Marillion.

Rush play the RPI Fieldhouse in Troy, New York, November 12, 1987. Support on the night came from the McAuley Schenker Group.

ABOVE: Buffalo's Memorial Auditorium, November 14, 1987.

LEFT: Geddy signing autographs for fans.

Buffalo's Memorial
Auditorium,
November 14, 1987.

A couple of *Hold Your Fire*-era ads from the author's collection.

Another shot from Buffalo, November '87.

SIDE A :

1. FORCE TEN
2. TIME STAND STILL
3. OPEN SECRETS
4. SECOND NATURE
5. PRIME MOVER
6. HIGH WATER

SIDE B :

1. LOCK AND KEY
2. M I S S I O N
3. TURN THE PAGE
4. TAI SHAN
5. T E R R I T O R I E S *
6. THE BIG MONEY *

* Taken From Album "POWER WINDOW"

Billboard
Reg. 150.053

BB - 10.654

RUSH
HOLD YOUR FIRE

RUSH
HOLD YOUR FIRE

BB - 10.654

Direct Metal
Dmm
Mastering
GIVES * EXCEPTIONAL SOUND TRANSPARENCY
* REDUCTION OF NOISE
* ELIMINATION OF PRE AND POST GROOVE ECHO
SETS THE STANDARD FOR SUPERIOR TOMORROW'S SOUND
TO GIVE YOU MORE PLEASURE
LICENCE No. 560/DJ/A/IUT-D.IV/NONFAS/XI/1986
Member of APNINo.27/APN/80
Made in Indonesia

00

Billboard

Rp 2500.-

12/88

Indonesian *Hold Your Fire* cassette. Note the inclusion of "Territories" and "The Big Money" from *Power Windows*.

Playable inserts from *Modern Drummer* and *Guitar Player*.

MARATHON

THE PASS

SUPERCONDUCTOR

An assortment of Rush singles from the 1980s.

ABOVE: Rare *Presto* promotional pencil.

RIGHT: *Presto* backstage laminate.

Geddy and Alex with Rush expert and collector Ray Wawrzyniak, at the mixing sessions for *A Show of Hands*, June 17, 1988, McClear Place studio.

Geddy with his softball team, Those Darn Fish, 1987.

CHAPTER 7

HOLD YOUR FIRE

"Well, it wasn't our best material . . . or was it?"

In 1986, Rush essentially had it all: another platinum record, robust tour receipts, an increasing sense of balance and a vigorous creative vitality, really, coming off their most radical album-to-album transformation as a band yet. Underscoring their professed sense of satisfaction with *Power Windows*, the guys made no major changes in the process toward what would become *Hold Your Fire*.

Perhaps we can frame this as a nice representation of the guys' growth as individuals, but after vacationing with their families, each of them began the creative process on their own, Neil at a cottage, Alex in his home studio, Geddy on the Digital Performer software loaded into his new Macintosh computer.

Getting together at Elora Sound Studios commencing September 27, 1986, the guys already had bits and pieces to the likes of "Time Stand Still," "Turn the Page," "Open Secrets" and "Mission." Creativity on the music end would be sparked by carefully cataloged ideas generated at sound checks on the *Power Windows* tour along with Alex's tapes. By November they had the brunt of the album fleshed out — "Force Ten" would be the last track to come, on the last day in Elora, December 14. The next month, they brought Peter Collins in. His most material changes were to "Mission" and "Open Secrets."

"First of all, I had just finished one of the worst projects of my life in between *Power Windows* and *Hold Your Fire*, which was a Billy Squier record," recalls Peter Collins, on being brought back by Rush for a second time. The album he is referring to is 1986's *Enough Is Enough*, which he worked on with Jim Barton. Following three platinum and multi-platinum records, *Enough Is Enough* stalled well short of gold. "That really brought me down to the ground with a resounding thump. That was the first time I had actually had a real failure — it completely tanked. Up to that point I had been like a rising star in rock music, and when I got the call from Rush to do *Hold Your Fire* it was really a huge shot in the arm for me, because I thought, well, my career is over with this Billy Squier record. When they called me, I was very, very pleased and had a great enthusiasm for diving in and doing it."

The heavy lifting began at the Manor in Oxfordshire on January 5, 1987, and utilized digital recording techniques for Geddy and Alex, while Neil was captured in analog with a later conversion to digital. *Hold Your Fire* was shaping up to be as glossy, hard, thin and high-strung as its predecessor.

"In terms of the direction, I don't remember any discussion about should the sound be any different," continues Collins. "I got the sense there was no problem keeping it in that direction at all, and they didn't have a problem using Andy Richards again."

Andy came into the picture when the guys transitioned to Ridge Farm, which is also where everything was converted to digital. Then, on March 1, it was back to Montserrat, and for the same purpose (other than swimming and drinking), namely Alex's guitar overdubs.

"It was not as difficult," says Peter, remembering the flare-up of Alex's skin condition on the previous trip. "We went back to Montserrat, and I don't think he had the same problems the second time. And we all had a better working relationship. By that time, we got his pedal board sorted out and the dynamic between all of us was much more comfortable. So he knew more what to expect and I think he was slightly more prepared, and we didn't have to go through all the guitar options. Having been through them on *Power Windows*, we knew more what would work quicker, so that was less stressful for him. Jimbo, the engineer, was more accepted by them. Having been through the process of figuring each other out during *Power Windows*, it was naturally going to be easier.

"I don't think we used Andy quite as much. Geddy stepped up more on *Hold Your Fire*. We had the power drill sound that Andy came up with, but I don't remember Andy doing a great deal on that record, certainly not as much as on *Power Windows*. It was getting toned down, the keyboard element. Alex was probably more vocal about us not needing as many keyboards. Also my son was born in the middle of that. I had forecasted for my son to be born in a certain week and we made that week a week off, and he didn't show up in that week so I had to leave in the middle of Andy's overdubs."

In terms of the record's sonics, the guys were looking to make one adjustment — get more bass.

"We had a very good engineer, James Barton on that," says Peter on the use of bass on the record. "Geddy was comfortable with James. But the bottom end was always an issue with Geddy, because it was coming more from an English sensibility where the bottom end is not as low as the American sensibility. Geddy was always worrying about the real low-end frequency. After *Power Windows*, we resolved to try to get more low end in on *Hold Your Fire* from a technical side. Geddy was definitely driving that, as I was — I became aware that we needed to address that. Part of Jimbo's sound though was that kind of mid-rangey thing; it didn't involve a lot of low end. Low end would come in at certain moments, particularly when Geddy was using the Taurus pedals, to distinguish itself from the regular played bass. But that was an issue, and an issue in mastering as well. But I was totally unaware of that. It didn't mean anything to me until I became much more aware of the American sensibility towards bass. And even to this day it's quite different between England and America."

As Peter alludes to, in the end, they didn't quite get where they wanted — *Hold Your Fire* was a notoriously trebly record, as bass-challenged as the one before it and the two after.

Geddy continued to show interest in all aspects of the recording process. "I would say definitely he was my co-producer. You know, it's always a co-production credit with the band, but Geddy had the greatest interest in production. He would be my go-to point of reference representing the band. But of course, with guitars and drums, the guys would speak up if they had a point of view. But in order of involvement on the production side, it would be Geddy, Alex and Neil."

"He has a nice balance of both spontaneity and careful application," reflects Neil, offering a rich explanation of Geddy's role in the band. "For instance, he and Alex can sit and just noodle away for a couple of hours. It's Geddy whose gonna sit there and sift through those ideas and assemble them into something. And when I bring him lyrics, I just give him a pile of stuff. It's not like, 'Here's my favorite new thing that I wrote.' It takes the pressure off both of us. He'll find lines that he likes, and he'll find a part of the song that they go with, and he'll take the time to work out things like that.

"And then of course having to work on so many levels, as part of the composition and arrangement, and the songwriting part of the band, he then has to think as the bass player, keyboard player and the vocalist. And it's interesting for the two of us, particularly, not only drummer and bass player, the tightest possible relationship in music, but lyricist and singer, the tightest possible relationship in songwriting. So, necessarily, we had to learn early on to be both considerate of each other's feelings and also so appreciative. That's why I feel inspired by Geddy liking something when I bring in lyrics, or a drum part. Because his standards are high, for himself, and necessarily, for all of us. If you have high standards, you're gonna apply them to everybody else.

"But that's one way in which the two of us are alike. Both of us are very methodical, and both of us aim for the highest possible standards on our instrument. The amount of time he's put in to just his bass playing, for example. I know he always likes to consider himself as — and I always list him in the credits as — bass player first. That's the most important thing. Then vocals and then the keyboards and stuff. All of us have tried to fill in for just being a three-piece. That's just a useful tool. Bass guitar is certainly his first passion."

But as Neil explains, Geddy also pays much thought and consideration to his singing and his respectful delivery of Neil's lyrics.

"When I bring lyrics to him that he has to respond to musically and emotionally, nowadays, with maturity, of course, there's a lot of dialogue possible. What he's looking for is the emotional essence of the words to get through. And sometimes he likes a phrase. He says, 'I don't care what it means; I just like the way it feels to sing, and what I can convey with that.' Everybody knows there is an impressionistic aspect to singing words — sometimes the words don't matter too much. But he has to feel that affinity with them, and as we work through the phrasing, a lot of little adjustments are made for the sake of the vocal performance. Melody and phrasing are one thing, but delivery is the other important part of vocalizing, and something he's incredibly attuned to.

"And I know he builds a persona, like an actor, to sing a song. He puts himself in a certain persona, and even adopts different attributes of that singer, that imaginary singer, that he would bring to that performance of the song, pretty much like an acting role. Something all three of us share a little bit is the comic acting. But the serious actor's also part of what we do, and how we interact together in our conversations. He's able to inhabit a song, and live that song, time after time.

"And we build that atmosphere between us, I would say, from the beginning, by getting the words he's comfortable with, sometimes not their meaning, but in their tonality, which is very important to him. A lot of times I'm tweaking words and tweaking lines just to fulfill a certain rhythm, a certain tonality he's looking to sing. That's a challenge for me — a welcome challenge. From the first time he says he likes something, I'm on board, right? That's all the inspiration I need. And if I have to go back and rewrite everything but those two lines — fine, you know? The fact that he likes it, or in Alex's case too, if they like a drum part or if they like the lyrics, then I couldn't be happier, and I'll do anything to make them like them more. Geddy brings that same dedication to all those analytical aspects of singing that only the singer probably has to know about. That's an important thing."

Neil elaborates on his point that Geddy does things only singers need to know about, saying, "When the art is concealed, it succeeds. It's part of what we've learned in technique over time, and he's learned as a singer. He's approached that very seriously. His singing and his voice, and the fact that his range has endured into forty years of working, is fairly superhuman. Alex and I have to recognize that if he couldn't do it, we couldn't do it. You know, if he was not able to sing — as happens to singers, especially when they sing with that kind of brio — we'd be done. If the singer can't sing, then the band can't play."

But Neil doesn't try to second-guess what Geddy wants in terms of singing methodology. That all comes later. "A lot of times when I'm handing in the lyrics, maybe a couple of lines or a verse is gonna survive out of them, so I try not to be that precious about it. When I'm writing lyrics, I have a tempo and often a melody in mind, but I don't tell Geddy or Alex that, because I want to see what they do. And many wonderful surprises happen that way. Sometimes if Geddy's having trouble with phrasing, for example, it's something I'm thinking of in syncopation as a drummer. I say, 'Well, I sort of saw it falling like this kind of phrasing.' Phrasing is one element that the two of us do discuss. If I have a way that I think a line can fall, during vocal recording, even, if we're working together, there's quite a lot of interplay around phrasing. If he's having trouble with a line, I might suggest a back-phrasing solution or rewrite it. You know, whatever it takes."

With respect to Neil's other role in the band, namely his status as "the world's greatest drummer," Peter says that during this period, Peart was full-on into the possibilities afforded the melding of old-fashioned acoustic and newfangled machine tooling.

Still, it was Geddy who was most interested in the guts of making records. Collins quipped that during the production of *Hold Your Fire*, "Neil would be off doing an eight-mile run or something, pushing himself to the limit," adding that, "he presented us with his sounds, and it was up to us just to record them.

Some of his electronic sounds were very odd to us because we thought we were the masters of electronic sounds in England, and what do these North Americans know? We thought they were quite backward. And some of the sounds sounded, to be honest with you, just not hip. But Neil was very positive: 'Well, if you don't think this is hip, what do you think it should be?' And it was up to us to offer some other suggestions, which sometimes he'd take and sometimes he didn't. But basically, by the time we got in the studio, as you probably know, he was absolutely one hundred percent rehearsed on exactly what he was going to do and what his sounds were going to be. There was very little wiggle room once we were in the studio."

"Neil listened to a lot of English music," says Peter. "He spent quite a lot of time in England in his, teenage/early adult years. I think he worked in Carnaby Street. So he was very plugged into the English sound. He was excited that we were incorporating some of the British sensibility into their music, and the cutting-edge technology and the new reverbs. We used a lot of effects on his drums and he was really happy. We would try things, and some got used, some didn't. But big reverbs, the effects, the really highly compressed snare drum . . . he seemed to be thrilled with it at the time.

"But I think they were more interested in establishing their sound — they certainly didn't want to chase anybody else's sounds. They never said, 'Why can't we sound more like this?' Or gave me an example of something they thought they should sound like. That never happened, like it happens with a lot of bands. They bring in their favorite band — 'Why can't our bass sound like this?' No, they were interested in establishing a genre of sound."

A genre of sound. Quite telling, since Rush were essentially alone across the rock spectrum in the types of records they were making at this time. Nobody from the '70s had loaded up on the electronics this radically, and no one this electronic had the grounding in original heavy metal that Rush had. It was a marriage of two wildly divergent worlds. Was it a shotgun marriage? Something that didn't exactly work? Many fans think as much. Pretty objectively, *Power Windows* and *Hold Your Fire* sound extremely dated, wholly of the '80s, where Rush's '70s material has become unassailably hip, and probably never again to be seen as anything but. If and when the '80s ever become hot again, these records might see renewed respect.

But the band maintains a brave defense of this period. "*Hold Your Fire* was a good record," affirms Alex. "We were sort of coming to the end of our foray into the world of keyboards. *Power Windows* was so layered with keyboards and *Hold Your Fire* was a bit of a relief; we kind of pulled back a bit on the use of keyboards. But it was part of the '80s thing; that was the sort of headspace we were at then." On the subject of that headspace, Alex takes a break to have a chuckle over press shots of the band back then, pointing out the bright new wave outfits, pageboy haircuts and Geddy's big glasses. Stopping at one of many live shots of himself in various *Miami Vice* suits and tuxes, he offers, "Yeah, and right after this, I ask the crowd, 'May I take your order?'"

Post-Montserrat, the band and their entourage would return to Toronto, specifically to McClear Place Studios, for more overdubs and some fancy orchestral stuff. Done by April 24, the record was then mixed at William Tell Studio in Paris, France. After mastering in New York, *Hold Your Fire* had been assembled in five different countries.

For an album cover, the band went with something as austere as the music enclosed, but that wasn't initially going to be the case. The much more action-packed photo used on the inner sleeve, of a man juggling three flaming balls, was painstakingly assembled with the intention that Hugh and photographer Glen Wexler were making an album cover. References to past albums are in the shot, and indeed, the guys had originally brought back Neill Cunningham from *Power Windows* to peer through a window. Instead, they went with the less gratuitous shot of the three floating red balls, which is indeed photography, with red painted billiard balls and even the Rush logo fashioned then photographed. Wexler had also designed the cover for Black Sabbath's *Reunion* double live package and Van Halen's *Balance* album, the record that was issued when Ray Danniels was managing the band.

Like the album's production, after twenty years, the juggler photograph looks dated, the whole thing an orgy of computer-generated imagery. But it was a physical, painstakingly assembled set, basketballs coated with rubber cement and lit on fire, actors (Dennis Hopper was supposed to be part of the scene, but they couldn't get him scheduled), painted bits, meticulous Frankensteining of parts by a highly skilled photographer.

As for the fit of the cover to the record's ostensible themes, it's a stretch. Originally, *Hold Your Fire* was going to be about time, spurred on by early composition "Time Stand Still," but then the word *instinct* became operative. But it's still all a bit nebulous. *Hold Your Fire* indeed lines up with the juggler photograph, but the balls on the cover are neither on fire nor juggled. And other than a pervasive and saturated red, there's no fire. It's been vaguely explained that one instinctually fires first and asks questions later, but that's a stretch as well.

The album opens with a curious collage of industrial sounds before "Force Ten" shuffles into view, stage right — of note, this would be the first song delivered to radio. Fairly rocking for this period, it demonstrates the band's will to diminish the use of keyboards and fill some of that space with Alex, although his tone is still astringent, anemic even. Geddy, inspired by friend and fusion bass wizard Jeff Berlin, plays bass chords on the song. The lyric uses the Beaufort scale to measure storms as a device to discuss the whirlwind of an active life, although the lyrics are fairly obscure, Peart also intimating that it's about having the courage to fail in the face of endeavor. This is his second co-write with Max Webster lyricist Pye Dubois, who collaborated with Neil on "Tom Sawyer." As is their process, it's less a collaboration and more like Neil taking sketches and aphorisms Pye has provided and sculpting them into shape, adding along the way.

Next is what would be the record's biggest song, "Time Stand Still" serving as a moderately successful single in the U.S. and the U.K. The song got full-on video treatment, Zbigniew Rybczynski directing the band floating across the screen somewhat comically, not intentionally so. The song is distinguished by a vocal cameo: 'Til Tuesday's Aimee Mann was called on for angelic contrast to Geddy's plaintive yet wistful sentiments on the passage of time (Mann also appears in the video).

"They were always interested in maximizing the songs," reflects Peter Collins, considering the housewifey pop of "Time Stand Still," "and getting them across in the most powerful way possible. On 'Time Stand Still,' we had virtually finished mixing it, and I had an idea to just create a one-beat pause in the song, and it meant remixing it and going to a lot of trouble to do it, but we did it and it worked very well. A lot of other bands would have been, 'Ah, let's just move on,' but they were interested in exploring all ideas. And that's how we pursued the record. I didn't think, 'We have to change the sound, we have to change gears.' The songs dictated the treatments."

Concerning Aimee's guest cameo, Peter says, "The guys really liked her voice [specifically on the 'Til Tuesday track 'What About Love'], and we brought her up to do it. One of the things

I remember, she was doing her vocal and I got on the talkback, and because she was kind of hippie-ish, I said, 'Aimee, could you give a bit more attitude?' And she goes, 'What kind of attitude?' I'd have to say it was Geddy pushing for the duet idea. Geddy is always thinking about new possibilities; not that the others aren't, but Geddy's probably more vocal than the other two."

Mann was paid $2,000 for her guest cameo on the track. Also considered for the part were Chrissie Hynde and Cyndi Lauper — Lauper of course had already covered this sort of wistful emotional area on "Time After Time," a smash hit for Cyndi from three years earlier.

Regarding "Time Stand Still," Peter says, "I thought it was a single, and they all laughed. They said, 'Well, we've never had a hit single.' So, they were very skeptical. They weren't weird about it. They wanted to have that, but they weren't prepared to compromise anything. You know, should it come about, great. But they weren't going to compromise what the song demanded or their sensibility to go for a single. They write really strong melodies, and if the form doesn't have to be too long to establish the song, then you have a chance of getting a commercial track out of them. I always thought 'Limelight' had a lot of potential as a single. That is another example to me of when you have strong melodies and strong lyrical ideas, and they come together and can be established in three or four minutes, then you've got an opportunity for a single with them. They were certainly comfortable doing it. They had broken the ice with *Power Windows*, and this was a natural extension of that. The song just demanded that sort of treatment, as far as I was concerned. And there was no fighting involved. It just turned out extremely commercial."

"Pop is a funny word," pondered Geddy at the time, speaking with Chris Jones of *Now*. "It means popular, and in that sense, we've always been a popular band — we've always been popular enough to sell and in good quantities. But because our music is unconventional and hard to categorize, it's been almost a sort of cult pop. I would say this record is probably our least aggressive and most melodic, and yet it's probably had the least AM radio success of any record we've ever made. I think our arrangements are still too unusual and our music is still too off center to be considered mainstream."

The "Time Stand Still" clip would result in a lot of snickers over the years — such are the pitfalls of always wanting to be right at the front edge of technology, even if it's not quite cooked yet. Justifiably, Geddy seemed a little wary of the medium. Truth be told, by this point, Rush's success with the genre had been mixed at best.

"I think we've survived the video age," Geddy told Jones, "if a little uncomfortably. We're not the kind of band that goes into any project easily, especially one where you're forced to work so closely with someone else, like a director. They always want us to act, and we don't see ourselves as actors. We're musicians, so the challenge is always to make each performance clip more interesting than the last. Videos are such a strange medium. They're not for sale, so you can't justify spending a fortune on them; they're like commercials. It's weird because they're not movies and yet they're movie-like, and they're not art yet they are artful. So it's always a sort of uncomfortable balance between a band performing their song and a director realizing his own creative ideal. It's very hit and miss."

Introduced by a spot of jazz fusion, "Open Secrets" is an obscure bit of up-tempo pop, airy and energetic, pressing forward all the hallmarks of this era, including ethereal keyboard textures and Alex pinched and commentating alongside a song that is dominated by bass, vocal and the lyrical sentiment, which is relationship related, caught in flummoxed temporal flux between "Different Strings" and "Cold Fire." Indeed, the lyric comes from a conversation between Neil and Geddy about people they know who let problems fester — helpfully, by song's end, Neil tries to offer a solution. Alex took it upon himself to create a guitar solo that sounded suitably frustrated and alone.

"Second Nature" finds Neil pleading for the expeditious in place of the perfect, compromise as progress. As he told Malcolm Dome from *Metal Hammer*, "Personally, I remain essentially an idealist and haven't been totally disillusioned. As soon as I started to realize that it wasn't a perfect world, I decided to try and make at least a part of it perfect. Yet that does become such a painful and one-sided, fruitless crusade after a while. The rest of the world is skeptical at best and usually cynical, so there has to be a meeting ground if I want any improvements and this stretches from musical morality to environmental consciousness.

"'Second Nature' expresses such a belief, because to me it seems so obvious that we should wish our cities to be as nice as our forests and that people should behave in a humane fashion — yet this is also clearly a naïve and laughable assumption. I want a perfect world and can be bothered to do something about it, yet I can't do it on my own. So, even if you don't want the things that I do, at least let's make a deal and go for some improvement. But you shouldn't just scream about it in a song. If you really care about a cause, then get involved with people who are doing something about it, people who are self-actuating and are actively working to improve things. That's what I do in my own time, without any clarion call for publicity. I go out into the dirty world."

Peart's words of wisdom are framed across a spectrum that is somewhere between pop and ballad, with a soft tribal lilt from Neil, definitely keyboards to the fore in the stead of Alex, something of which Geddy was all too cognizant.

"Yeah, we started having a bit of a territorial thing going on, because I was writing more on keyboards. I was getting more comfortable. I was taking piano lessons at the time and it really is a different sound. There's so many more ways you can approach the same chord. It was just different you know, an angle. As a songwriter you're always looking for an angle to come into it, to give you something fresh. When you're tired of the same devices, you bring a new device in and it gives you different angles, so it sparks your creativity. Keyboards for me were a creative spark."

Geddy says indeed that on this record, he and Alex butted heads over keyboards, adding, "And some, it was warranted, some of it wasn't. Some of it was ego, some of it was music-based. But at the end of the day it wasn't worth fighting for because I wasn't happy with the direction anyway, where it was taking me, so we started putting these limitations on us, and I think that was the best thing we ever did. I think it returned us to the spark of what we do best, really."

And when there's trouble, being a trio helps three people find a way out of tight spots, which is somewhat what "Second Nature" is about, essentially seeking a path out of inertia. "I like three," says Geddy. "It's a good number for us. Three is a good number because there's no fractions in three. If you have an innate sense of right and wrong, three is a good number because two against one is not fair. And if you're acutely aware of alienating the other person, then you always bring that person back into the fold.

"Whereas when there's four, it's us and them — five and it's chaos. And I like the fact that the three of us can have dinner together every night and that's our own moment of bonding. There's so much about our lives that is separated and work related. But we've got that fifteen minutes or so when Frenchie brings our dinner in and we're all sitting around a coffee table, just, 'What's up?' You know, 'Where did you go last night?' Find out what Neil read. 'What'd you do on your day off?' You know, who are you today? 'What's going on with you — are you sick?' 'Oh, you've got a cold?' And I mean it used to be every time there was a dinner on a day off or something like that we'd get together. Now it's usually at the venue. I like that number — works good for us."

But as we've discussed — another lesson of "Second Nature" — the guys were learning to extricate themselves from each other just enough so that decisions could and would continue to get put on the board and then knocked down efficiently. Rush 2.0, making music well out of any semblance of mainstream and then to boot, not touring it as hard as they used to, had to find a way to keep some sort of forward-flung critical mass. And at this point, that meant personal development and perspective.

"Sure, but that's out of necessity," ponders Ged about taking time apart from the guys. "Because you spent so much time together that when you get home, doesn't matter how much you like the guy, you just spent four intense months with the person, five, six intense months, I don't want to see that person for a while. I don't want to see Neil and I don't want to see Alex even though I love them both. I'm happy to see them but I don't really want to. I need to get away from it and everything they represent, and that works well. It's just like getting away from writing after we've had a long writing session or whatever. You can't just go in and write another record. I mean, we could, but I think we do better work when we're hungry for it. And I approach the same thing in terms of our personal relationships. When I really start to miss Alex, that's when I want to see him and I want to hang with him. I don't see him much in the off-season. Although as we get older, I do see him more because he only lives two blocks away and we play tennis together and all that stuff. But somehow that's okay. Still, we just need to get out of each other's face for a while."

"Prime Mover" seems to be the song on the record that explores the stated concept of instinct most thoroughly, with the largest number of definitions or proposals. Of note, Neil was a big fan of *The Twilight Zone*, and "Prime Mover" is the name of an episode Neil had known from his youth — he would have been nine when it came out. Not about playing dice like the episode, and not about God, "Prime Mover" seems to champion instinct as the prime mover, the urge toward the first move. And the music? Pert pop, sometimes dominated (but never driven) by Alex, sometimes by Geddy, with prominent bass lines. Like so many of the songs from this period, Neil winds up and lets fly signature and expected fills, but if there's no drama to accentuate, what's the point, really?

"Lock and Key" pairs nicely with "Prime Mover," defining one form of instinct most thoroughly, namely the instinct toward violence and how society has evolved to keep it tamped. This one's fairly up-tempo and rocky, with lots of rainy guitars from Alex, sparring with *Power Windows*–type keyboard stabs. Melodically speaking, the track is dark, even threatening, in keeping with the fraught subject matter. As a trivia note, Geddy put aside his regular four-string Wal for this track and used a five-string (also a Wal), with the fifth being a lower B string. The idea was that synth technology had advanced to the point where it was competing with the lowest of lows on basses, and at least for this track, he was looking for a little extra firepower, even if the brief was still very much hard articulation over low, warm bass tones.

The first words of the album's tour de force, "Mission," are "Hold your fire," which makes sense, given that the song is grand enough to be the record's title track, through ambitious construction and a particularly poignant and insightful lyric from Neil.

But it could have been even grander, says Peter. "Yes, well, I wanted the band to use a brass band on it, from the mining districts in England, basically like the Salvation Army band. And I had it arranged, and it was done, and ultimately we didn't use it. But that was another great thing about Rush — they'll try anything. If somebody's got an idea that sounds like it has some possibilities, they'll go for it."

Geddy is in agreement that "Mission" is one of the special moments across the expanse of *Hold Your Fire*. "It's a very ambitious album, a dark horse, full of textural changes, dramatic rhythmic changes. And it's quite a romantic album in some ways, melodically. But 'Mission' is really a song I'm proud of in terms of melody and a kind of boldness. That record was influenced a lot by Peter Collins in the sense that his love of melody and what we'd gone through on *Power Windows* was still resonating with us. Some of those were very, very difficult songs to put together, texturally.

"'Mission' was a song Peter Collins just loved," continues Lee. "And at some point in Britain, when we were working on it, he really wanted to do what he called the full monty — put orchestra and choir on it. And there's a particular sound of an English brass band, which I guess was something he grew up with that we had no feel for, the kind of band you saw in the park on Sunday playing the gazebo. He was kind of obsessed with finding an authentic one.

"And he tracked one down in the north of England and he wanted them to play on this track. We were really working hard on that record, and there was this weekend where this band was available. We were all supposed to fly up there to record them, and we just said, 'Look, Pete, you go. You know what you want, we're pooped, why don't you go and record them? This will be a treat for you.' And he did. And he brought it back, and he was all excited about it, of course. And we never really shared the same enthusiasm for it. And in the end, the version of the song that we released was kind of stripped down; I don't think we used the brass band very much. We didn't use the whole arrangement. So there is another version of that song I hope we'll release, that has the full monty on it."

There's a bit of old Rush trickery to "Mission" as well, which elevates the song and ties it to Rush's rich tradition of math rock. As Neil told Tim Ponting of *Rhythm Magazine*, "I play in four over the five pattern that Geddy and Alex are playing. I either pick up the odd beat when I need to, or just wait until it comes around to me. It owes a lot to the R&B or funk idea, where the pulse is most important and you want to make it feel like four, much as for instance Peter Gabriel did with 'Solsbury Hill' — it's in a long seven pattern, but all the casual listener feels is the quarter note pulse. You can tap your foot comfortably to it. And that's a magic thing that we've been able to learn — that these things don't have to feel odd to an audience. Odd time is not truly 'odd'; it has a lilt to it, a flow, a human cadence, but it just has to be learnt. Our audience don't know how to count out seven, but they accept that those quirky little twists are part of our music. It would be presumptuous to say that we educate our listeners; rather, we let them grow accustomed to us of their own volition.

"I just soak up everything I hear," continues Peart, concerning his approach to the wider album. "Anything new that creeps into pop music is bound to creep into my drumming by an osmosis effect. It's something that I'm far from being ashamed of — I'm proud of the fact that I'm a big fan of music and I want to respond to it and adopt every style as a part of mine. It's an acquisitive-ness, I guess, that's almost equivalent to greed. I've been very conscious of what the drummers of the world are doing, and I've tried to stay in touch with the most esoteric music that I can ever get to hear, whether it's from South America or China or some remote pocket of Africa. Any kind of rhythm gets my blood stirring."

Neil's passionate, multidimensional lyric for "Mission" really connects with Rush fans. If we can risk making generalities, ardent Rush supporters are an ambitious lot with all manner of dreams — creative ones, entrepreneurial ones — and this song covers all sorts of territory concerning dreams, from their idleness at one end through to the drive and obsession it takes to make them come true.

"Well of course it pleases me," ponders Neil, on the depth of the connection, leading to a look at "Mission." "To be appreciated, a lot of times I have to break things down to what almost seem reductivist terms. But it is that simple. Of course I like being appreciated — you know, who wouldn't? Whether it's the drumming or the lyric writing, yes, it's wonderful to connect that way. Of course there's a fringe that don't connect with the same signal that you're sending because their receptors are faulty. There's a little fringe like that, but that's so small, the tiniest of minorities. For most people the lyrics-writer is just part of the package of the imagery.

"I remember being a young music fan, a lot of times I wouldn't really listen to the words per se. I would hear the words as part of the tapestry, and those images would stay with me. And sometimes when I'm on my motorcycle riding along, some whole song will come back to me, all the lyrics and everything — how do I possibly remember the verses of 'Monster Mash' or whatever? Obviously they imprinted at the time. And many, many other songs — 'Good Vibrations' — songs that can go through my helmet and I can remember the words for or can eventually put it together as I ride along.

"Words can carry different weight for different people, of course," continues Peart. "But those who do have the sensitivity to pay the kind of attention to lyrics that I put into them, that's to a key part of the audience. On the drumming side too, you know, to feel that you're not playing down to anyone. We always had the impression that people are just as smart as we are. So if we can figure this stuff out, they can too. This music is sophisticated enough to please us, but we're not overreaching, or being that terrible damning word: pretentious. We're not pretending anything. This is really what turned us on this year that we chose to write about.

"Lyrically it's always been a reflection of my times and the times I observe. Every one is a reflection of me. But they can come out of conversations. Geddy and I have had conversations sometimes that lead to a song because I know it's something he would like to say. The collaboration between Geddy and me is intense, because I'm writing for his voice. So of course he has to feel not only comfortable with it, but inspired by it, and be able to mean it every time he sings it."

"Mission" was very much one of those songs in which Geddy was part of the mindspace from the start. Neil remembers the discussion that generated the lyric. He and Geddy spoke about how they both always had music as a mission, whereas many people go through life never feeling they have a mission at all.

"That song came out of a conversation he and I had in the mid-'80s, so we would have been in our mid-thirties," says Neil. "A lot of our other friends were at that crucial time of life when you're learning to settle, or making all those adjustments to go, 'Okay, I'm middle-aged now.' And we would talk to friends who would say things like, 'When did you know what you wanted to do?' You know, 'What age did you know what you wanted to do, and how did you figure it out?' and all that. Well, to us, of course, we knew what we wanted to do from age thirteen and spent our lives in the pursuit of it.

"But we realized there was this whole other group of people — among people we knew and cared for and respected and loved — fighting their way through life too. And again, a lot of times my lyrics reflect people I care about — I want their voice in there. So 'Mission' is sung in the first person but it's somebody else.

"So Geddy and I had the conversation about our friends going through that life crisis that we had been spared because we had a mission. I took that and put it in the words of someone wishing they had it. And also making the comparison — 'Be careful what you wish for.' There's a line toward the bridge of that song: 'We each pay a fabulous price for our visions of paradise.' And, 'If their lives were exotic and strange' . . . I was thinking of painter Paul Gauguin, when he went through the suffering he went through to do what he did. Because, 'Ah gee, I'd like to be a painter and move to Tahiti.' And, you know, it wasn't really like that. It never is, the fantasy. Of course *we* are living a fantasy to a lot of people, and I try hard not to trample on that unnecessarily. But my life ain't no fantasy, you know. It's for real. And my aches and pains and struggles and sorrows are real. I don't have to make them up or pretend them. And that's why even I might use fictional devices, like in a song like 'Mission.'"

"Turn the Page" finds the band continuing with this record's — and the previous one's — furtive, agitated, high-midrange pop rock sound, distinguished by Geddy's clacky, percussive bass and Alex's throttling of his guitar until it squeals and pings.

Alex agrees that these late '80s records took on a much different tone than those quickly crafted in the unadulterated power trio days. "From a guitar standpoint, my sound had really changed. It was much more wiry and brighter. Part of the reason for that is, again, there was such a conflict between all the keyboard stuff that was happening and where the guitar fit into that. The main part of the problem is, when we made those records, we decided to do all the keyboard stuff before we did the guitar stuff. And it was just a scheduling thing, more than anything. It was just more convenient to do the keyboards that way. When it came time to do guitars, it was hard to figure out where the guitar was going to fit in because there was so much of this going on. And I think with *Hold Your Fire*, we kind of reached a peak, and that was it. And then every album after that we just gradually started to thin out the keyboards."

Neil agrees with Alex's description of the guitar sound as "wiry," but with an asterisk. "Yeah, but that was his choice of the guitars and the guitar sound he was going for at the time, you know? No one to blame for it. And if you listen to other music from the time, there was a prevalent guitar sound. The Fixx and stuff was highly compressed. Processed, I call it, processed guitar sounds. That's what he wanted! You know, hindsight is a pretty useless thing. And drumming-wise, I always just wanted a great natural drum sound, with the addition of all the electronic effects and stuff. But that's been the linear pursuit for me, just getting a really great natural drum sound."

With respect to the "Turn the Page" lyric, Neil told Malcolm Dome that it "expresses the attitude: How sensitive can you afford to be? If you're watching the news or reading a paper, how much can you afford to feel? How much can you get involved in the world without wanting to kill yourself immediately? Another constantly recurring theme is trying to reconcile idealism with clear-sighted reality. I remain an idealistic person to this day, much to my pain sometimes. I grew up that way to the point where all life was then suddenly disillusioned to me. I'd imagined it as being so much nicer than it really is, and the hardness, the crassness and the inhumanity of it all really homed in on me. It was tremendously painful, and really hard for me to face. Thus the dividing line between youthful illusions and their subsequent loss with age is an attractive one to me. There are prices and rewards for that — you exchange your illusions and innocence for experience and the way things really are. If you weather it emotionally, that's a fair exchange. I went through this change in a very extreme manner, and a lot of the current album does face up to this dilemma."

"Tai Shan" is one of the band's travelogue songs, this one being a tribute to China, looking down from a sacred mountain vantage reached after seven thousand stairs. With its pan flutes and Chinese guitar figures from Alex, it's all a bit much, and the kind of thing that would be deemed cultural appropriation in this day and age. Also, the Buddhist vibe rings somewhere between hollow, insincere and patronizing, coming from these practical, no-nonsense atheists, the singer a cultural Jew.

On a technical note, Neil explained to Deborah Parisi that on the song he included "an antique Chinese drum which is far too fragile and valuable to think about using live. I brought it into our rehearsal studio and sampled it. I have a number of antique — especially Oriental and African — musical instruments that the only way I can use them is to sample them. So it gives you all that freedom. That's what I like the most.

"I'm not a pioneer by any means," added Neil on his level of comfort with the latest music technology. "I sort of take the Rolls Royce attitude of letting other people pioneer things and prove them and then adopt them — like Rolls Royce uses General Motors power steering because they make the best power steering. You don't have to pioneer if somebody else does it. You can still be just behind the leading edge but have the advantage of things that are reliable. And you avoid the trendy aspect of things like Syndrums, where in the early days every beer commercial had that sound on it, and you avoid having to wince about your past.

"When I finally figured that digital sampling had come of age and it was a tool that I really wanted to have and could no longer resist, I went to Jim Burgess at Saved by Technology and said, 'Here's what I want to do, and here's what I don't want to do.' And he recommended a setup and worked with me a lot to get the gear and the library of samples from my older records. It's good to have someone like that to steer you in the right way."

Hold Your Fire ends a robust fifty minutes after it began with what feels like a more successful version of "Tai Shan." "High Water" is tribal, atmospheric and at the lyric end, still somewhat spiritual. It's about the instinctual reaction we have to water, in the form of the ocean, mighty rivers, torrential downpours, redemptive rains, floods, mountain springs, even from "marble fountains." Sparse as it is, there are strong melodies and even some new (and better) keyboard sounds. A fresh idea occurs at the end additional to the unifying theme of the front 90 percent, namely that we share kinship with water because all those many moons ago, life first jumped out of the froth and wriggled on land — this turns out to be the "home" part of the equation. On an amusing musical note, the chords Alex plays at the 2:12 mark sound like a quote from "Bacchus Plateau" from way back on *Caress of Steel*.

So do we deem *Hold Your Fire* a success? For the rest of all Rush time, there will be debate about this period's overt '80s-ness

— that will never change. But indeed the band defends it, and its songs have lived on from the record in live and fan-fondness consciousness.

"At the end of *Hold Your Fire*, I was delighted with the record," reflects Peter Collins. "We mixed it in Paris, and it was a very enjoyable experience. And we finished it and it sounded wonderful. My only regret soon after was the fact it didn't go platinum. And I felt the responsibility for that quite heavily, and I expressed that to Geddy. I felt it was my fault somehow, you know, that it was the first album in a long time that had not gone platinum. From my point of view, why didn't this do as well as *Power Windows*? And Geddy subsequently, in later years when we had the discussion, said, 'Well, this album is loved by a lot of Rush fans. It's nothing to do with that. Nobody knows why.' But I took it very personally.

"And when Geddy called me to produce the next record, 'Well, Geddy you need somebody who can take you back up to platinum, or to the next level. I feel I've let you down on this record.' He didn't really accept that, but that's the way I felt. I felt they needed somebody with some fresh ideas.

"So yeah, I basically fired myself. Because by that time I had a deep affection for this band. And while I didn't feel I could call myself, you know, one of the brothers, I felt very close to them, and they all are very dear to me to this day. I truly wanted the best for them. I thought it would be better for them. After *Presto* also didn't go platinum, I thought, well, I guess it wasn't my fault, so when I got the call to work with them again, I was in there."

Further testimony that the band's drop in success wasn't really Peter's fault: with him gone, Rush really didn't change the sound much for two more records. "I think Geddy might have made that realization later on," says Peter, on the eventual idea to feature more guitars, essentially just idle threats, all the way up until

Counterparts two records later. For his part though, Collins reasserts that "one of the main sonic issues of course was the bottom end and also where the voice lay in the mix. Because coming from my background, I wanted more voice, and sometimes it was a struggle come mix time as to where the voice was going to land in the mix. That was really from my memory the only issues we had. The keyboard thing was never a big deal for me, as I remember. I wasn't anti-keyboards or had to have them. If we were going to have keyboards, I wanted them to be great."

Coming full circle then, to one of Peter's very first comments about the band, is the conundrum of Geddy's voice. Collins talks about what ultimately happened on this front, saying, "Well, I wanted to bring him more into a midrange, less of the high stuff, more toward the lower end of his vocal range. And you know, a lot of Rush fans hate me for that. And of course years later when I worked with them again and tried to get Geddy to sing up high, he had become more used to singing in the midrange. With the fullness of time, I now realize how key that sound was. But at the time I really didn't want him to sing like that. I just didn't like it. I since have changed my opinion on it."

But it was becoming obvious that changes needed to be made.

"We had tension," admits Geddy, when it came to Alex's role in the band. "Sometimes it was not overt. Sometimes it was swallowed up. You know, he was all in favor of the changes we were making, and he loves new sounds and he loves technology. He's a real technocrat, that guy. Guitar players in general are like that. He really loves gear, loves playing with it. It's like the old joke about a guitar player: when you're recording a guitarist and you tell him, 'That sounds perfect,' he goes, 'That's great, I'll change it.' You know, they love to fiddle.

"So he was not against bringing in synthesizers. He was not against sharing the sound. I think what happened with him was that after the record was finished, he was happy with it, and he would go with the flow, and then you know, he would go away, the record would sit there for a while, and then he would hear that part of his sound was pushed to the side a bit to make room for these keyboards. I think it was only later that it bugged him. Maybe he felt like he didn't speak up enough at the time, so the frustration built. It got to a point where he started putting his foot down, and he said I think these keyboards are really taking over our sound, and we should go back. It was his way of saying I don't like the way my guitar has to struggle all the time to be heard.

"So it was fair enough. Synthesizers and technology . . . it's fun, and it's not fun. In that time period, it was all new and exciting to throw this sound into a band that's been around a long time. It forces you to go in a different direction. It doesn't matter what the sound is, it just sparks you. Whether that is good or bad, only time can tell. So you know, twenty years later, you look back and, okay, we went in that direction and because we started experimenting with electronics, you go, 'Well, it wasn't our best material . . . or was it?'

"The bad thing about electronica is that it's like wrestling with an eel," continues Lee. "The sound gets everywhere. Once you start adding layers of synthetic sounds, it just takes all the air out of the sound, so it's always a battle. That's when we started changing producers; that's when we started looking for new sounds and new ways of looking at music. I mean, I'm really pleased we went through all that because it makes for some interesting music on those various records. If you listen to *Power Windows*, which to me is the most successful marriage of guitar and synthesizer of all the records we've made, that's what we were after: a more angular use of synthesizers, still plenty of room for the guitars to shine. But it kinda became a bee in his bonnet for a while. And even when there was enough guitar, he was like, 'Well, you just better make sure there was enough guitar.' And that was a dangerous thing, but I understood it.

"It made the working relationship difficult, but we never really took it home with us. We would come in and lock horns over ideas, and sometimes I was right and sometimes he was right. And Neil was always the objective third party about that stuff. And you have a producer, and that's why we always have a producer. Because you need that referee and that person you can turn to when you're not sure. Or when you're not sure that your own personal desires are superseding the desires of the band: 'Am I taking my opinion too far?' Because sometimes in the band, the loudest voice wins. It doesn't mean it's the right voice. And you learn how to do that with each other, how to get your way.

"As for me, I know I can get my way, but I'm not sure it's the right way. So I want to have a producer to say to, 'Look, am I crazy?' Or 'This thing I'm pushing for, is this the right thing we should be doing here? Does it make it a better song?' That's always part of the process, that whole to-ing and fro-ing. There has to be some argument and there has to be some tension, otherwise the thing is not alive. People paint this picture of our relationship because we're friends and we laugh, and it's like, 'No, after you,' 'No, do whatever you want.' It's not like that. There are times when you have to fight for your ideas, and there are times when you need to have a discussion about it to make sure you are doing the right thing in the right way."

"*Hold Your Fire* was another that's not hugely popular but people that love it, really love it," summed up Neil. "And I count myself among them — I love that record. It still sounds so great, and there's so much passion in that record too. But it's strange and I can understand why people don't; like with *Grace Under Pressure*, I totally understand why it's not for everyone. *Hold Your*

Fire too is not for everyone. *Power Windows* was, I think, much more open. Yeah, extroverts — that's probably the difference. Where *Hold Your Fire* is a bit introverted, even sonically for some reason. Although we worked with the same co-producer and the same people and all that, there was a difference in the character of those, interestingly. There are probably a thousand reasons why that should be. But our live shows stayed the same. People would come because they know they didn't like the last record so much but like the previous one a lot and our old stuff, so they would still come and see us. We maintained and continued to build an audience for the live show, which in these times especially is the key to our survival and probably anyone's."

CHAPTER 8

A SHOW OF HANDS

*"He's very dramatic in how he plays the
lighting board as an instrument."*

With four more studio albums under their belts, it was time for another double vinyl live album. *A Show of Hands* would feature material mostly from the tour for *Hold Your Fire*, but two *Power Windows* dates, March 31 and April 1, 1986, at the Meadowlands Arena in New Jersey, would also be represented, yielding the tracks "Witch Hunt" and "Mystic Rhythms."

The *Hold Your Fire* campaign opened with Rush once again promoting a small local act in the opening slots of their shows. The guys had heard about Chalk Circle while they were writing and recording for their last album at McClear Studios in downtown Toronto. Geddy and Neil had talked about how it was refreshing having their ear to the ground once again, feeling the pulse of their city, after all those pilgrimages to rural settings to cook up Rush songs.

After a handful of Atlantic Canada tour dates, it was off to the States, supported by the McAuley Schenker Group — one bit of Rush lore had Neil and Geddy pondering putting together a project with blond bomber Michael Schenker back in the early '80s, but it never came together. When asked if he actually played with Geddy and Neil, Michael says, "No, we just discussed it, and they said they wanted to do it. I think I may have blown it because I made a joke and said that Alex could be the coffee boy. Maybe I went too far, I don't know. I can't remember actually what happened or why it didn't work out."

The Atlantic Canada shows were the result of a petition campaign much publicized at the time to get Rush to play there. It's always been notoriously hard for bands to make the economics work for shows in Nova Scotia, Prince Edward Island, New Brunswick and Newfoundland. But Ray made it happen, with Rush playing Moncton, New Brunswick, two shows in Nova Scotia and two dates at Memorial Stadium in Newfoundland and Labrador's capital, St. John's, October 29 through November 4 of 1987, all dates supported by Chalk Circle.

Into December, Rush again toured with a former heavy hitter now onto a career as a solo artist: Tommy Shaw from Styx supported the band through to March of 1988. After this, it was back to Canada with Chalk Circle. Three shows in January and February of 1988 would be recorded for use on the new live album. Three additional shows would be recorded in April, all in Birmingham, U.K., as the band conducted a short European campaign, wrapping up May 5 in Germany, Wishbone Ash as support. Birmingham would be captured on film for the platinum-selling video release of the album.

Rush's stage presentation was both massive and classy by this point, but very much reflective of '80s style.

"Howard had really developed his skills as a lighting director," recalls Lifeson of Mr. Ungerleider, now in his fourteenth year with the band. "And I gotta say, the way he sees things, it's just unbelievable. He has such a creative ability. The colors are liquid; the application of the lighting is so dramatic and so unique and exciting. I've been to some other shows that have looked amazing, but there is something about his style and the way he sees things that are so deserving of the awards he's gotten.

"We spend a lot of time talking about aspects of the production. I mean obviously, the lighting is something he brings to the table, and he makes suggestions, and he's always got a fixed idea of how he wants to change one tour to the next to the next to the next. We try to reel him in a little bit budget-wise, or at least, our road manager, Liam Birt, does. He's got this idea, and then we talk about some of the other signature things we want based on what we're promoting on that tour, which album it is, or what point in the tour it is. And then we work together on these concepts. And he often brings things from a technical standpoint. He always brings in really great visual moments.

"He's been there since 1974," continues Lifeson. "He knows the music as well as we do. He's heard those songs as many times as we've heard them. So he knows them inside out. And if you've ever been out in the house to watch him work, you see that he's very dramatic in how he plays the lighting board as an instrument. It's very, very effective. And as a technician he's amazing; he directs that show. I don't know how he does it, because you're working with different people every night, different spot operators, different countries. Some of them don't speak the same language. It's a real challenge at times, and he always pulls it off."

As for how in the world it turned out that Howard ended up with the band from 1974 through to this point (and actually to the end), Alex says, "Well, we love each other, for one thing. We're great friends. It's always been a part of the way Rush operates. We get close with our crews, and we become friends. And it has an impact on how the whole show comes up and comes down and how it works, and how obligated everybody feels to put on a good show, whether it's their station or someone else's. You know, something happens across the production, everybody is there to help. And it's an amazing thing to witness on our shows. And Howard's just been there from the very beginning. We're like brothers. So I couldn't imagine it any other way, really. And he's such a character. He is absolutely the greatest storyteller I've ever heard. He can tell a story in such a way that you're crying, in tears. And quite often he'll tell stories of things, situations that I've been at, and it's completely different from what happened. But who cares? They're just awesome stories.

"In the world of lighting, things change so quickly. There are big tours that go out with unlimited budgets. They get the latest equipment, they get the great people working these shows, and they're such a visual extravaganza. You have to find your way in that sort of stuff. And I think Howard has a real good sense of not competing with those big shows, but to do something on another scale that's very emotive, or, you know, powerful and profound. Some of his movements are just astonishing. When you see them up front. I mean, I don't really get to see too many Rush shows, but during rehearsals, when he's doing a full production, he'll show us some of the stuff he's doing. Or if we videotape it, we get a chance to see the kind of action that's going on."

"I love multimedia," says Howard, who was obviously so much a part of the live presentation by this point. "To me when I sat in an audience watching Pink Floyd when I was young and I saw all this eye candy happening, you know, it's really great that you can deliver something like that. It helps to tell a story. The first thing I ever did with Rush is use these Kodak S-AV projectors and put together the owl from *Fly by Night*. We made it flap its wings. To me back then, I was like, wow! Look at that — we can flap its wings, and the audience went crazy when it would do that. But looking back it was such a simple effect. I sort of developed it from there."

Howard offers a glimpse of what was involved as the show evolved. He says, "Video walls weren't out yet, so we used a lot of projectors. And then we used thirty-five-millimeter projectors, and then to get bigger I created a monster because we got together with a friend of ours in Toronto named Norm Stangl, who worked for a company called Nelvana Films at the time. And we'd do prints from New York to develop some content, and I came up with this wacky idea: let's take three projectors and take three rolls of film, and let's feather them together and do it like pseudo IMAX, but not IMAX.

"And I didn't realize what a nightmare I was creating for myself at the time, but three rolls of film all have to be in sync. All the edges were soft, all the sprockets must be counted on the film, and they need to have a starting point so that when the projection edits the film, we don't lose track of where we are. But more important than that, we never even realized we needed encoders — a piece of equipment that goes on a projector to make sure each individual projector runs at the same speed. We found out that everything was running out of whack, and this projector guru from New York said, 'You need to put encoders on your machines.' And then we finally tightened that up and were able to do some really nice widescreen projections."

The band felt it was necessary to get this grand with their shows for a few reasons. First off, as any trio will tell you, an audience requires distractions, at the base level, because you are looking at only three guys. As a trio, you often have your hands full, so it's hard for the band members to put on a show. In Rush's case, two of the three also have to play bass pedals.

"I just think it's an entertainment thing," adds Howard. "Very few people were doing it, and it's something that adds another dimension. You have some great music happening, so why not tell the story through visuals? It delivers a message. I can always remember the visuals that I saw when Pink Floyd did "One of These Days" from *Meddle*. They had that quiet part, the ethereal part, then they exploded a concussion prior to the voice saying 'One of these days I'm going to cut you into a million pieces,' and then the police car lights come on and these towers lifted. Every time I heard that song on the radio, that's what I saw in my mind. So I think visuals help recreate the experience of a live show. When you hear the song on the radio when you're not at the show, in your mind you might actually see the picture of what you remember — that's what I think is important."

And by *A Show of Hands*, Howard says, "It was like when you put on a high school performance and then you take it to Broadway. We had the ability and the money and the crew to pull it off. It's not easy putting together a show that is multimedia. You are dealing with animators, actors, amazing editors and conceptual people, and with Rush it's a brain trust. Geddy is really into the visuals, his brother Allan spearheads our productions, and Geddy and myself and Alex sit down and we brainstorm ideas. Geddy has a lot of amazing ideas and then they take it to the film houses that we hire, and they have on-staff people who will add to those ideas. It becomes a collaboration."

Just as we've heard with the production of the records, Geddy was heavily involved in the production of the show. "They all care about the show, but Geddy in particular," says Ungerleider. "He's playing the music, but now he has a handle on what's going on behind the music as well. It's sort of interesting and fun. We look at this as a fun project. Although it's a lot of work, it's a lot of fun, because who gets the chance to dream of something and your dreams come true? A couple tours ago, I was up on a patio at a cottage in Northern Ontario looking at wind chimes, and I said, 'Wow! It'd be great if those wind chimes were LED video pixels.' And I designed my next video rig to be hanging like wind chimes. So it's all these ideas you get. I'm driving in the middle of the night and I'm going through the forest and there's the moonlight coming through the mist, and it just looks like something from a science fiction movie. I would want to try to recreate that onstage, get that same look.

"But Geddy, yeah, the beauty about him is, he's a hands-on guy, but he gives you the respect and the freedom to do what you want to do. He'll never come and say, 'You know, I hate that.' But we discuss everything. He's not even a micromanager; he just knows specifically what he wants, but always asks your opinion. You can't expect that everyone knows everything. I had a fan come up to me once, 'You should be putting those lights in the back in blue, because I think it would look better in blue, and you're using them now in red — I don't think it's working.' So I listened to what he said and I'm thinking, all right, I'll do them blue. Next day I put them into blue, checked it out and said, 'Yeah, I like them in blue — I'll leave it there.' So I'd take people's advice, just so long as it's not stupid. And I think when you give somebody creative freedom, there's a trust there. The band has always given me the creative freedom to design lights. They've never told me, 'No, you can't do this, you can't do that.' Well, they've told me, 'No, you can't spend that much money,' but they never said we hate what you're doing or we don't believe it works — they trust you."

Though his job is dealing with all this technology on the road, Howard of course also deals with the guys themselves. Taking a run at their personalities, he figures, "Alex is one of the most generous, friendly guys you ever want to know. There's no way you are going to have a boring time hanging out with Alex; he's a party waiting to happen, basically. And he's a great guy, and he's involved and into a lot of things. Al is Al — he's outgoing and out to have a good time. I mean, they all are. When Neil gets going he's classic, he's a fun guy to be around. But he's very serious too. And Geddy is very serious only because he feels the responsibility of keeping everybody focused. But once in a while, we have fun. Ged gets loose too; everyone in the world gets loose — it's just when. People think you get out on the road and get out of your mind and every day is a party. It's not true, because we'd all be dead if that was the case.

"The secret with Rush is consistency," affirms Howard. "Great songwriting, putting together great productions, keeping a team of people you trust around you to support you. And the machine rolls — the machine rolls smooth. You know, you buck the odds for so many years, you've never had a bona fide hit single . . . Rush have never been a Top 40 act, but they've succeeded despite everything. Everyone used to say this band will never succeed. You don't have a hit single, you don't appeal to commercial audiences. Instead they developed an underground following that is staggering. By bucking the odds for all these years and going against the grain, this is what you have. You have a solid three generations of fans, which I'm seeing at the shows every night. It's pretty amazing.

"How many bands out there are still doing this? There's not a lot. There's a handful of true artists. When you go see a David Bowie or an Elton John, you realize there's talent. You see Rush, you realize there's talent. When you get your fans to come see it, and word of mouth spreads, that's why they're still able to write spectacular music and move ahead. It really upsets me when I hear fans say, 'Oh, I just want to hear the old stuff.' Yeah, you do want to hear the old stuff, but they should be thankful the band is writing new material and pushing forward and giving them more than the old stuff. I mean, I can always say to someone,

'Why don't you go and act the way you did when you were eighteen even though I know you are thirty-five now. Act the way you were when you were eighteen — I liked you better then.' You know, that's what it's like."

Thinking more about the band's unique appeal, Howard comments, "Maybe you can call them a cult band, because they do have an underground following. Is it a commercial following? Maybe it turned into that. But I think it's more of a hard-core cult following. A lot of people don't go around humming Rush tunes in their head. They know them."

For his part, Geddy agrees with Howard's statements about how the two work together. "Yeah, I'm pretty involved in the visual presentation as far as the films go. But the lights are Howard's, ninety-nine percent. I might give him an opinion at the end, but I trust Howard implicitly with the lights, and I only get involved when there's a budget that has to be crunched. Because what he always wants is the moon. And I like to give him the moon, but I have other people who don't want him to have the moon. So I have to put myself between the bean counters and Howard and figure out the creative alternative so it works for Howard and it works for them.

"But the fun part of it for me — and it's always been the fun part of it for me — is the film stuff and the animation. I've always been fascinated with film; I've always been a huge film buff. One of my private lives was dreaming of being a movie director at one point. I gave that up a long time ago, but this satisfies a lot of that because I get to work with some great creative people, put a great team together. My brother is very helpful in that regard. He's a talented producer and finder of real talented people. And there's a number of people I've worked with for years, and we just keep finding these new artists, these young animators that are interesting, and we give them a song to work on. We try to find different, fresh approaches to making films for the rear screen, and that's great fun. You learn a lot and you get to meet some really fabulous animators and talented people."

And live, of course, is the where and when for Rush in terms of really getting to interact with their fans.

"I bless their hearts every single day," says Geddy. "But they're hard to analyze as a group because they're so different. We have these hard-core fans, the old fans who have been there from the beginning, and they're usually male, and they are really intense about the band. And then you get this new wave of female fans we keep seeing, and they're driven a lot by the lyrics, I think. Then you get these fans who are so young, all young players, and they're just air drumming. So you've got musicians in there, and then you've got people who've been really touched by the sentiment of a song that has some profound effect on their everyday life, their optimism. If anything is a connector between a lot of them it's that something Rush has done musically or lyrically has had a connection with them that has impacted their life in an optimistic way, and that has made them indebted in some crazy way.

"I'm always amazed when a fan holds up a sign that says thank you. I think that's all wrong. I'm the guy who says thank you, you came to see me, you've invested your life in something I've done. Yet they're saying thank you to me. That is the most common thing fans say to me. It always takes me aback. It blows my mind that they're thanking me for what we've done. It means I've given them something they've really needed or really wanted in some way. That it has offered them some comfort, maybe escape, but something that's been interpreted as a positive thing to their lives.

"And so I am so appreciative of our fans, and I'm not just saying this in a pandering way. Every night I'm out there I cannot believe they're there for us in those numbers. It really does touch me every night. It makes me want to play the best show I can possibly play. I can't think about it past that because it distorts your sense of yourself. In a way, it's not my business. Their relationship with me is their business. My relationship with them is my business. And to ponder it . . . like I know there's some guys in our organization who go on these chat lines and blogs, and I can't do that. I feel like it's not meant for me. I feel like I'm eavesdropping on a conversation that I shouldn't really be a party to.

"I still have the most beautiful miniature pair of basses that a fan made," continues Ged on his relationship with his fans. "An exact replica of two of my basses. It was done with such care, in a little glass. I've kept it ever since, and it's always on my desk. It's one of the most touching gifts a fan has ever given me.

"I was given a ring, which I wore for over twenty years. A fan came up to me at the Edgewater Hotel in Seattle. This was on maybe the second tour, and it was a female fan, and no I didn't sleep with her. A female fan just came up to me out of the blue and said, 'I want you to have this ring.' And it was a little ring that had a lyre on it, you know, a little medieval musical instrument. I thought it was such a sweet little thing. Anyway I put it on my finger, and I don't know whether I thought of it as a good luck thing or some sort of icon or totem of some kind, but it stayed with me until just last year when finally because of the fatness of my baby finger I had to remove it. I keep meaning to wear it around my neck. I have no idea what the person's name was."

And the fans are so dedicated. Eventually they even created RushCon.

"Well, Kiss, *Star Trek* and Rush — those are conventioneers, right?" figures Ged. "I don't know, I can't think about that either. It just blows my mind. I don't know how it came to be like that for them. There was a magazine in England called *The Spirit of Rush*. They talked about all kinds of stuff, and every time we came to England, they gave us copies. I think the guy who originally started it passed away — nice fellow. But they used it as a means of collecting all these like-minded people, and then they talked about other music and other bands and other things these people might like. It was like a coming together. I guess the internet has made that obsolete now, but it was like bringing a community together."

The Spirit of Rush was first published in the summer of 1987 and ran sixty-four issues, closing shop in the spring of 2003. Its founder, Mick Burnett, died of a heart attack in July of 2002. The band sent a bouquet of flowers to his funeral.

"It goes back to that whole sense of comfort," continues Lee, "and offering some optimism at a time in their lives where they need it. Everybody needs that, and you get it from wherever you can. You get it from your friends, you get it from your family, you get it from the books you read, you get it from films. I mean, film has a powerful effect on me. And I think for these fans, our music has that effect on them. I think if it were a poem, it would be less effective, but in the right surrounding, and if we've done our job properly in constructing the music to go along with Neil's lyrics, then we're delivering this message in a more emotional fashion.

"Some magazine — is there a magazine called *Paste* or something? — said that a Geddycorn is a semi-mythical creature, usually or always female, that comes to a Rush concert, sings all the lyrics, without a significant male other. And I was telling the story about how I saw a guy holding up a sign saying, 'My wife is a Geddycorn, and she doesn't use earplugs,' which I thought was great. But that's a new trend now — we're getting more Geddycorns."

Back to the business of 1989 and *A Show of Hands*. "Our productions got incredibly complicated at that point," explains

Geddy, reiterating the band's intense reliance on technology, as can be heard all over this slick live spread.

"It was the beginning of the nightmare years for me. We started bringing in banks of samplers and sequencers to try to reproduce all these things we had now put on our records. So you take a record where maybe the biggest difference was that there was an extra guitar in a song or a little bit of keyboard here and there, and now we had orchestras and choirs. How do you go onstage and reproduce that? Play that song suddenly without the orchestra and choir? So we had to figure out a way to do all that. And the only way to do that was to bring in these sequencers and samplers. And at that point, they weren't like they are now. Now you can hold down a cluster of keys and you can play the whole fucking song — it goes forever. In those days there was only a certain amount of sample time you had per piece.

"To avoid having to play to a click track and just automate the whole thing — we didn't want to do that; we wanted it to be performance-based — we would have these sequences assigned for each note or each chord part of the song, and in order to play them live and still play them as a band would play them, I would have to play them in time. That meant playing bass pedals to keep the bottom end there, not playing bass in a particular part of the song and triggering either the chord pattern or the sequence, whatever it was. And in a lot of those songs, there were layers, so you're playing a string part, and you're adding a little accent on the other hand. It was very complex and required a lot of technology and required us to have somebody offstage loading a separate bank of sequencers and samplers for each song.

"And we had to design a fail safe too," continues Ged. "What happens if the sampler goes out? It's electronic technology; it's very buggy. At that stage, computer technology also was very buggy. So we designed this whole system that was literally duplicated.

Every song was loaded twice, and we had this giant switch that if one bank of sequencers went down, Tony Geranios, who does my keyboards, could hit this switch and instantly it would switch to the other bank of samplers. And some of it was just too much for me to handle, so we would split some off to Alex and he would trigger some stuff. And then we'd split some off even to Neil, because he was using electronic drums, although he had his own sampling nightmare going on back there. But sometimes if we had an extra sample that none of us could trigger, we'd give it to him, and he'd stick it on his [laughs]. So we became really trapped in this complex arrangement of keyboards."

The video version of *A Show of Hands* (VHS and LaserDisc, with DVD to follow in 2006) would include a number of selections not on the double LP album or single CD, namely "Prime Mover," "Territories," "The Spirit of Radio," "Tom Sawyer" and the "2112"/"La Villa Strangiato"/"In the Mood" medley used as an encore. "Lock and Key" showed up on first pressings of the U.S.-issued LaserDisc.

"*A Show of Hands* to me is a very fine album," says Geddy, despite the computer-borne challenges. "That style of recording a live album, basically taking a handful of shows and choosing the best you've got, is a very good representation of that kind of live album. In terms of the construction of it, I think it was down to Paul Northfield and myself mostly."

You can hear the band's cartoony intro music (including "Three Blind Mice") before the vista-wide entrance of "The Big Money," which closes in less grand fashion, using the heavy metal riff from Cheech & Chong's "Earache My Eye." Offering value for the money, the album contained only two pre-*Signals* selections, "Closer to the Heart" (included because of its explosive climactic finish) and *Moving Pictures* deep track "Witch Hunt," which appeared on a live album for the first time. Neil's drum solo, which had begun going by the name "The Rhythm Method" on the *Hold Your Fire* tour, was not supposed to fit but did after all, even if it is presented in abbreviated form, with the edits decided by Peart himself.

Though Geddy was involved with nearly every aspect of the band and tour, he might have been driven nuts if he didn't have non-rock things to do on the road to keep him sane. Inquisitive as he is — as all three of them are — falling deep into their hobbies came naturally.

"Yes, baseball became a way of distracting me during a tour," explains Lee. "I would get up midday after getting in at four or five in the morning on the road, and I'd order my breakfast, after arguing with the room service person as to why they should still serve me breakfast at one in the afternoon. I'd turn on the tube as I'm eating my breakfast and in that time period, there was nothing on except for soap operas — and the Cubs. So I used to look forward to watching the Cubs during breakfast every day.

"And the more I watched them, I got hooked. Always have a fondness for the Cubs for that reason, even though I'm a local fan. But I guess that was the late '70s, early '80s. And so as soon as I came home after that tour, I got myself Blue Jays tickets and I was off as a baseball nut. It became a way of keeping my mind off of what I'm doing, off of the seriousness. You know, you can make yourself believe that what you're doing is so important that you become this obnoxious creature. I don't like to do that. I don't want to think that what I do is so important. I'm just a musician. I'd much rather get excited about something else. It's a survival mechanism for me. So baseball is great, and now that I'm a complete freak for rotisserie baseball and fantasy baseball, it's never-ending and it's wonderful. So I can hide in a room full of people and I can escape from whatever the band has to do by just pondering my fantasy team.

"The more hobbies you have, I believe, the more interesting life is. Art became an interest, as did photography. Wine is interesting stuff; it's interesting to know how it's made, it's interesting to learn about where it comes from. I'm more interested in European wine, particularly French wine, and that has taken me to spend my summers overseas more, bring the family and summer in the south of France whenever I can and investigate different parts of the world. And that suits me, and it suits my wife. She loves to travel, I love to travel, and I like my kids to be well traveled because I want them to feel they can live anywhere in the world. I think I love everything that my wine collecting has brought me more than I love the wine itself. I've learned a lot about a lot of places, I've met some great people, and that's what that passion is kind of all about.

"And art goes on forever. I mean, you can never learn enough, or get tired enough. I think in my secret heart of hearts, I wish I had that to do as my expression more than music; I think that's my deep secret. Because it's solitary and I really admire the solitary artist. I think it's wonderful. And I'm sure if you talk to a solitary artist, he'll tell you the exact opposite. But I love the fact that he doesn't need any partners — studio, committee, production manager — to do what he needs to do. He just needs some available light and his technology, which is paint. It's a fantasy. We always want to be someone else, I believe. I haven't met anyone who's so satisfied with their moment that they haven't imagined being something else — I always do."

And Geddy has other dreams to add to this list. "I wanted to be a major league pitcher for a couple of years there," he says. "And I fantasized about that, but that wasn't going to happen. Baseball's so interesting; so many games within the game. And I love that it's an eighteenth-century sport. That's why people can't watch it now, because it's a complete anachronism. I mean, it is out of time; it has no business being played in the twenty-first century. But that's what I love about it. I love that no two games are the same, I love what's going on between the pitcher and the catcher, I love that whole game of outfoxing the hitter. I love the fact they're all trying to steal each other's signs. I love that there's a different defensive alignment for every pitch and that every player on the field is thinking about what to do when the ball comes to him.

"But yet when it's orchestrated and it's all working in a great team, it's such a beautiful ballet of athleticism. It's just endlessly fascinating to me and the whole side of me that loves numbers. Baseball is a great game for number crunchers — it's just so full of ridiculous numbers. Plus I love to collect things, and I love to find undiscovered things in all my various hobbies. And fantasy baseball is like that, finding the player that no one else has gotten hip to yet, finding a photograph in an auction that nobody else has found, unearthing the diamond in the rough."

CHAPTER 9

PRESTO

"The six right answers."

N ot that you'd know it from the recorded evidence, but 1988 was a year of transition for Rush, symbolized by their break with Mercury Records. Strongly branded, with considerable control, through their unique situation on their own label at home, Anthem Records, Rush nonetheless had commitments and deadlines when it came to their American situation. Having felt Mercury was no longer working hard for them, Ray and Rush made a break, moving over to Atlantic. The live album and this business rending allowed the band to take an unprecedented six months off as they planned their next set of songs and a sound to go with them. The band had actually finished the record before inking a deal with Atlantic's Doug Morris, who for years had wanted to sign the band. He wasn't going to let them get away without an attractive package.

"We were changing wonderfully, and I choose the word carefully," reflects Neil, on the making of what was to become *Presto*.

"That was a wonderful decade for us, all the changes we went through, and then we changed again coming into the '90s with *Presto*. It's a really different kind of record, and the one that all of us would like to do again, because we don't think it reached the potential it had.

"There's a funny distinction among us and the way we think about the work. I'm very much instant gratification — my favorite part of recording is the demos. Because we work on the lyrics and we go back and forth, and the other guys will suggest things, and I'll get excited because that means they like it enough to suggest ideas. So I go back and work on the lyrics some more and then the song develops and then I'll work on a drum part. Then one day you hear a brand-new song for the first time, and that, for me, that's the end. The rest of it is just making it true, making it real.

"Whereas Geddy refers to mixing, the last process of making a record, the final mix, as the death of hope. Because he kept thinking, 'Oh, this is going to be better.' There is that striving and you can't know at the time. We're always doing our best. We're always totally heartfelt, making the best record we possibly can, with all of those influences and all of our progressions along the way, all that we've learned and all that we want to do and our ambitions. That remains constant. But you can't predict the result in something you know as transitory, as a period of time and a piece of music. *Presto* was a bizarre one."

After two records with Peter Collins, Rush would change things up again with respect to production. Feeling a strong urge toward self-production, they decided nonetheless that having that outside opinion would be valuable. In that role would be yet another Englishman — every Rush producer to this point had been English — Rupert Hine. Prog enough in his (obscure) credits through the '70s, Hine would work with the likes of

Howard Jones, Thompson Twins, Bob Geldof and the Fixx in the '80s, along with baby Rush band Saga, on two of that band's bigger records. His last collaboration before Rush would be with Stevie Nicks on her record *The Other Side of the Mirror*.

Rush had a history with Hine, having wanted to work with him back at *Grace Under Pressure*. "That's true," begins Hine. "It didn't really compute to me that they would want someone like me, who was doing synth pop records at that moment in time. Not that that was a conscious thought for me, but Thompson Twins, Howard Jones, the Fixx . . . these were rather electro-oriented pop bands. I really didn't see the connection. So it was a puzzling request to me. I mean, I was far too busy at that time to do it, so it didn't manifest until much later. It came through management and record companies. It wasn't a very direct request. I found out later, of course, why they asked me, but I didn't know at the time."

It turns out, Hine explains, that Rush wanted someone with a "different background. And I wasn't really up to speed. I hadn't realized they'd already transgressed from the obvious heavier rock side into this new thing. When I did listen, I suddenly realized they were more like the Police than a heavy rock band. And I thought, 'Good Lord, that's not what I thought Rush was.' But that was a bit later, after the first request, maybe a year or two later."

Also part of the connection, much to Rupert's surprise, was his solo work. "It was very much Neil's liking of my own solo albums as opposed to my productions, which is the last thing I thought would be true. My own albums were relatively successful in northern Europe, and to some extent England, a little bit in Canada, but nothing in America. I just didn't imagine he would have even known I made records on my own. It was interesting to me later on when I found out that was the connection for him. He thought, 'Well, if Rupert can make those sorts of records, and write those kinds of songs, and do those kind of arrangements and play pretty much everything himself, that's the kind of influence I'd like to see rattling around inside the Rush machine.'"

With Hine on board, or at least willing to entertain working with the band, it was time to roll up the sleeves and get down to work.

"I was invited up to a rehearsal space that was maybe an hour or an hour and a half outside of Toronto. It was a studio in itself, but they were treating it as a rehearsal room, and they could stay up there if they wanted to. It was leisurely, which I later realized is very much a Rush modus operandi — you move into a place and take it over and are free to move around with no time constraints. But it was ostensibly a rehearsal space.

"I'd said yes in principle but thought we should at least get to grips with whatever it is they're hoping to do on the album and talk about and listen to it. As I'm always saying to people, I can't say yes on the basis of your history. I can only say yes on the basis of what it is you're hoping to do now. And a lot of big acts think that's a bit insulting. They sort of think, 'Look, I'm just asking you to make my next record — we'll figure out what it is later.' And what if I didn't like the songs? What would be the point of me sitting there recording, arranging songs I don't like?

"I distinctly remember on the first day hearing Rush playing for me. It was this extraordinary band playing me their songs, already sort of brilliantly arranged, in immense detail, this very Rush-like detail, and I sat listening to it. Normally this would be sketches of songs, maybe finished songs, but with no or little attention to detail at that point; that would usually come later. It felt sort of so already done. And they would say to me, 'What do you think of that?' And I said, 'Well, excellent, it sounds just like Rush. What do you want me to do?'

"I was used to arranging records I work on a lot of the time and sometimes, as with the Tina Turners, you know, writing the songs too. Mostly I work with writer/artists, but never do they come so completely worked out. So I said, 'I'm not sure. It seems to me like you want more just a purely sound guy here. You know, how am I going to adjust Rush songs? Rush songs do what Rush songs do — that's why people love them. I would feel forced to make changes to make my presence worthwhile.'

"We listened to the songs and had that kind of dialogue. And then Neil reminded me of the kind of atmospheric tones and qualities of my own albums, this trilogy I did for A&M Records between 1980 and 1983; he particularly liked those. And I realized it was going to go far beyond just commenting about arrangements and details and songs and text. It was going to be more conceptual. And of course, that is immediately ten times more interesting to me as well. And the conceptual stuff, you know, originates certainly with Neil."

What intrigued Rupert was the marriage of Rush's past with what was now cutting edge in the industry. "I hadn't realized they had progressed from heavy rock, which wasn't a genre I was that interested in. I didn't keep my eyes on them, really, in that sense. And yet, of course, they are brilliantly, absolutely, the epicenter of progressive rock. And to me, the idea, at the end of the '80s, of doing something that technically was progressive rock and yet pop-oriented was strangely fascinating. How one could make that feel contemporary without losing the essence of what Rush are."

Rupert realized the band wanted to work with him at a high-concept level and were interested in what he as an artist could bring to the table. Rupert says, "I think it's primarily a Neil concept although the three of them can operate like one organism anyway, really. A lot of Neil's thinking fires up the others to think along the same lines, and then they throw things about. It wasn't as if they were asking me to come in and do a Rupert Hine sound, whatever that might have been. I never got that impression. It was more 'let's put this ingredient in the mix and see what happens.' And because they knew I was also a writer, someone who had made, by then, seven or eight albums of my own as an artist, they liked that idea of putting an artist in the mix, someone who could also really get into the nitty-gritty of the notation and the arrangement, if required, who could at least comment on it and be very sharp to it."

As for Rupert's impression of the guys? "Astounding musicians — there's no doubt about it. And I don't think I've ever produced a record with any band — believe it or not, even punk bands I've worked with — who haven't cited at least one member of Rush as in their all-time top three or four musicians on the planet. Not one band, of any kind of genre, and as far apart as you can get. Far and away the winner of course is always Neil — he seems to be considered the world's best drummer. Of course, there's a million kinds of best drummers, but on a technical level he is astounding. I don't think I could find another player who can match Neil's extraordinary abilities as a drummer. It's almost magical.

"So here I was on their thirteenth album, and both Alex and Geddy still refer to Neil as the new boy. They'd turn around every now and then and say, 'Well, what does the new boy think?' He only didn't play on one album, right? By the time the second album came, that was the combination and it's been there ever since, but they still refer to him as the new boy. So there's that lovely, close kind of ribbing you only get away with when you really love each other.

"And Geddy has got this very broad view about creativity, and a well-read, well-educated creative mind. It's just a delight to talk to him, particularly about movies and that side of his creative passion. Alex was always easygoing, reactive, you know, reactive to the others. He could really bounce between the other two, and that became sort of an issue later for me to tackle, because I realized that sometimes musically that was exactly what was going on. That he was somehow tossed between Neil and Geddy — they sort of played with him. And I tackled that issue."

Rupert clarifies what he means here, explaining that everybody seems to always have an opinion about what the guitar player should be playing. "It became an issue. It almost took my breath away to start with the first time I experienced it, how the guitar parts were sort of manufactured by all three of them. And when it came to solos and things that were supposed to be — I thought — much more personally expressive. I always think that soloing is something that should just be there for that moment. And it was so not that. It was handed round the party and everyone had some. Alex was included, but it seemed like everybody was doing the guitar solo. I felt very frustrated by that; I mean, frustrated for him as a player, and I wondered how many years or how many albums this had been going on. I wondered what he would play if he was just left to his own devices. I'm making it a little more extreme than it was, but that's how it felt."

Hine sensed Alex was frustrated by the situation too, but it was never overtly talked about. "And I think the reason we didn't was that it didn't really become necessary. I manufactured this little device, this little ploy. He had an eight-track machine in his bedroom at the studio we were recording in, in Morin Heights in Canada. And he would practice ideas and come up with parts, literally in his bedroom, even when we were in the studio. And then he'd play everybody the parts, and everybody would sort of dive on them and sort them out.

"And one time," continues Hine, "I asked him in advance, 'If you're going to do some stuff for that solo, can you just play it to me in the morning?' And I tried to leave it not sounding too pointed. So he played it to me. He had a rough mix, just over a stereo track, and he'd done these guitar solo ideas, and they were really excellent, they were just fantastically Alex. So I just spooled them onto our main multi-tracks, just copied them straight over. I think maybe we did an edit between a couple, but we weren't compiling; it was pretty much as was. I sunk it into the track, and then I put the track away and we carried on with whatever we were going to do when the rest of the guys arrived.

"So the next time we got that track out, everybody's sitting there, and out popped this guitar solo that Alex had done apparently invisibly. I said, 'Oh, we just did that; it was something Alex did, and I just thought it sounded so great; I wanted to use the one he'd done upstairs.' And I could see them both thinking, 'Hmm, the one he'd done upstairs?! But fidelity-wise, that's just a funny little tape machine thing — we've got to do it again.' And I just said, 'I think it sounds fantastic just as it is.' And they both agreed; thus a new methodology was born.

"From then on, I just got Alex to do all the parts upstairs that involved free playing, free expression. Sometimes we would redo it, but by then it was so clear. As far as solos went, we often used the ones he recorded, just on his own without any input. And the rest of the guys were fine about it. It took them a minute, but they became sold; they loved the parts too."

And then there was Geddy's singing, another area where Rupert aimed to have impact.

"By *Roll the Bones*, Geddy had started to include the idea of singing much lower, and I think there are a lot of songs on both albums that are beautifully fresh within the Rush world because we can hear Geddy, the man — and he's an interesting man — you can hear that in the voice. And we can hear the text, Neil's text, more clearly. It sort of tumbles out rather than us having to work it out because it's so high and shrill — we can't really understand the words at that pitch.

"The other thing was the keyboards, or lack of. A third and most important thing was the fact they wanted to book me for a year, or fifteen months or something, to make the first album. I said I hadn't ever spent more than three months making a record, ever, with anybody, and that includes multi-platinum records. 'Well, we don't work like that. We have a pace that is very much Rush.' And after much bartering, we settled on six months, which to them felt like half a dozen days. I mean, they were just completely panicking, saying, 'Well, don't book a project right off the back of that six months. Can't we just have sort of a gray area?'

"In the end, we did it in just over four and a half months, which for them was a shock. They thought that was a massive plus. At the end of it, they actually really enjoyed not having to live with this album for the usual year. And the second album, just to finish that line of thinking, they said, 'Well, we don't want to put in just four months' . . . and they did it in three months — *Roll the Bones* was three months."

Geddy, when asked what he was going for musically when it came to *Presto*, and with hiring Rupert specifically, says, "One of the reasons I wanted to work with Rupert was that I felt he was a very good producer of singers, vocalists. And that was very attractive to me, to try to work on developing and improving different ways of using my voice. The projects he's associated with are always strong melodically, and I thought that was a good thing for us. It certainly plays into where my interests lie as a writer — it's always my default point of interest, the melodic side of things. For me personally, apart from the band, that was one of the big motivators to use him. And going into the record, there was a lot of experimentation in the writing, for me, of melodies, chorus melodies, and he's terrific to work with from that point of view, and I learned a lot. From an arrangement point of view, we were just looking at trying to perfect that whole idea of how much can we accomplish in that shorter time frame, five minutes, six minutes, as opposed to ten or twenty. And I think melody was a key to that."

Specific to the transition of Peter Collins to Rupert Hine, Geddy figures, "Well, it's interesting. I found working with Peter very, very satisfying. And Rupert is a person of interest, always, and we almost worked together so many times in the past that he was kind of a natural choice. I'm not sure I can recall exactly what my motivation was, and what the band vision for that album was, at the time. But I know there was definitely a strong desire to focus on songwriting and certainly, for me, stronger choruses. That's a craft; it's all part of that craft, you know? For us, as time goes by, being players is one thing, but when you sit down to make a record, you know that the playing is going to be fine, that kind of comes to us naturally. But to wrestle with the songwriting to try to get a new take on it, and to try to make that palatable in the context of three hyperactive musicians, that's always the thing.

"And the fact that Rupert was a keyboardist as well and had all this experience with very hip keyboard sounds and different ways of recording with the Fixx and bands like that . . . he was all about keyboard expertise, plus his vocal expertise and his songwriting and arranging expertise. That's what I wanted out of Rup. And I think he delivered that for us. He's quite a nice man to argue with too, because he's completely unflappable. So if you have a difference of opinion, it's the most gentlemanly difference of opinion you can imagine. Which suits us fine, because that's kind of how we operate anyway.

"To me it was just moving forward," says Geddy, in terms of his general impression of the character of the resulting collaboration. "There was a shift away from the super-busy digital-sounding keys, back to kind of more analog sounds and using it more as a textual tool and an orchestrating tool, as opposed to a showcase. That was toned down, and that was probably much more exciting for Alex than me. I guess we were of two different lines about that. I mean, he was obviously stressed over his previous experience, so this seemed like a monumental shift to him, where to me it didn't really seem like that big of a shift. His guitar is always big and ballsy and present in our music. It's never really gone away. But I think to a guitar player, a subtle difference between eleven and nine [laughs] is huge."

And it was never much of a problem because Alex is Alex. Geddy says, "He's very good at disguising his feelings, because he likes to keep everybody vibey. But then he's very bad at it, you know? He's got a typical Eastern European Serbian attitude; like, he'll freak out. So he'll swallow it, swallow it, swallow it and be really quiet, and then all of a sudden he'll go nuts on you and have this explosion of emotions. And everybody will just go, 'Okay, let's pick up the dishes and figure out what happened.'

"But generally, he's pretty interior in that regard. He's not the kind of guy who will talk for the sake of talking, unlike myself. He's not a big talker in the studio, unless something is really bothering him, or he's really excited about something. He's happy to let Neil or me push the session along until something is going in a direction he really disagrees with, or if he has some fresh thinking he wants to try. He does keep it in, but he will also explode in a way that Neil and I will never explode. He's got that emotional reaction, and he'll [makes explosion noise] freak out and you think, 'Geez, what the hell just happened?' And then he'll be fine. So it's like a quick storm and then it's gone.

"I think he's been guilty of that a few times," explains Geddy. "Like I think all through *Signals* . . . the thing about Al that is so frustrating in a way is that he's going along with it, he's into it, he's playing, he's digging it, he's loving it, and then a month after the record comes out, he'll express his frustration with the way it went! It's kind of like a delayed reaction with him. He loves to experiment, first of all. He's the first guy in there to want to keep experimenting. And I don't know if that's typical of guitar players, but the ones I've known in my life are very much like that. They love to fiddle, they love to tinker with the sound. He loves to play with the toys, he loves to get his hands dirty with the electronics, and so he does have a real willingness to experiment. He's adventurous. So he'll go along with whatever everyone else is excited about, and this has happened a few times in our career, where albums are really experiments. We're not one hundred percent sure what record we're going to make 'til it's finished, so it's a living thing, our albums. With *Signals*, we loved it in the end! And then a month later he was kind of bummed about it because he felt the guitar was moved out of the focus, in a way it hadn't in the past. Which is true. There was still guitar, but its role had changed. So he comes into that next session with a bit of that pent-up thing, 'Okay, I can't let that happen, because that bugged me.' Then we'll go and make another record, and he'll walk away, and it will be something else that maybe he internalizes. Again, there's that delayed reaction.

"And that's normal for a musician, I think. It's not how I operate, but maybe I spill my beans as we're going, you know? I'm very vocal, very verbal, and if I go home at the end of the session and something is wrong with the track, I'll be up all night. I'll be listening to it, I'll be thinking about it, I'll be driving myself nuts. And then when Alex and I go to the studio the next morning, I'll drive him nuts, and I'll be listening over and over and over again, and that's our partnership. And we bounce off each other like that. But I think that's why it's less frustrating for me, because I know what we're doing in the moment. I'm more aware of the changes that are going on, and sometimes he kind of goes with the flow, and then a little bit later wasn't so satisfied."

"I think we were looking for a different angle," says Lifeson, on the *Presto* experience, "working with a different producer who again came from a different background. Funnily, we always worked with English producers. And Rupert had seemed quite interesting. The work he had done with the Fixx, for instance, sonically, was something I thought was quite interesting. The guitar sounds and the arrangements were always great on all the work he had done. He had a background in more of a keyboard thing, and he was a player himself, and at the time it was a very interesting approach to shift to somebody like that.

"My guitar sound was transitioning from that active, bright sound that I used for previous records because of the density of the keyboards. I think with *Presto*, we had a combination of the two. There's a bit more acoustic stuff on that record, and there is a lot more air around the production. There's a lot of room, there's a softer sound. I think in the end, it was softer than I hoped for, than we had anticipated. But it had an interesting dimension to it. So in the whole volume of our work, it's a record that stands out.

"The previous two records were real experiments in the keyboard aspect of the band, and we were coming to the end of that," affirms Alex — though it doesn't seem, listening to *Presto* now, that his guitars are really all that much more forthright. "And *Presto* really steps back from the density of keyboards, with a lot of emphasis placed on melody and the interaction between guitar and vocals and the band. But it seemed to me to be a cleaner sound — that was sort of a goal. Not quite the thickness those other records had. And working with somebody different, working with different engineers, everybody has a different approach. Geddy and I had gone to more of a sort of straightforward way of writing, and that seemed to suit us at that point as well.

"Still, I don't think that record sounds like a power trio. It's definitely not a hard rock record. It's not heavy in any way, really. But Rupert thinned the keyboards more than anything, bringing back the guitar and making it more three-piece, you know, that sense of Geddy and me standing beside Neil and playing together. It was part of the revitalization. We had the break and had some family time and some rest, and then falling into *Presto*, recording in England, recording in Canada, mixing in England, moving around a bit — that was a lot of fun."

Dismissing any serious sense of conflict with Geddy about his role, Alex figures, "We've always been on the same page. You might be at other ends of that page, but we're always on the same page. And that's why our relationship works, why our partnership works. We might not agree on all things, but we wanted to go in that same direction, and that's the synergy that works between us. We get better results for it. Looking back, I'm not so sure that was the start of getting closer. Not that there was any distance, you know what I mean? I think we've gradually worked our whole songwriting relationship closer and closer. It's a matter of trust. Feeling confident that you can step away and you know it's still going to be great, or it's still going to go in a good direction. I think that's something we've achieved through the years, particularly through the last ten or twelve years.

"And it's trusting yourself," continues Lifeson. "You think you know everything, and your ideas are the most precious ideas and your ideas are the best ideas. It takes maturity and experience to accept that your ideas aren't always the best. And you can better your ideas by solid input and by inspiration from your partner.

And that's something we've worked on, not consciously over the years, but have grown into. We were both like that. We were both very, I don't know, pushy when it came to wanting our ideas to move forward. Like most relationships. Now I don't go in for a day. I just leave Ged to do his thing, and he does his thing, and typically when we work, he likes to work to about six o'clock and then goes home and has dinner with his family. I don't mind working late. I work 'til eleven. I work with Neil on his drums, while we're writing, so there is this fantastic trust that we have. Like, 'I'll see ya tomorrow. I can't wait to hear what you do — go for it.' And I think we've done our best work that way."

Presto was issued on November 21, 1989, in a classy yet amusing sleeve featuring rabbits proliferating out of a magic hat, a concept initiated by the band and instantly nailed by Hugh Syme. The idea grew bombastically when it came to tour visuals, but here the overall presentation is quite restrained, even refreshing, given the continued deliberate lack of a Rush logo and open field of typographic possibility. The title itself was a holdover, having been on the table for the just-passed live album. The upscale photographic portraits of the band on the back cover were taken by Andrew MacNaughtan, who then took on a prominent photography role with the band, directing videos for them as well and joining them on tour. Inside the original vinyl LP was an inner sleeve, one side with the lyrics in tiny type, the other, simple band credits and "rock paper scissors" game illustrations that tie in to a song on the album called "Hand Over Fist."

The record opens in memorable fashion. "Show Don't Tell" announces itself with a rhythm flourish, a brief Rush instrumental, before a calming as the verse starts. This album-announcing music barrage is a perfect example of Rush making math rock weirdly hooky: for any fan with a modicum of rhythm, this part got stuck in the head, helping to push the song to the point where it became a crowd favorite, featuring in the set list for the tour of this record, as well as the next two, before dropping out forever.

Though the song hit #1 on the (secondary) Hot Mainstream Rock Tracks chart, Rupert says in no way did the guys aim for such a result. "It's hard not to chuckle because I have never, ever, before or since, sat with a band whose primary member said to me — on the first meeting, and this of course being Neil — there are just two words we don't mention in Rush-land. I was thinking, what kind of swear word was he going to come out with? 'Singles and videos. We don't talk about them.' We went back to the next point on the agenda and that was it. We didn't talk about it then and we never did — it was a simple and bold statement."

Nor did singles or videos become a topic of discussion between Rupert and Ray Danniels. "No," he says when asked. "I mean unless it was so brief and fleeting that I can't remember it. But there was no conscious discussion or decision about direction at all. I mean, other than the ongoing process, when we hit on a new sort of idea, or a way of going about things, that would be discussed and talked about, usually over dinner. But it was never in a commercial perspective — never. They were this wonderful, rarefied entity that had reached a point where they sustained a remarkably good living doing exactly what they wanted to do. Why on earth would you topple that? By trying to become something that others need of you, not just in terms of trying to preempt an audience, which you'd never do, but you know, pleasing the shopkeepers."

True to form, "Show Don't Tell" is a single that breaks all the rules. Still, it's insidiously catchy, through fleeting tips and tricks like bass licks, vigorous acoustic guitar strumming and a sturdy chorus that repeats the title dependably (albeit approximately). Lyrically, Neil explores the concept of action, not words, couched in the metaphor of a courtroom, creating with Ged a nice call and response come chorus time.

"I'm a great believer that the best record you can make is the record only *you* can make," continues Hine, "and Rush is a fine example of that. There are no Rush would-bes, although there may be Rush wannabes. But Rush is such a rarefied zone. It's beautiful. I mean, it is what it is, and I see no point in changing it. Early on to me it was peculiar, because I couldn't really fully understand why I was there. I didn't feel like changing anything. I thought, 'Well, I'm just going to sit here and smile while these guys make a great record.' Every time they turn to me, I can only say, 'Wow, sounds like Rush.' You know, what do you want me to say?"

Rupert comments further on the words *single* and *video*: "I think they're bad words for any artist. A single, to me, these days there's no such thing. I think there is what I tend to refer to as the jewel track, which is something that so intensely represents everything that artist is about. It's a real synthesis; it's a trailer, if you will, but one that is wholly acceptable unto itself, not just chopped-down bits. But it synthesizes all the best idiosyncratic individual elements of that artist. You can do that now because you can find a great visual to go with it. And if that pops up on YouTube, then you have exactly what you need — you have a jewel that's flying round the planet like brushfire. So we don't need singles anymore; we need something that's just an intense example of what we're doing at that moment in our lives, and I've always felt that. But even by the time I worked with Rush, already the single was a piece of advertising, in a bad way."

But the concept was a moot point with Rush, because as Rupert explains, "they'd reached a point where their fan base was big enough to sustain the machinery of their lives, and they realized how fortunate they were. And if they continued to make really great Rush records, and didn't throw anything away, made sure every track was as beautifully done as every track is, their fans would stick around because it was sort of already proven to be timeless music. They were already out of fashion, because in a sense they were never in fashion. That's one of those wonderful areas that if you can maintain that place . . . Peter Gabriel did it for years, for instance, until 'Sledgehammer' ruined everything for him. People say, 'What do you mean? It was a fantastic huge hit and everything else.' But it stopped him. It stopped the flow of creativity and in the twenty years after that he only made two albums."

"For 'Show Don't Tell' I adopted an attitude and character," Peart told Nick Krewen, from *Canadian Musician*. "I took a stance and a good attitude and developed it. I think it's just a sense of growing power in my own confidence and ability. I hope it reflects growing technique. I find a trend for us since *Grace Under Pressure* has been cutting off abstractions."

"Chain Lightning" makes a similar statement to "Show Don't Tell," with the band moving forward with less keyboards, albeit maintaining the same band-in-matchbox sound. Avows Rupert, "As I say, even before we got to rehearsal, I wanted to get those keyboards out of there. And I just said to them, 'I'm a keyboard player; I'd be the first to want to put keyboards in there. But I want to take everything out.' And they had already put some keyboard parts in the songs themselves, but we really kept them minimal. And I said I'm not going to bring an armory of my keyboards. I don't want you to dig out every keyboard you've got. If we have any keyboard parts on this record, let them be minimal, and let's just choose one synth or two synths, tops, that we're just going to call on, and not look at this mound of technology to get lost in.

"So it really was getting them back to the three-piece. I just said I thought it was so crazy that a guitar, bass and drums trio should be smothered in keyboards. And then watching how they do it live, which of course is acrobatic madness — everyone's got their Taurus pedals, everyone's got a keyboard within reach, Neil's triggering all these keyboard things — it's mad. Get a keyboard player or be a power trio. So we did. On both albums, it was very crucial."

As to whether the guys were receptive to the idea, Hine says, "Yeah, completely. I mean they were sold by the idea. It was already in Geddy's mind. But certainly, my priority right from the very first meeting was get those keyboards out of there. I was probably also a bit sick of it myself. That was good timing. The '80s had been so keyboard driven, particularly in England. In Europe it was almost forbidden to have a guitar on anything. It got that extreme — if you had a guitar on something it was, 'Ah, how old fashioned — what are you doing?' So here we were sort of rediscovering guitars. But of course with Alex, you're going to get a wide palette of sounds anyway. I just said to them, if we want kind of a keyboard-like sustain, let's try to get it out of Alex first for the record, so that the sustain will be sort of transparent and modulating and abstract."

Hine makes a good point. Alex is still a source of angular stabs, of texture, of chorus and reverb. What Rupert indicates is that the idea was to have Alex stay with the harshly modern guitar presence he had since 1985, but to just give us more of that, in a mathematical and methodical crowding out of a few keyboard bits. This transition is subtle, which is why one wouldn't be at fault for not noticing that *Presto* and *Roll the Bones* weren't radically different from *Power Windows* and *Hold Your Fire*.

"He was looking like sort of dribbling," says Rupert. "You know, he was not just going to play the guitar parts, but he was also going to be playing the keyboard parts — on guitar."

In terms of its musical architecture, "Chain Lightning" finds Geddy hitting a few bass chords and then transitioning into ska come chorus time — as a spot of temporal congruity, the verse approximates a polite, guitary new wave derived from punk rock. Indeed the most prominent keys are some innocent washes in the intro, which return later but never cut in. At the lyric end, the Professor, a professed weather fanatic, gives us a weather report, like a more action-packed "Jacob's Ladder." Like that song as well, it's not just clouds; there's musing about using all this stuff for inspiration.

"The Pass" turned out to be *Presto*'s finest moment, or at least this era's lasting contribution. It's an encouraging and hopeful anti-suicide number, considerably researched by Peart. Despite being about teen suicide, this song might be viewed as a cautionary tale to a Tom Sawyer–type character with his spark for defiance waning, resulting in a late-in-life epiphany. Aligning with Neil's themes around self-reliance and responsibility, his lyric suggests finding the character building amidst trauma.

"'The Pass' is one of the best songs we've ever written," agrees Geddy, who has proven the band's appreciation for it by featuring it proudly in the set perennially. "I just love that song. There's something about the atmosphere and the nature of the lyric; it's some of Neil's best writing, and I still think it holds true. It deals with a really difficult issue in a very positive way. That song has stayed with me. I love playing it, I love singing it, and I think it's just one of those accomplishments, as a writer. You know, fans view us differently than we do. They look at us as a band of players, to a large degree. But from the inside looking out, the victories that I look back on usually are when I had a breakthrough as a writer, or when I was able to approach something from an arrangement point of view that was new for me. And that's one of those songs."

Indeed there's reason for Geddy to linger over the architecture of "The Pass." It's a sturdy song of pop melancholy, with much of the band's itchy, agitated playing of this period put aside. Nonetheless his bass chords are back, and Peart still plays stadium rock come chorus time, bringing the Rush-ness to sober vocal, bass and guitar parts.

Neil is also justifiably proud of the song, realizing it's a pillar of the album, and one of the reasons he'd love to re-record *Presto* if he could. Having worked long and hard on the track because of its sensitive topic, Neil also went so far as to massage in a nice literary reference: an Oscar Wilde quote from *Lady Windermere's Fan*, namely, "We are all in the gutter, but some of us are looking at the stars." The character portrait in the song comes more from stories Neil gathered of university students rather than high school students. At the end of the song, Neil very deliberately and carefully wants to be a bit steely eyed about suicide, gently proposing that there's nothing heroic about it.

"War Paint" sticks to recurring *Presto* themes, including minimal keyboards, quiet verse with tribal drums, in total, rocked-up REM. Lyrically, Neil is talking about the war of the sexes, boys and girls both working their way through the rituals in terms of making themselves attractive, with an amusing suggestion at the end from Neil to "paint the mirror black," followed by a gratuitous "paint it black."

"With all the songs from *Presto*, I had a rough demo made to the drum machine," explained Peart, in conversation with J.D. Considine from *Musician*, concerning "War Paint." "I had the opportunity to sit down by those demos by myself and work out the parts and refine them all. But I tend to work backwards. I put everything in and then subtract what doesn't work; that's why it's better to me to work by myself. I'm not driving everybody else nuts. I basically like to start with a clean sheet of paper and play the song through, jotting down everything I can think of that will fit in that tempo or that rhythmic structure. Then I see what feels good to play, go back and listen to it and see what sounds right, and then just start eliminating stuff.

"Sometimes I am forced to play things that are simple to the point of moronic, but if that's what works, I have to accept that reality. But I find ways to balance it out. 'War Paint,' the intro and the bridge sections are moronic, just so simple that they drive me nuts. But the chorus sections allow me to stretch out and play some really satisfying stuff. I was able to find ways to play something complex but make it sound simple, make it fall right into the flow of the song. As I'm thrashing my way through the moronic part, I know there's a really cool part coming that I'm going to love playing. If it's a simple part rhythmically where all it requires is a beat, then I'll play the beat and find some cool little inflections that I can do with an opposite hand, or something to make it hard to do, something to make it interesting or difficult. It's not just the record I'm thinking about in a context like this. With touring on the horizon, I have to play that song again and again and again. That does become a part of the thinking, rightly or wrongly."

"Scars" puts Rush in Shriekback terrain, wholly European, atmospheric, agitated pop from start to finish with icy, expensive chord changes and Neil hitting all manner of futuristic surfaces. Peart, for his part, was influenced by a rhythm he heard while cycling in Africa, and he spent a day building a procedure and system to be able to play this, combining traditional percussion and electronics. Alex as well hauls out a pile of effects, pleased that Rupert let him indulge, while Geddy plays a post-punk funk pattern, robotic and erudite. Another point of comparison here might be Talking Heads, records three through five.

Explains Rupert, who pulls out all the stops: "I like to think of producing as a combination of consulting. You bring your experience of working on a lot of other genres, and with lots of different artists, and you can come up with ideas and little goody bags to drop in the mix, like a therapist. Not so important with Rush I have to say, but usually very important. You're there to figure out what it is they're really trying to say. And that's hugely important because you can lose focus halfway through an album, halfway through a song. You need to be reminded of how you want to leave your audience changed four minutes later. If you leave them as you found then, what's the point in doing it?

"By focusing on how it is we want to change them in those four or five minutes, what we're really doing is getting to the heart of what it is we're doing. And that gets everybody off their twiddly, twiddly bits for the sake of twiddly, twiddly, or the clever, clever bits for the sake of clever, and you can get the focus back to how we're meant to feel at the end of it as an audience — there's those capacities.

"And there's being an editor, which is actually one of my favorite comparisons, in the book publishing sense. Editors are there to provide resistance for a writer to push against. So when they say things like, 'This character that comes in, in chapter four, you know, I keep finding him unbelievable; I don't see why . . .' The writer will be, 'What?! He's crucial. The whole idea is . . .' So what that writer realizes, even as he's just pontificating, is there's something about that character that's broken at the moment. Note to self, must fix it, right? That's the sort of resistance the artist can push against. I think I did that quite a bit with Rush, just to see how much things needed to be done, how clever they needed to be, which is part of Rush. And I wouldn't use the word *clever*, but you know what I'm getting at. That beautiful sort of smart playing is definitely a really strong character of the band. But as with everything, it's a question of how much you use it, you know, using it at the right moment for the right effect."

Neil's "Scars" lyric marks a swift transition from the idea of physical scars or indeed the idea of a scar being wholly negative. Instead he's talking about both positive and negative imprinting from experience — both emotionally and intellectually — acquired primarily, through his travels.

Presto's title track is an early example of Alex's predilection for layering acoustic tracks over his electric parts, although most memorable is the naked acoustic that accompanies the opening verses, amidst minimal bass and drums. Again, keys are there only to add a little color as arrangements unfold and evolve. This song closed side one of the original vinyl issue of the record. Of note, *Presto* would be the last Rush album that could be said to come from the vinyl era, given the wholesale changeover about to occur in 1990. But the band had already made the transition to offering a higher quantity of music, with side one of *Presto* a whopping twenty-nine minutes in length. In fact, the band found it necessary to add a note at the end of the credits indicating, "Side I is much longer than Side II, therefore is not as loud. So turn it up!"

Explained Neil, to Nick Krewen at *Canadian Musician*: "The song 'Presto' reflects me and life as a theme, although I invented the scenario." Peart adds that "irony is also a tool I used on this album. Most times I was careful not to dramatize the situation. When you step into true fiction, you use the fiction to explain the truth and reality. I'm still learning how to say personal things in an effective way — and I see this vast ocean in front of me. Initially, lyrics were never that important to me, internally or externally. But dealing with words changed the way I read and introduced me to some new worlds. It's also important that you see different points of view. I've read a lot of American literature from the '20s and '30s, and what was interesting was that all the authors of the time — Hemingway, Steinbeck, Fitzgerald and

Faulkner — saw it all so differently. Yet they manage to strike at some universal theme. It's important to be conversant with other people's views, even if you don't agree with them."

There was no attempt to push this song as a single, despite its title track status. In fact, the song was not played live until the Time Machine tour of 2010.

Opening side two of the original record was "Superconductor," a song warning about the emptiness of superficial entertainment. It's a quick rocker, as rocky as possible, that is, given this tooling and schooling. But yes, this was about as power-trio-like the band would get on the record, with only almost inconsequential keyboards, most prominent at the reggae-like break.

"We certainly did not want to go the full Andy Richards route," says Geddy, reiterating the clear mandate for *Presto*. "We didn't want to have the big show of keyboards. I think there was still a role for keyboards there, but they were being pulled back. The question was being asked: Do we need them here? What do they contribute here? They weren't disappearing. They were still a big part of it, but I think we were looking for different ways of using them, not so much of the upfront dynamic, tour de force that the Andy Richards show produced on *Power Windows*. By virtue of not taking the approach we took with Andy Richards, giving keyboard so much latitude, filling so much space before we even put guitars on, by that token, yeah, it was a more traditional approach. But the keyboards were still there, present but not as ostentatious."

Whether this helped his relationship with the band's guitar picker, Geddy says, "I'm trying to put myself back to that time. My relationship with Al is fairly indescribable. It's very brotherly, in the sense there is a certain amount of abuse that goes on between us, but we don't really regard it as abuse, the same way you would to your brother or sister. It's just kind of like elbow room. I don't remember any overt attention, but Alex keeps things in sometimes. So maybe he was more uptight about the guitar role, after the experience of the past two records. I only recently realized how frustrated he was during that period. But maybe that's just me not wanting to think about that. I'd forgotten that maybe there was more tension than I cared to recall."

And again, from Rupert's way of thinking, something like "Superconductor" is indeed a type of hard rock, but it's likely most fans would disagree.

"I was all the time trying to concentrate Rush on making the maximum Rush album," says Hine, "which meant the least interference from outside. I really wanted to push them into the most intensely Rush combination, what would have been the more hard rock tracks. Those are on those records. Not the classic kind of very heavy, thick guitar sounds, but rather these sharper, edgier sounds that I'd had a liking for and developed in a big way with the Fixx, which I know they also liked."

"Anagram (for Mongo)" is another mid-tempo pop rocker with guitars, although there are a few more keys and even a few spare classical piano chords. As for the title, Geddy explained to a caller on *Rockline* that it's a reference from Mel Brooks's comedy *Blazing Saddles*. "There's a scene, if you recall the film, where — I can't remember the name of the actor who plays the lead — he dressed up as a candygram delivery man and knocks on the door of the saloon and goes, 'candygram for Mongo, candygram for Mongo.' And Mongo takes the candygram, and of course it explodes in his face. That's where it comes from."

Framing Neil's lyrics on the record more generally, he adds: "I think it's hard to describe all the things that make you want to write about the things you write about. I know for Neil, he's a person who's driven by what's going on around him and what's going on in the world. He's constantly traveling and thinking and examining, and he goes through many different things, as we all do; and it's hard to say where these things come from. And yes, there are some songs that are angry, and some subjects that, I think, require anger from time to time — and I always think that makes for good rock music anyway. So it's hard to say where the inspiration comes from in any of those songs."

Neil's lyric is indeed rife with partial and full anagrams. There are key words in each line that use letters from larger, other key words or, roughly speaking, each line uses the same set of letters twice. The most instructional bit to lead the reader to what they are suspecting is "There is tic toc in atomic." Most clever is "Image is just an eyeless game" because *image* less the *i* leaves you the letters for *game*. Geddy excuses Neil's less than coherent messaging across the aggregate of the song, amused that this type of word game results in very singable lyrics. After all, along with the narrative of less keyboards, the ear of Rush with Rupert Hine, figures Geddy, is about singing, an increased sophistication of vocal phrasings — this song is almost *about* phrasing, where despite the little fortune cookies delivered to each place setting, the game itself shouts any other meaning down.

"Red Tide" is a straightforward 4/4 rocker with dark, sophisticated chord changes, distinguished by a crazy guitar solo from Alex, who deliberately wanted to match the anger of Neil's lyrics. Of note, it was never played live. Although most of the song is about various forms of ecological degradation, the first verse is about AIDS. By the end of the song, Neil is approximating the famous words of Dylan Thomas, "Do not go gentle into that good night," his point being it's time to turn the tide on the likes of red tide before it's too late. Indeed, pollution has been a concern ever since the dawn of the industrial revolution — nothing surprising there — but by 1989, there had already been scientific warnings about global warming, so decades later, Peart's words take on new weight. Even if taken literally, his final missive seems to reference then-popular theories about a coming ice age. Also somewhat dark is "Hand Over Fist," at least for the verses, against a hooky, happy resolve come chorus time. Alex tries out a few additional tones — light funk and pretty distorted — over a spare beat and generally quiet arrangement.

As Neil told Keith Sharp from *Music Express*, "If there is an identifiable lyrical trait here, it's my use of irony, which is injected by acting a character out through the lyrics. For example, in 'Hand Over Fist' there are two people walking down the street arguing, and the lead character is saying things which are supposed to be ironic. I was conscious that maybe a couple of the last albums were a little on the heavy side, lyrically speaking. With *Presto* I took a little looser approach to things. These songs have their own stories and messages without necessarily being linked by some overall theme."

Peart makes an amusing and salient point, speaking with Keith, about manufacturing Rush material at this juncture. "We can't be more creative than locking ourselves away in a farmhouse. I know there is such a thing as inspiration, but I know how to take advantage of it. When we're not rehearsing or writing, I collect ideas and prepare myself for when we do start writing. By the time we're ready to work on a new album, I'm fully prepared. I've got pages and pages of notes to work from. Call us efficient, call us mechanical. The point is, when we have to get something done, it's done. That's the only way we know how to work. Maybe we're exceptional in that way. To our mind this is simply being professional."

Noted Geddy, speaking with Bob Coburn on the link to the simple game to which the lyric alludes: "It's kind of an abstraction. The kid's game or what you want to call it, that you play with making your fist and making your two fingers into scissors and paper . . . paper covers a rock, that whole little game. It turned into a nursery rhyme that we put together as a chant. I guess there's lots of different analogies you can make with that kind of a thing. What represents a stone in your life, what is paper and all these different things. But basically it was — for me anyway — just a rhythmic thing that the whole sound of that chant, to me, was a very strong rhythmic thing to write music to."

In essence, here's Geddy again, working with Neil to get to a lyric that rolls off the tongue effortlessly and with logical rhythm, although, in fact, "Hand Over Fist" had initially been crafted to appear as an instrumental.

Presto finishes strong with the enigmatic "Available Light," another song that begs for re-recording, a fattening. Even though this is somewhat a ballad, it grooves nicely. In fact, Geddy applies proper, deep bass tones while the song accentuates the piano part, played by Jason Sniderman, Blue Peter keyboardist and son of Sam Sniderman, the Sam in Canadian record store chain Sam the Record Man. Lyrically, Neil presents an odd mix of weather — sun and sea imagery — against some of the preoccupations a photographer has to ponder and solve. Both are tied together by the concept of "available light," which then also serves as a life credo, the desire to live in available light.

And that was it for *Presto*. The record went gold in the States almost immediately, but then never got its platinum designation. In truth, Rush were continuing to operate well at odds with any sensible direction that might have them aligned with any kind of musical movement.

But the goals with this band were inscrutable. Reflects Geddy, "I think that phase, those two records we did with Rupert and Stephen [Tayler, the engineer], were very much songwriting experiments — learning how to be better songwriters in a more concise period of time. *Presto* was the first one, but I found that when we finished *Presto*, I was a little unsatisfied, somehow. I like the sound of the record a lot. I thought it was a good production, but I didn't feel we really nailed the songwriting on that album, aside from a couple of tracks that stand out, and have, I think, endured. I don't think it's our strongest work as writers, and I think the next record we did with Rupert was almost the exact opposite. I think it's one of our strongest pieces of writing, and maybe not our strongest sounding record. So you can't always have it all.

"But yeah, I think the songwriting, in retrospect, on the whole of *Presto*, was weaker than I thought it was when we were working on it. In retrospect, *Roll the Bones* is much, much stronger. In fact, I think you can make an argument that it's our strongest album from a songwriting point of view, but not from a sonic point of view. 'The Pass' stands out on *Presto*, and I can't think of any other titles off the top of my head. 'Red Tide' is an interesting song. They were interesting songs, but I don't think they were profound in terms of writing."

"I think the other guys have gone on record as saying it's one they really wished they could redo," adds Neil. "Of course, there are so many elements that come together in a record — the composition, the instrumentation, the sound, orchestration, producer, all of that. And *Presto*'s one that strikes me too; it didn't live up to its own potential even, never mind our potential. Or the potential that was in the material there, for whatever reason. That's what we feel. But it's pointless to say that because someone who likes that record would go, 'What are you saying?! What do you mean?!' That's a lesson we learned long ago. Don't dare to criticize even your own work because somebody's going to take you to task for it. Okay, you know best!"

"I thought it was a very exciting direction," says Alex. "And I was happy with the results. I just think it's a lighter record than what perhaps we intended it to be. But there's some really good playing on it, and there are some good arrangements, I think, good songs. But I don't know, for me, the record was a good catalyst for feeling fresh and excited again. We'd come from a very difficult phase in touring. We were on the road for a long time the previous tour, and we decided to take our longest break — about seven months, I think. And we were recharged and came back into the project feeling very positive and excited, and that carried through with the tour. I think when we were in our rehearsal mode and getting ready for the tour, we were quite excited about getting on the road and playing again. That was important, because we finished the '80s feeling pretty exhausted and not that interested in really touring anymore.

"And I think *Presto* was maybe the starting point of that. As I said, there was never friction, but there was pulling and pushing. And I think coming to the '90s, that was a transition, that we had our nice break, to close off the whole chapter and move into something new. All those records have their own particular mood. Generally they are pretty positive. I think we talked about *Grace Under Pressure* as a very stressful record to make, as it was. And *Moving Pictures* was just a real great experience, lots of fun. But my recollection of *Presto* was very positive. Rupert was a wonderful energy to be around. He was very positive all the time, quite humorous, and we really worked well together. Very gentlemanly."

"At the end of *Presto*," ponders Rupert, "probably at the very end of the last mix, I said to them, 'I'm not really sure I've been great value for money for you guys. I've had a whale of a time — don't get me wrong — but what do you think I really did?' And once again it was Neil who voiced it clearly: 'You were there to answer questions.' I sort of jokingly said, 'What, oh yeah, the six questions,' and, 'Yeah, and the six right answers,' he said.

"People have asked me since, 'Well, what were those six questions?' And I said, 'Well, there weren't really six.' They were things like a conversation I had with Geddy, very early on, a difficult one to have with a singer, which was, 'Why didn't you produce us before, when we asked?' And I said, 'Well, mainly lack of availability, and I didn't think I was really the guy for rock records,' and mumbled a bit like that. And then I said, 'And I also had a problem with your voice. But I'm doing the album. This is not a reason why I'm not doing the album. But when you're up on the fucking ceiling the whole time, I want to pull you back down so we can hear your personality, so we can get to grip with what Geddy is like' — because now I'm understanding him as a human being — 'I think there's a lot that never comes out of your voice because we don't hear it when you're stuck on the ceiling the whole time. Why can't we do something where we drop you, not a couple of keys, but a whole octave? Let's just take the song exactly as it stands now, for instance, and drop a whole octave.' And Geddy said, 'Well, that would just sound like me humming probably.' 'Well, let's try it, and then we can soar up the octave when we want impact.' So, in the end, that conversation affected a lot of that album, and even more so *Roll the Bones*."

Rupert has a different attitude than Peter Collins about whether the producer should be concerned with how many units the record goes on to shift after being put in the stores. "No, it's all about being in the studio," he says. "The second you've made the best record you can possibly make with your artist, it's unfortunate, but the record producer then has to hand it over to the next in line, the promotion and marketing people. When I tried to go with the tapes, and I have on a couple of occasions stayed with the finished album and tried to become part of its promotion and marketing in an effort to really make sure it's pushed all the way through, normally it only happened with an unknown artist. You are kind of elbowed out of the way. You're very unpopular if as a record producer you get out of the studio and start sticking your nose into other departments, which is in the end why a lot of producers do try their own record label.

"I think we pulled it off," figures Hine. "I do remember feeling very happy at the end of it, that it was a really great balance of all these ideas we'd talked about on the way. Not that we started out with this clear plan — we just wanted to experiment. And within that experimentation and focus we got a great balance over those songs between all the different aspects of the band. And I do think it was very cohesive, like a capsule of where the band were at that time in every way, right from Neil's text through to Geddy's greater range in his vocals and the nature of the flow of the songs, through the whole record. I remember being very happy with it, and thankfully so were the guys.

"When three guys have already made as many records as they had, it's tough," continues Hine, on this constant search he saw in the guys, which included the use of different producers. "We've seen how few bands can make it, you know. And three people is not many, which is both a strength and a weakness. Its strength is that three people is the most open, flexible format for a band. I mean, classically, all the great, madly improvisational bands have been three-pieces — Cream, Hendrix Experience. Where all three can play as madly as they like and no one's going to tread on anyone else's foot; it's just a basic design truth, the three-man group.

"As soon as there is a fourth, you've always got an argument between the guitar and keyboards. You've got to have some agreement as to who does what, and right there the improvisational idea is gone out the window. So this is the essence of a trio; this is why the word *power* so easily fits in there, because all three members can create a very powerful, entirely improvisational force without it being a mess. And that I think is something they wanted to really sustain, even though they'd just been through this departure by having a fourth shadow member, keyboard player, who didn't actually exist. They'd been through that sort of romance and they had come out of it with, 'Well, that was a bit of a holiday.' And now they were back to the day job of being a power trio and wanting to keep it fresh.

"And it is when you come back to making a new album, you are standing there, the three of you with your drum kit, your bass guitar and your guitar. And to keep that fresh, over that many albums and that many tracks, requires some inspirational thinking. And probably rather than trying to rely on the same three guys to come up with inspirational thinking, the best thing is to get someone in the mix who can shake it about. They don't have to come in with the great idea, but they do have to come in with a provocative role. And that sort of provocation can be on some very subtle levels; it doesn't have to be confrontational, although that can be good too. But that sort of provocative, constantly teasing, constantly moving things around, freshens it up for them. I sensed that very early on, that they wanted things to be pushed about a bit — by someone from outside."

And now it was time to take it outside, to go earn for the guys, their families and all the staffers and crew, the income that wasn't really going to come from these offbeat records made for no one in particular but Geddy, Alex and Neil, and maybe Rupert.

Only five songs from the album — "Superconductor," "Show Don't Tell," "The Pass," the Police-like "War Paint" and "Scars" — were played on the *Presto* tour, a five-month jaunt that would cover all of America and large Canadian markets only. The band was determined not to be on the road too long.

The Toronto stand would raise $200,000 for the United Way; staff back at the office printed up "I Survived Rush Playing

Toronto" shirts because of the demands put on the band for complimentary tickets and such. Mr. Big, featuring Buffalo bass legend Billy Sheehan (also of Talas and David Lee Roth), would provide most of the support. "Good friends, good musicians, good people," says Neil, with Geddy adding that "Billy Sheehan was a terrific bass player. I was always aware of him, and he's still just a monster bass player."

"I've got pictures of Neil practicing archery with Pat Torpey," laughs Billy, referring to the Mr. Big drummer, sadly deceased in 2018 at the age of sixty-four. "There's a photo of me with Jeff Berlin and Geddy backstage. Yeah, we had a wonderful time with those guys. I'd met them a couple times here or there over the years, but I never knew them that well, and then when we were on tour with them, we didn't know what to expect. They're a little intellectual, so we thought this wasn't going to be much fun at all. But we had a riot. And they were just so generous and nice. Great, great experience."

Voivod (Rush with fangs?) was called on to play in Quebec and Toronto. Of note, that band's acclaimed *Angel Rat* album from 1991 would be produced by none other than Terry Brown.

"In 1990 we toured with Rush for *Nothingface*," recalls Michel "Away" Langevin, explaining what had been the band's fondest career memory, until, that is, Voivod won a Juno of their own in 2018. "And of course Rush being a huge influence, and Terry Brown also, we wanted to try out recording with him, although the album turned out to be a bit mellow for the average Voivod listener, both in the mix and the performance. We got the gig through our management, who in the *Nothingface* days worked for Donald K Donald, a big promoter who books the stadium shows here in Montreal. And our management was in touch with Rush management, and the song 'Astronomy Domine' was doing really good on MuchMusic and MusiquePlus, and so we were offered two shows at Maple Leaf Gardens, one show at the Forum in Montreal and then another show at le Colisée in Quebec City. It was an amazing year for us, 1990, with that song getting us these Rush shows and also a North American tour.

"Both managements had a meeting arranged for us," continues Michel. "We met the band, and of course they were our heroes, so we were pretty intimidated. But they were really, really nice. We also had, on the first show, a bottle of champagne backstage with a note signed by the three members, which we gave to Piggy [guitarist Denis D'Amour, deceased from colon cancer in 2005], because he was the biggest Rush fan ever."

Voivod is considered the thrash metal Rush, in the same way that Victoria trio Nomeansno is considered the punk Rush. But Langevin isn't too sure if the Rush guys saw any of Voivod's math metal performance at these shows. "Well, they probably caught some of it. I seem to remember Blackie [the bass player] saying he saw the members watching on the side of the stage. But I never really saw them at all. I was very focused, and these were big crowds for us, and we were a bit nervous. I had seen some bands get booed off the stage opening for Rush. But when we played 'Astronomy Domine,' at every show, the crowd was louder than the music, which was a new experience for us."

Michel talks about what it was like to see how the pros took care of business. "I remember Neil came from behind the stage and Geddy came from the right and Alex from the left, and so they seemed to have their system down very precisely. It was a huge machine to observe, and of course, attending all the shows, watching Neil go at it on the drum kit."

But typical baby band woes almost sunk the band's shot at making a big impression. "Yes, when we went to the show in Toronto, we left from Montreal and stopped in Kingston to get gas, and the van never started after. And so we were pretty nervous because the show was the same night. The gear was already on its way to Toronto, and so we jumped into a bus in Kingston that was going from Montreal to Toronto, and we had to stand in the aisle of the bus the whole way, but we made it. We were lucky the driver let us stand. It was totally full. We left the van in Kingston, to be repaired. After the second show in Toronto, we were in the back of the Maple Leaf Gardens, and fans were there, and we were signing some stuff, and then we jumped in the back of the cube van we had rented to move the gear and we closed the door. They could not believe that. With no explanation. It was just a joke. But we were actually traveling on top of the gear, in a rented truck, a moving truck, and had to drive back to Kingston to pick up the van. It was funny to see the faces of all the fans watching us jump into the back of the truck and close the door."

"The most memorable thing was the big bunnies, the giant inflatable bunnies," says Neil about the *Presto* tour, which turned out, by all accounts, to be a most enjoyable trek. "That was amusing, the good bunny and the bad bunny. Because the title was *Presto*, which I had used in an ironic sense, wishing I had magic powers to make things right in the song. I really just liked the word. So we chose that as the title, and I think Hugh Syme came up with the idea of the bunnies making themselves come out of hats. So in the production design for that tour, we were playing off of that as a prop and we got two inflatable bunnies, forty feet tall or something. There was the good one and the bad one, and there was an animated movie of the bad bunny shooting the good bunny, who collapses. It was the theater absurdo."

But the specific plot around good bunny versus bad bunny, Geddy explains, didn't come until later.

"The bunnies were the big deal on that tour," says Geddy. "Everybody loved the bunnies. They were just a matter of coming up with the idea and having them executed and working on the timing with respect to inflating them and deflating them. After we used them for a couple of tours, it was hard to put them away because people loved them so much. But after we used them on two, it was like, 'Guys, we can't just keep trotting these bunnies out.' And somebody said, 'It's time we killed the gag.' And I said, 'Yeah, why don't we do that?'

"I have this group of people who are involved in the preproduction every year — Norm Stangl from Spin Productions and a few other people — and every year he helps me create a team of animators or visual people that we discuss ideas with for rearscreen films. We were sitting around talking. 'Is there something we can do with the bunnies?' And we decided we would go all evil on the bunnies, make one an evil bunny and make one a good bunny, and we would literally kill the gag by having one of the bunnies pop up and suddenly, instead of being a sweet cuddly thing, be this evil one with a gun. He would raise the gun and fire a bullet, and the bullet would hit the screen and be animated, and we would go on this little animated journey with this bullet, looking for the good bunny.

"And it actually turned out to be a really clever bit of animation; it's one of my favorite pieces. In the end, the good bunny rises, then the bad bunny comes up, fires the gun, a puff of smoke, and this cartoon starts, where there's this bullet that has a personality, and it goes through all kinds of wacky . . . it was really loony tunes. And then it hits the good bunny, which deflates. Well, you could hear the crowd go, 'Ooh.' I mean, they didn't like us killing the bunny [laughs]. It was a really bizarre little gag that came out of the dark corners of our creative ability. And to this day, I can remember people being so disappointed that we actually shot the bunny onstage."

The bunny joke was taken a step forward. In each city, the band's production office would order up some impromptu, unofficial

"Playboy" bunnies, who would emerge from side stage and give Alex and Geddy a peck on the cheek, a wipe of the brow and serve them both some much-needed refreshments. In terms of visuals, the band also carried with them a full laser setup, most impressive for the running laser man of "Marathon." "The Pass" used excellent black-and-white rear-screen imagery. "Subdivisions" featured the classic video footage from seven years previous.

It was Andrew MacNaughtan's job for the *Presto* tour — along with being the official photographer, acting as personal assistant and taking on various additional video duties as time went on — to "keep the band entertained."

"Yes, we would get a bunch of wonderful films, comedies, foreign films, just really great stuff, to watch on the bus," recalled MacNaughtan, in an interview with the author before his death in 2012 at the age of forty-seven. "And stupid films too. We would wear silly hats on the bus. And I remember, on the *Presto* tour, there was the movie called *Moon Over Parador*, with Richard Dreyfuss as the South American president or something. And he had these drinks called punas, and they're basically cocktails that are fruity and delicious. And I remember they were served in the very elaborate puna glass or puna cup. My mission was to get interesting glasses we could drink these drinks from. So we always had unusual drinking attire, and of course we all had to be wearing silly hats. Just things to sort of help pass the time on the bus. You would go a little stir-crazy.

"Also for *Presto*, Alex always insisted on bringing his paint set. I schlepped that to his room every night, but of course he never used it once. So that was kind of funny. Also for *Presto*, Alex and Geddy played tennis virtually every day off. But then for *Roll the Bones*, Alex started picking up golf.

"As for Neil, during the *Presto* tour he rode his bicycle everywhere," continues MacNaughtan, "from show to show. We would all be in a bus together, and the bus would stop about an hour outside of the next city we were arriving in, and he would be dropped off at a really inexpensive motel. It was almost like a game for him, more of a challenge for him. He was on this mission to find the most inexpensive motel room in America. He got it down to like $26 one night. Anyway, we would drop him off in the middle of the night, an hour outside the next city we were driving to on the bus. And we would continue on, and we would get into the hotel about five in the morning or whatever. And then Neil would spend the whole day, on the day off, riding his bike to get to that next city.

"I remember one time on the *Presto* tour, we dropped him off an hour outside of Salt Lake City. When he got there, it was already dark out, like around seven at night. And it was so hard for him to ride. He actually rode through snow. He went up through the mountains on his bicycle and it was just an absolute nightmare for him. He was so exhausted. But I'll never forget that. I just thought it was really strange to be wanting to ride up and actually go through snow, over a mountain. That was his pastime.

"And then with *Roll the Bones*, they started doing a couple of different things. Alex is definitely full-time golf at that point. Geddy was starting to do some golf with him; I think Alex sort of turned him onto it. Neil was still doing his bicycle thing, but he started doing archery with various guys from the crew. They would set up a big archery target at one end of the arena, down a hallway or outdoors, and they would target practice, which I took pictures of. Those pictures appeared in the *Counterparts* tour book, him doing his archery. We stayed in a castle in Birmingham, and he set up a target at this big castle and he did that all afternoon. But golf: Alex actually played at Turnberry, the famous golf course outside of Glasgow. It's on the ocean, and we stayed there on the day off before we played in Glasgow. Alex played golf with the soundman, Robert Scovill, and I swear to God, we were on the ocean and it was March and it must have been close to zero degrees. It was so cold and so windy."

Robert Scovill was responsible for the surround sound system Rush was using. Says MacNaughtan, "Correct. It was *Presto* and *Roll the Bones*. I don't know if it was every show, but that was pretty much the thing. And where you would really hear the full effect is in 'Force Ten.' It has an echoey, weird electronic drum sound at the beginning, and that's how the song ends as well. You would hear that at the front of the stage, and then all of a sudden, Robert would make it 360 around the entire stadium with that echoing drum thing. Actually a better example would be in Neil's drum solo. He triggers this electronic sound, when his drum kit is turning, and that sound he triggered, which would be repeating — bang, bang — went 360 degrees around the arena.

"Also during *Presto*," continues Andrew, "Neil and Geddy took me to a couple art galleries. I remember we went to one in Richmond, Virginia, that was really cool. So we would do a lot of art galleries. And for *Presto* and *Roll the Bones*, Geddy and I collected fine art photography. We would go to art galleries to actually purchase photographs. Of course, he had way more money than I did, and he purchased a lot of great art photography, all from the great masters.

"For *Presto*, they used footage from the video for 'The Pass,' black-and-white rear-screen imagery. And they had a big curtain that was painted to look like a vaudeville show, with an old man in a top hat. For 'Time Stand Still,' there would be Aimee Mann footage from the 'Time Stand Still' video, her singing her line. 'Subdivisions,' I think they used the same footage from many years ago, on all the tours. I could be wrong. 'Marathon,' they had a running laser guy. They had a full laser setup on both tours.

And the hired Playboy bunnies, that was for *Presto*, of course, every town. They'd have a girl in a bunny outfit come out and bring them drinks. These weren't official bunnies. I think this was arranged by Rush's production manager. His name was Nick Kotas. I'm not sure what his title was; he basically worked in the production office."

Then there were the books. "Yes! Neil and Geddy are both big fine art book collectors." But not first edition literature. "No, nothing like that. Neil has a couple of those, but it's not really his thing. But the fine art books, because we would always be going to these galleries, yes, they collected a lot of art books. Of course Neil is a great reader. He would read a book every two days, basically; it's crazy. Oh, the other pastime during *Presto* and *Roll the Bones* — their favorite, favorite, favorite thing — Neil insisted he had to have the *New York Times* at his door every Sunday. No matter what. No matter where we were, Buttfuck, Nowhere, I had to get him his Sunday *New York Times* so he could do the crossword puzzle. Geddy would do it as well."

It was a lot of living packed into a mere six-month tour, all of it in North America, all of it supported by Mr. Big. Following the last show on the tour — in Irvine, California, June 29, 1990 — Rush wouldn't play live again for another year and four months, more deeply taking that time they'd vowed to take, for family, for themselves, for personal enrichment.

There was one lone show, however, stuck in the midst of this personal development time away from being Rush. On September 15, 1990, Alex and Geddy performed as part of the Music & Tennis Festival at the North Ranch Country Club in Westlake Village, California, alongside a bunch of other old-timers like Eddie Money, Kansas, fellow Canucks Saga, and REO Speedwagon's Kevin Cronin, plus their warm-up act from the *Presto* campaign, Mr. Big. It would be as close to the professional circuit these childhood friends in tennis whites would ever get. But they could always dream . . . as Alex would continue to dream about becoming a pro golfer, as Geddy would dream about being a major league pitcher. But of course, there would be more Rush to come in the '90s, followed by a series of tragic events for Neil Peart that would turn the band's dreams into a sorrowful, seemingly never-ending nightmare.

DISCOGRAPHY

A few notes: I've provided the greatest level of detail for the studio albums, then less for live albums (most notable, no song timings). Note that this is a U.S. discography, with U.S. chart placements, U.S. certifications and, when we get to singles, official U.S. singles only.

Side 1 and Side 2 designations are provided for everything here, *Presto* being the last Rush album before the pronounced shift from LP to CD around 1990. Where possible, I've endeavored to reduce repetition (i.e., for live albums that were issued both in audio and video format). Catalogue numbers are the originals, as are the issues or editions.

Summing up, the idea was to limit this to the core, relevant discography (and, yes, videography). Also, I've skipped chart placement for videos. I figure the only chart measure that carries enough significance to mention is the actual Billboard 200, for albums. One other thing — and I'm sure there are a few more of these gremlins — originally and then occasionally, it's "Freewill" and other times it's "Free Will."

A: Studio Albums

Permanent Waves
(Mercury SRM-1-4001, January 1, 1980)
PEAK U.S. CHART POSITION: #4
U.S. RIAA CERTIFICATION: Platinum
PRODUCED BY: Rush and Terry Brown
SIDE 1: 1. The Spirit of Radio 4:54; 2. Freewill 5:23; 3. Jacob's Ladder 7:50
SIDE 2: 1. Entre Nous 4:37; 2. Different Strings 3:50; 3. Natural Science — I. Tide Pools; II. Hyperspace; III. Permanent Waves 9:27

Moving Pictures
(Mercury SRM-1-4013, February 12, 1981)
PEAK U.S. CHART POSITION: #3
U.S. RIAA CERTIFICATION: 4 x Platinum
PRODUCED BY: Rush and Terry Brown
SIDE 1: 1. Tom Sawyer 4:33; 2. Red Barchetta 6:07; 3. YYZ 4:23
SIDE 2: 1. Limelight 4:18; 2. The Camera Eye 10:55; 3. Witch Hunt – Part III of 'Fear' 4:43; 4. Vital Signs 4:45
NOTES: First Rush album issued on CD.

Signals
(Mercury SRM-1-4063, September 9, 1982)
PEAK U.S. CHART POSITION: #10
U.S. RIAA CERTIFICATION: Platinum
PRODUCED BY: Rush and Terry Brown

SIDE 1:   1. Subdivisions 5:33; 2. The Analog Kid 4:46; 3. Chemistry 4:56; 4. Digital Man 6:20

SIDE 2:   1. The Weapon 6:22; 2. New World Man 3:41; 3. Losing It 4:51; 4. Countdown 5:49

NOTES: Last Rush album issued on eight-track tape. Second Rush album issued on CD.

Grace Under Pressure
(Mercury 818 476-1, April 12, 1984)
PEAK U.S. CHART POSITION: #10
U.S. RIAA CERTIFICATION: Platinum
PRODUCED BY: Rush and Peter Henderson
SIDE 1: 1. Distant Early Warning 4:59; 2. Afterimage 5:04; 3. Red Sector A 5:10; 4. The Enemy Within (Part one of *Fear*) 4:34

SIDE 2: 1. The Body Electric 5:00; 2. Kid Gloves 4:18; 3. Red Lenses 4:42; 4. Between the Wheels 5:44

Power Windows
(Mercury 826 098-1, October 29, 1985)
PEAK U.S. CHART POSITION: #10
U.S. RIAA CERTIFICATION: Platinum
PRODUCED BY: Peter Collins and Rush
SIDE 1: 1. The Big Money 5:36; 2. Grand Designs 5:05; 3. Manhattan Project 5:05; 4. Marathon 6:09

SIDE 2: 1. Territories 6:19; 2. Middletown Dreams 5:17; 3. Emotion Detector 5:10; 4. Mystic Rhythms 6:08

NOTES: First Rush album to be issued on CD as a new release.

Hold Your Fire
(Mercury 832 464-1, September 8, 1987)
PEAK U.S. CHART POSITION: #13

U.S. RIAA CERTIFICATION: Gold
PRODUCED BY: Peter Collins and Rush
SIDE I: 1. Force Ten 4:28; 2. Time Stand Still 5:07; 3. Open Secrets 5:37; 4. Second Nature 4:35; 5. Prime Mover 5:19
SIDE 2: 1. Lock and Key 5:08; 2. Mission 5:15; 3. Turn the Page 4:53; 4. Tai Shan 4:14; 5. High Water 5:32

Presto
(Atlantic 82040-1, November 21, 1989)
PEAK U.S. CHART POSITION: #16
U.S. RIAA CERTIFICATION: Gold
PRODUCED BY: Rupert Hine and Rush
SIDE I: 1. Show Don't Tell 5:01; 2. Chain Lightning 4:33; 3. The Pass 4:51; 4. War Paint 5:24; 5. Scars 4:07; 6. Presto 5:45
SIDE 2: 1. Superconductor 4:47; 2. Anagram (for Mongo) 4:00; 3. Red Tide 4:29; 4. Hand Over Fist 4:11; 5. Available Light 5:03
NOTES: First album under Rush's new U.S. deal with Atlantic, all previous albums being with Mercury. Also last album of the vinyl era. Only Rush album issued on vinyl in Uruguay. Original CD issue was in longbox format.

B: Live Albums

Exit . . . Stage Left
(Mercury SRM-2-7001, October 29, 1981)
PEAK U.S. CHART POSITION: #10
U.S. RIAA CERTIFICATION: Platinum
SIDE 1: 1. The Spirit of Radio 2. Red Barchetta 3. YYZ
SIDE 2: 1. A Passage to Bangkok 2. Closer to the Heart 3. Beneath, Between & Behind 4. Jacob's Ladder
SIDE 3: 1. Broon's Bane 2. The Trees 3. Xanadu
SIDE 4: 1. Free Will 2. Tom Sawyer 3. La Villa Strangiato
NOTES: "A Passage to Bangkok" was omitted from the original CD issue, but re-added when CD capacity was raised to eighty minutes.

A Show of Hands
(Mercury 836 346-1, January 10, 1989)
PEAK U.S. CHART POSITION: #21
U.S. RIAA CERTIFICATION: Gold
SIDE 1: 1. The Big Money 2. Subdivisions 3. Marathon
SIDE 2: 1. Turn the Page 2. Manhattan Project 3. Mission
SIDE 3: 1. Distant Early Warning 2. Mystic Rhythms 3. Witch Hunt – Part III of 'Fear'
SIDE 4: 1. Force Ten 2. Time Stand Still 3. Red Sector A 4. Closer to the Heart
NOTES: Only Rush album issued on vinyl in Yugoslavia.

C: Selected Singles

Singles is perhaps the department where it most bears reminding that this is a U.S. discography. The singles story for Rush is pretty dull, given the complete lack of non-LP (studio) tracks from the lads. A further note: I've included all commercial U.S. releases but only select promos, as some of the promos are slight variations of each other, or slight variations on the official release (beginning with same catalogue number). PS denotes picture sleeve.

7" Vinyl Singles
The Spirit of Radio / The Spirit of Radio (76044) promo
The Spirit of Radio / Circumstances (76044)
Entre Nous / Entre Nous (76060) promo
Entre Nous / Different Strings (76060)
Limelight / Limelight (76095 DJ) promo
Limelight / YYZ (76095)
Tom Sawyer / Tom Sawyer (76109) promo
Tom Sawyer / Witch Hunt (76109) PS
Closer to the Heart (live) / Closer to the Heart (76124 DJ) promo
Closer to the Heart (live) / Freewill (76124)
New World Man / New World Man (76179 DJ) promo; brown
vinyl, PS
New World Man / New World Man (76179 DJ) promo; PS
New World Man / Vital Signs (live) (76179) PS
Subdivisions / Subdivisions (76196) promo
Subdivisions / Countdown (76196)
Red Sector A / Red Sector A (PRO 319 7) promo; red vinyl
The Body Electric / The Body Electric (880 050 7 DJ) promo
The Body Electric / Between the Wheels (880 050 7)
The Big Money / The Big Money (PRO 383 7 DJ) promo

The Big Money / Red Sector A (live) (884 191 7) PS
Mystic Rhythms / Emotion Detector (884 520 7)
Time Stand Still / Time Stand Still (888 891 7 DJ) promo
Time Stand Still / High Water (888 891 7) PS

12" Vinyl Singles, EPs, LPs (all promo)
The Spirit of Radio / The Trees / Working Man (MK-125)
Entre Nous (edit) (MK-137) PS
Rush N' Roulette (MK-185) PS
A Passage to Bangkok / Freewill (MK-188) PS
New World Man / Vital Signs (live) (MK-216); clear vinyl
Distant Early Warning / Between the Wheels (PRO 276-1)
The Body Electric (PRO 290-1)
Red Sector A (edit) / The Enemy Within (PRO 320-1); red vinyl
The Big Money (PRO 382-1)
Mystic Rhythms (PRO 400-1)
Force Ten (PRO 532-1)
Marathon (live) (PRO 689-1)

Cassette Singles
The Pass / Presto (4-87986)

CD Singles
Time Stand Still / Time Stand Still (edit) (CDP 05)
Show Don't Tell (PR 3082 2)
Show Don't Tell (edit) / Show Don't Tell (PR 3125 2)
The Pass (edit) / The Pass (PR 316 2)
The Pass (PR 3175 2)
Profiled! (PRCD 3200-2); fifty-five-minute interview
Superconductor (PRCD 3331)

D: Videography

Exit... Stage Left
(Polygram PMV 60285, 1981)
U.S. RIAA CERTIFICATION: Gold
   1. Limelight 2. Tom Sawyer 3. The Trees 4. Xanadu
   5. Red Barchetta 6. Freewill 7. Closer to the Heart
   8. YYZ 9. Medley: By-Tor & the Snow Dog, In the
   End, In the Mood, 2112
NOTES: Originally issued on Beta, VHS and LaserDisc by
   RCA/Columbia Home Videos. In 2006, the set was
   issued in DVD form as part of *Replay X 3*, followed by a
   stand-alone release in 2007. Recorded March 27, 1981, in
   Montreal. Almost entirely different performances from
   the *Exit... Stage Left* live album.

Through the Camera Eye
(Polygram PMV 60466, 1985)
U.S. RIAA CERTIFICATION: n/a
   1. Distant Early Warning 2. Vital Signs 3. The Body
   Electric 4. Afterimage 5. Subdivisions 6. Tom Sawyer
   (live) 7. The Enemy Within 8. Countdown
NOTES: This forty-four-minute video collection was originally
   issued on VHS and LaserDisc (PMV PA-85-112) by
   RCA/Columbia Home Videos. In 2006, the set was
   issued in DVD form as part of *Replay X 3*, followed by a
   stand-alone release in 2007.

Grace Under Pressure Tour
(Polygram PMV 60607, 1986)
U.S. RIAA CERTIFICATION: n/a

1. The Spirit of Radio 2. The Enemy Within 3. The Weapon 4. Witch Hunt 5. New World Man 6. Distant Early Warning 7. Red Sector A 8. Closer to the Heart 9. YYZ 10. The Temples of Syrinx 11. Tom Sawyer 12. Vital Signs 13. Finding My Way 14. In the Mood 15. Bonus: The Big Money (production video)

NOTES: This sixty-nine-minute video is culled from a concert at Maple Leaf Gardens, Toronto, September 21, 1984. It was originally issued on VHS and LaserDisc (CDV 080 103-1) by RCA/Columbia Home Videos. In 2006, the set was issued in DVD form as part of *Replay X 3*, followed by a stand-alone release in 2007. An audio version was also included in the *Replay X 3* package and then issued as a stand-alone CD in 2009.

A Show of Hands
(Polygram PMV 041 760-3, 1989)
U.S. RIAA CERTIFICATION: Platinum
1. The Big Money 2. Marathon 3. Turn the Page 4. Prime Mover 5. Manhattan Project 6. Closer to the Heart 7. Red Sector A 8. Force Ten 9. Mission 10. Territories 11. The Rhythm Method 12. The Spirit of Radio 13. Tom Sawyer 14. 2112 / La Villa Strangiato / In the Mood

NOTES: This ninety-minute video is culled from a concert at the National Exhibition Centre, Birmingham, U.K. It was originally issued on VHS and LaserDisc (PMV 082 575-1) by Polygram. In 2006, the set was issued in DVD form as part of *Replay X 3*, followed by a stand-alone release in 2007.

CREDITS

Canadian Composer. "Surviving with Rush" by Nick Krewen. April 1986.

Canadian Musician. "*Presto* Change-O" by Nick Krewen. April 1990.

CHUM-FM. Interview with Geddy Lee by Rick Ringer. February 11, 1981.

Free Press. "Interview with Alex Lifeson" by Andrew MacNaughtan. June 1984.

Guitar Player. "Playback: The Making of an Album — Rush *Grace Under Pressure*" by Alex Lifeson as told to Jas Obrecht. August 1984.

Guitar Player. "Alex Lifeson of Rush: The Evolving Art of Rock Guitar" by Jas Obrecht. April 1986.

Hit Parader. "Leaps & Bounds" by Andy Seeber. March 1983.

Innerview. Interview with Neil Peart by Jim Ladd. June 11, 1981.

Innerview. Interview with Geddy Lee by Jim Ladd. February 1983.

Innerview. Interview with Neil Peart by Jim Ladd. 1984.

In the Studio with Redbeard. Show #28. Week of January 2, 1989.

Kerrang! "The Pressure Principle" by Geoff Barton. No. 67. May 3–16, 1984.

Kerrang! "Pane and Pleasure" by Mark Putterford. No. 107. November 14–27, 1985.

Metal Hammer. "All Fired Up" by Malcolm Dome. April 25, 1988.

Modern Drummer. "Notes on the making of *Moving Pictures* — Part I" by Neil Peart. December 1982.

Moving Pictures tourbook. "A Rush Newsreel" by Neil Peart. 1981.

Music Express. "Neil Peart: New World Man" by Greg Quill. September/October 1982.

Music Express. "A Parallax View" by Keith Sharp. December 1985.

Music Express. "Something Up Their Sleeves" by Keith Sharp. Vol. 14, No. 144. 1990.

Music Technology. "Fire in the Hold" by Deborah Parisi. February 1988.

Musician. "Rush Screwing Up Pop — On Purpose" by J.D. Considine. April 1990.

Now. "Time Rewards Rock's Underdogs" by Christopher Jones. March 3, 1988.

Record Mirror. Permanent Waves record review by Malcolm Dome. January 26, 1980.

Rockline. Geddy Lee interview by Bob Coburn. December 4, 1989.

Rhythm. "Neil Peart: Mystic Rhythms" by Tim Ponting. August 1988.

Signals radio premiere. September 1982.

Signals tour program by Neil Peart. 1982.

ABOUT THE AUTHOR

Martin Popoff has unofficially written more record reviews than anybody in the history of music — approximately 7,900 across all genres (with over 7,000 appearing in books). Additionally, Martin has penned eighty-five books on hard rock, heavy metal, classic rock and record-collecting. He was editor in chief of the now retired *Brave Words & Bloody Knuckles*, Canada's foremost metal publication, for fourteen years and has also contributed to *Revolver, Guitar World, Goldmine, Record Collector*, bravewords.com, lollipop.com and hardradio.com, with many record label band bios and liner notes to his credit as well. Additionally, Martin has been a regular contractor to Banger Films and worked for two years as researcher on the award-winning documentary *Rush: Beyond the Lighted Stage*, on the writing and research team for the eleven-episode *Metal Evolution* and on the ten-episode *Rock Icons*, both for VH1 Classic. Additionally, Martin is the writer of the original metal

genre chart used in *Metal: A Headbanger's Journey* and throughout the *Metal Evolution* episodes. Martin currently resides
in Toronto and can be reached at martinp@inforamp.net or
martinpopoff.com.

MARTIN POPOFF — A COMPLETE BIBLIOGRAPHY

Empire of the Clouds: Iron Maiden in the 2000s (2020)

Blue Öyster Cult: A Visual Biography (2020)

Anthem: Rush in the '70s (2020)

Denim and Leather: Saxon's First Ten Years (2020)

Black Funeral: Into the Coven with Mercyful Fate (2020)

Satisfaction: 10 Albums That Changed My Life (2019)

Holy Smoke: Iron Maiden in the '90s (2019)

Sensitive to Light: The Rainbow Story (2019)

Where Eagles Dare: Iron Maiden in the '80s (2019)

Aces High: The Top 250 Heavy Metal Songs of the '80s (2019)

Lettin' Go: UFO in the Eighties and Nineties (2019)

Judas Priest: Turbo 'til Now (2019)

Born Again! Black Sabbath in the Eighties and Nineties (2019)

Riff Raff: The Top 250 Heavy Metal Songs of the '70s (2018)

Unchained: A Van Halen User Manual (2018)

Queen: Album by Album (2018)

315

Iron Maiden: Album by Album (2018)

Welcome to My Nightmare: 50 Years of Alice Cooper (2018)

Sabotage! Black Sabbath in the Seventies (2018)

Judas Priest: Decade of Domination (2018)

Popoff Archive — 6: American Power Metal (2018)

Popoff Archive — 5: European Power Metal (2018)

The Sun Goes Down: Thin Lizzy 1977–83 (2018)

The Clash: All the Albums, All the Songs (2018)

Led Zeppelin: All the Albums, All the Songs (2017)

AC/DC: Album by Album (2017)

Lights Out: Surviving the '70s with UFO (2017)

Tornado of Souls: Thrash's Titanic Clash (2017)

Caught in a Mosh: The Golden Era of Thrash (2017)

Rush: Album by Album (2017)

Beer Drinkers and Hell Raisers: The Rise of Motörhead (2017)

Metal Collector: Gathered Tales from Headbangers (2017)

Hit the Lights: The Birth of Thrash (2017)

Popoff Archive — 4: Classic Rock (2017)

Popoff Archive — 3: Hair Metal (2017)

From Dublin to Jailbreak: Thin Lizzy 1969–76 (2016)

Popoff Archive — 2: Progressive Rock (2016)

Popoff Archive — 1: Doom Metal (2016)

Rock the Nation: Montrose, Gamma and Ronnie Redefined (2016)

Punk Tees: The Punk Revolution in 125 T-Shirts (2016)

Metal Heart: Aiming High with Accept (2016)

Ramones at 40 (2016)

Time and a Word: The Yes Story (2016)

Kickstart My Heart: A Mötley Crüe Day-by-Day (2015)

This Means War: The Sunset Years of the NWOBHM (2015)

Wheels of Steel: The Explosive Early Years of the NWOBHM (2015)

Swords and Tequila: Riot's Classic First Decade (2015)

Who Invented Heavy Metal? (2015)

Sail Away: Whitesnake's Fantastic Voyage (2015)

Live Magnetic Air: The Unlikely Saga of the Superlative Max Webster (2014)

Steal Away the Night: An Ozzy Osbourne Day-by-Day (2014)

The Big Book of Hair Metal (2014)

Sweating Bullets: The Deth and Rebirth of Megadeth (2014)

Smokin' Valves: A Headbanger's Guide to 900 NWOBHM Records (2014)

The Art of Metal (co-edit with Malcolm Dome; 2013)

2 Minutes to Midnight: An Iron Maiden Day-by-Day (2013)

Metallica: The Complete Illustrated History (2013); update and reissue (2016)

Rush: The Illustrated History (2013); update and reissue (2016)

Ye Olde Metal: 1979 (2013)

Scorpions: Top of the Bill (2013); updated and reissued as *Wind of Change: The Scorpions Story* (2016)

Epic Ted Nugent (2012); updated and reissued as *Motor City Madhouse: Going Gonzo with Ted Nugent* (2017)

Fade to Black: Hard Rock Cover Art of the Vinyl Age (2012)

It's Getting Dangerous: Thin Lizzy 81–12 (2012)

We Will Be Strong: Thin Lizzy 76–81 (2012)

Fighting My Way Back: Thin Lizzy 69–76 (2011)

The Deep Purple Royal Family: Chain of Events '80–'11 (2011); reissued as *The Deep Purple Family Year by Year Volume Two* (1980–2011) (2018)

The Deep Purple Royal Family: Chain of Events Through '79 (2011); reissued as *The Deep Purple Family Year by Year (to 1979)* (2016)

Black Sabbath FAQ (2011)

The Collector's Guide to Heavy Metal: Volume 4: The '00s (2011; co-authored with David Perri)

Goldmine Standard Catalog of American Records 1948–1991, 7th Edition (2010)

Goldmine Record Album Price Guide, 6th Edition (2009)

Goldmine 45 RPM Price Guide, 7th Edition (2009)

A Castle Full of Rascals: Deep Purple '83–'09 (2009)

Worlds Away: Voivod and the Art of Michel Langevin (2009)

Ye Olde Metal: 1978 (2009)

Gettin' Tighter: Deep Purple '68–'76 (2008)

All Access: The Art of the Backstage Pass (2008)

Ye Olde Metal: 1977 (2008)

Ye Olde Metal: 1976 (2008)

Judas Priest: Heavy Metal Painkillers (2007)

Ye Olde Metal: 1973 to 1975 (2007)

The Collector's Guide to Heavy Metal: Volume 3: The Nineties (2007)

Ye Olde Metal: 1968 to 1972 (2007)

Run For Cover: The Art of Derek Riggs (2006)

Black Sabbath: Doom Let Loose (2006)

Dio: Light Beyond the Black (2006)

The Collector's Guide to Heavy Metal: Volume 2: The Eighties (2005)

Rainbow: English Castle Magic (2005)

UFO: Shoot Out the Lights (2005)

The New Wave of British Heavy Metal Singles (2005)

Blue Öyster Cult: Secrets Revealed! (2004); update and reissue (2009); updated and reissued as *Agents of Fortune: The Blue Öyster Cult Story* (2016)

Contents Under Pressure: 30 Years of Rush at Home & Away (2004)

The Top 500 Heavy Metal Albums of All Time (2004)

The Collector's Guide to Heavy Metal: Volume 1: The Seventies (2003)

The Top 500 Heavy Metal Songs of All Time (2003)

Southern Rock Review (2001)

Heavy Metal: 20th Century Rock and Roll (2000)

The Goldmine Price Guide to Heavy Metal Records (2000)
The Collector's Guide to Heavy Metal (1997)
Riff Kills Man! 25 Years of Recorded Hard Rock & Heavy Metal (1993)

See martinpopoff.com for complete details
and ordering information.